THE INQUISITION

Nihil Obstat.

THOMAS J. SHAHAN, S.T.D.

Imprimatur.

✠ JOHN M. FARLEY, D.D.,
Archbishop of New York.

NEW YORK, June 24, 1907.

THE INQUISITION

A CRITICAL AND HISTORICAL STUDY
OF THE COERCIVE POWER
OF THE CHURCH

BY

E. VACANDARD

TRANSLATED FROM THE SECOND EDITION BY
BERTRAND L. CONWAY, C.S.P.

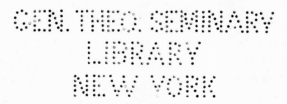
LONGMANS, GREEN, AND CO.
91 AND 93 FIFTH AVENUE NEW YORK
LONDON, BOMBAY, AND CALCUTTA
1908

First Edition, February, 1908
Reprinted, May, 1908

The Plimpton Press Norwood Mass. U.S.A.

PREFACE

THERE are very few Catholic apologists who feel inclined to boast of the annals of the Inquisition. The boldest of them defend this institution against the attacks of modern liberalism, as if they distrusted the force of their own arguments. Indeed they have hardly answered the first objection of their opponents, when they instantly endeavor to prove that the Protestant and Rationalistic critics of the Inquisition have themselves been guilty of heinous crimes. "Why," they ask, "do you denounce our Inquisition, when you are responsible for Inquisitions of your own?"

No good can be accomplished by such a false method of reasoning. It seems practically to admit that the cause of the Church cannot be defended. The accusation of wrong-doing made against the enemies they are trying to reduce to silence comes back with equal force against the friends they are trying to defend.

It does not follow that because the Inquisition of Calvin and the French Revolutionists merits the reprobation of mankind, the Inquisition of the Catholic Church must needs escape all censure. On the contrary, the

unfortunate comparison made between them naturally
leads one to think that both deserve equal blame. To
our mind there is only one way of defending the attitude
of the Catholic Church in the Middle Ages toward the
Inquisition. We must examine and judge this institution objectively, from the standpoint of morality, justice,
and religion, instead of comparing its excesses with the
blameworthy actions of other tribunals.

No historian worthy of the name has as yet undertaken
to treat the Inquisition from this objective standpoint.
In the seventeenth century, a scholarly priest, Jacques
Marsollier, canon of Uzès, published at Cologne (Paris),
in 1693, a *Histoire de l'Inquisition et de son Origine.* But
his work, as a critic has pointed out, is "not so much a
history of the Inquisition, as a thesis written with a strong
Gallican bias, which details with evident delight the
cruelties of the Holy Office." The illustrations are taken
from Philip Limborch's *Historia Inquisitionis.*[1]

Henry Charles Lea, already known by his other works
on religious history, published in New York, in 1888, three
large volumes entitled "A History of the Inquisition of
the Middle Ages." This work has received as a rule a
most flattering reception at the hands of the European

[1] Paul Fredericq, *Historiographie de l'Inquisition,* p. xiv. Introduction
to the French translation of Lea's book on the Inquisition. This work of
Marsollier was republished and enlarged by another priest, the Abbé Gouget,
who added a *Discours sur quelques auteurs qui ont traité du tribunal de
l'Inquisition.*

press, and has been translated into French.[1] One can
say without exaggeration that it is "the most extensive,
the most profound, and the most thorough history of
the Inquisition that we possess."[2]

It is far, however, from being the last word of historical
criticism. And I am not speaking here of the changes
in detail that may result from the discovery of new documents. We have plenty of material at hand to enable
us to form an accurate notion of the institution itself.
Lea's judgment, despite evident signs of intellectual
honesty, is not to be trusted. Honest he may be, but
impartial never. His pen too often gives way to his
prejudices and his hatred of the Catholic Church. His
critical judgment is sometimes gravely at fault.[3]

Tanon, the president of the Court of Cassation, has
proved far more impartial in his *Histoire des Tribunaux de
l'Inquisition en France*.[4] This is evidently the work of
a scholar, who possesses a very wide and accurate grasp
of ecclesiastical legislation. He is deeply versed in the
secrets of both the canon and the civil law. However,
we must remember that his scope is limited. He has of

---

[1] *Histoire de l'Inquisition au moyen âge*, Salomon Reinach. Paris, Fisch-
bacher, 1900–1903.

[2] Paul Fredericq, *loc. cit.*, p. xxiv.

[3] The reader may gather our estimate of this work from the various criti-
cisms we will pass upon it in the course of this study.

[4] Paris, 1893. Dr. Camille Henner had already published a similar work,
Beiträge zur Organisation und Competenz der päpstlichen Ketzergeschichte,
Leipzig, 1890.

set purpose omitted everything that happened outside of France. Besides he is more concerned with the legal than with the theological aspect of the Inquisition.

On the whole, the history of the Inquisition is still to be written. It is not our purpose to attempt it; our ambition is more modest. But we wish to picture this institution in its historical setting, to show how it originated, and especially to indicate its relation to the Church's notion of the coercive power prevalent in the Middle Ages. For as Lea himself says: "The Inquisition was not an organization arbitrarily devised and imposed upon the judicial system of Christendom by the ambition or fanaticism of the Church. It was rather a natural — one may almost say an inevitable — evolution of the forces at work in the thirteenth century, and no one can rightly appreciate the process of its development and the results of its activity, without a somewhat minute consideration of the factors controlling the minds and souls of men during the ages which laid the foundation of modern civilization."[1]

We must also go back further than the thirteenth century and ascertain how the coercive power which the Church finally confided to the Inquisition developed from the beginning. Such is the purpose of the present work. It is both a critical and an historical study. We intend to record first everything that relates to the sup-

[1] Preface, p. iii.

pression of heresy, from the origin of Christianity up to the Renaissance; then we will see whether the attitude of the Church toward heretics can not only be explained, but defended.

We undertake this study in a spirit of absolute honesty and sincerity. The subject is undoubtedly a most delicate one. But no consideration whatever should prevent our studying it from every possible viewpoint. Cardinal Newman in his Historical Sketches speaks of "that endemic perennial fidget which possesses certain historians about giving scandal. Facts are omitted in great histories, or glosses are put upon memorable acts, because they are thought not edifying, whereas of all scandals such omissions, such glosses, are the greatest." [1]

A Catholic apologist fails in his duty to-day if he writes merely to edify the faithful. Granting that the history of the Inquisition will reveal things we never dreamt of, our prejudices must not prevent an honest facing of the facts. We ought to dread nothing more than the reproach that we are afraid of the truth. "We can understand," says Yves Le Querdec,[2] "why our forefathers did not wish to disturb men's minds by placing before them certain questions. I believe they were wrong, for all questions that can be presented will necessarily be presented some day or other. If they are not presented fairly by those who possess the true solution or who

[1] Vol. ii, p. 231.   [2] Univers, June 2, 1906.

honestly look for it, they will be by their enemies.   For
this reason we think that not only honesty but good
policy require us to tell the world all the facts. . . .
Everything has been said, or will be said some day.
. . . What the friends of the Church will not mention
will be spread broadcast by her enemies.   And they will
make such an outcry over their discovery, that their
words will reach the most remote corners and penetrate
the deafest ears.   We ought not to be afraid to-day of
the light of truth; but fear rather the darkness of lies
and errors."

In a word, the best method of apologetics is to tell the
whole truth.   In our mind, apologetics and history are
two sisters, with the same device: *"Ne quid falsi audeat,
ne quid veri non audeat historia."*[1]

[1] Cicero, De Oratore ii, 15.

CONTENTS

xi

CHAPTER IV

FOURTH PERIOD (FROM GRATIAN TO INNOCENT III). THE INFLUENCE
OF THE CANON LAW, AND THE REVIVAL OF THE ROMAN
LAW.

CHAPTER V

THE CATHARAN OR ALBIGENSIAN HERESY: ITS ANTI-CATHOLIC
AND ANTI-SOCIAL CHARACTER.

CHAPTER X

CRITICISM OF THE THEORY AND PRACTICE OF THE INQUISITION.

APPENDIX A

APPENDIX B

THE INQUISITION

CHAPTER I

FIRST PERIOD

I-IV CENTURY

THE EPOCH OF THE PERSECUTIONS

ST. PAUL was the first to pronounce a sentence of condemnation upon heretics. In his Epistle to Timothy, he writes: "Of whom is Hymeneus and Alexander, whom I have delivered up to Satan, that they may learn not to blaspheme."[1] The apostle is evidently influenced in his action by the Gospel. The one-time Pharisee no longer dreams of punishing the guilty with the severity of the Mosaic Law. The death penalty of stoning which apostates merited under the old dispensation[2] has been changed into a purely spiritual penalty, excommunication.

During the first three centuries, as long as the era of persecution lasted, the early Christians never thought

[1] I Tim. i. 20. Cf. Tit. iii. 10–11. "A man that is a heretic, after the first and second admonition, avoid, knowing that he, that is such a one, is subverted and sinneth, being condemned by his own judgment."

[2] Deut. xiii. 6–9; xvii. 1–6.

of using any force save the force of argument to win back their dissident brethren. This is the meaning of that obscure passage in the *Adversus Gnosticos* of Tertullian, in which he speaks of "driving heretics (*i.e.* by argument), to their duty, instead of trying to win them, for obstinacy must be conquered, not coaxed." [1] In this work he is trying to convince the Gnostics of their errors from various passages in the Old Testament. But he never invokes the death penalty against them. On the contrary, he declares that no practical Christian can be an executioner or jailer. He even goes so far as to deny the right of any disciple of Christ to serve in the army, at least as an officer, "because the duty of a military commander comprises the right to sit in judgment upon a man's life, to condemn, to put in chains, to imprison and to torture." [2]

If a Christian has no right to use physical force, even in the name of the State, he is all the more bound not to use it against his dissenting brethren in the name of the Gospel, which is a law of gentleness. Tertullian was a Montanist when he wrote this. But although he wrote

[1] "Ad officium hæreticos compelli, non illici dignum est. Duritia vincenda est, non suadenda." *Adversus Gnosticos Scorpiace*, cap. ii, Migne, P. L., vol. ii, col. 125. On the different readings and sense of this text, cf. Rigault, *ibid.*, note. The Scorpiace was written 211 or 212.

[2] "Jam vero quæ sunt potestatis, neque judicet de capite alicujus . . . neque damnet, neque prædamnet, neminem vinciat, neminem recludat, aut torqueat." *De Idololatria*, cap. xvii, P. L., vol. i, col. 687. This work was written 211 or 212.

most bitterly against the Gnostics whom he detested, he always protested against the use of brute force in the matter of religion. "It is a fundamental human right," he says, "a privilege of nature, that every man should worship according to his convictions. It is assuredly no part of religion to compel religion. It must be embraced freely and not forced." [1] These words prove that Tertullian was a strong advocate of absolute toleration.

Origen likewise never granted Christians the right to punish those who denied the Gospel. In answering Celsus, who had brought forward certain texts of the Old Testament that decreed the death penalty for apostasy, he says: "If we must refer briefly to the difference between the law given to the Jews of old by Moses, and the law laid down by Christ for Christians, we would state that it is impossible to harmonize the legislation of Moses, taken literally, with the calling of the Gentiles. . . . For Christians cannot slay their enemies, or condemn, as Moses commanded, the contemners of the law to be put to death by burning or stoning." [2]

St. Cyprian also repudiates in the name of the Gospel the laws of the Old Testament on this point. He writes

---

[1] "Tamen humani juris et naturalis potestatis unicuique, quod putaverit, colere, nec alii obest aut prodest alterius religio. Sed nec religionis est cogere religionem, quæ sponte suscipi debeat, non vi." *Liber ad Scapulam*, cap. ii, P. L., vol. i, col. 699; written about 212.

[2] *Contra Celsum*, lib. vii, cap. xxvi.

as follows: "God commanded that those who did not obey his priests or hearken to his judges,[1] appointed for the time, should be slain. Then indeed they were slain with the sword, while the circumcision of the flesh was yet in force; but now that circumcision has begun to be of the spirit among God's faithful servants, the proud and contumacious are slain with the sword of the spirit by being cast out of the Church."[2]

The Bishop of Carthage, who was greatly troubled by stubborn schismatics, and men who violated every moral principle of the Gospel, felt that the greatest punishment he could inflict was excommunication.

When Lactantius wrote his *Divinæ Institutiones* in 308, he was too greatly impressed by the outrages of the pagan persecutions not to protest most strongly against the use of force in matters of conscience. He writes: "There is no justification for violence and injury, for religion cannot be imposed by force. It is a matter of the will, which must be influenced by words, not by blows. . . . Why then do they rage, and increase instead of lessening their folly? Torture and piety have nothing in common; there is no union possible between truth and violence, justice and cruelty.[3] . . . For they

[1] Deut. xvii. 12.

[2] "Nunc autem, quia circumcisio spiritalis esse apud fideles servos Dei cœpit, spiritali gladio superbi et contumaces necantur, dum de Ecclesia ejiciuntur." *Ep.* lxii, *ad Pomponium*, n. 4, P. L., vol. iii, col. 371. Cf. *De unitate Ecclesiæ*, n. 17 *seq.*; *ibid.*, col. 513 *seq.*

[3] Cf. Pascal, *Lettre provinciale*, xii.

(the persecutors) are aware that there is nothing among men more excellent than religion, and that it ought to be defended with all one's might. But as they are deceived in the matter of religion itself, so also are they in the manner of its defence. For religion is to be defended, not by putting to death, but by dying; not by cruelty but by patient endurance; not by crime but by faith. . . . If you wish to defend religion by bloodshed, by tortures and by crime, you no longer defend it, but pollute and profane it. For nothing is so much a matter of free will as religion." [1]

An era of official toleration began a few years later, when Constantine published the Edict of Milan (313), which placed Christianity and Paganism on practically the same footing. But the Emperor did not always observe this law of toleration, whereby he hoped to re-store the peace of the Empire. A convert to Christian views and policy, he thought it his duty to interfere in the doctrinal and ecclesiastical quarrels of the day; and he claimed the title and assumed the functions of a Bishop in externals. "You are Bishops," he said one day, addressing a number of them, "whose jurisdiction is within the Church; I also am a Bishop, ordained by God to oversee whatever is external to the Church." [2] This

---

[1] "Nam si sanguine, si tormentis religionem defendere velis, jam non defendetur illa, sed polluetur, sed violabitur," etc. *Divin. Institut.*, lib. v, cap. xx.

[2] "Vos quidem, inquit, in iis quæ intra Ecclesiam sunt episcopi estis; ego

assumption of power frequently worked positive harm to the Church, although Constantine always pretended to further her interests.

When Arianism began to make converts of the Christian emperors, they became very bitter toward the Catholic bishops. We are not at all astonished, therefore, that one of the victims of this new persecution, St. Hilary, of Poitiers, expressly repudiated and condemned this régime of violence. He also proclaimed, in the name of ecclesiastical tradition, the principle of religious toleration. He deplored the fact that men in his day believed that they could defend the rights of God and the Gospel of Jesus Christ by worldly intrigue. He writes: "I ask you Bishops to tell me, whose favor did the Apostles seek in preaching the Gospel, and on whose power did they rely to preach Jesus Christ? To-day, alas! while the power of the State enforces divine faith, men say that Christ is powerless. The Church threatens exile and imprisonment; she in whom men formerly believed while in exile and prison, now wishes to make men believe her by force. . . . She is now exiling the very priests who once spread her gospel. What a striking contrast between the Church of the past and the Church of to-day." [1]

vero in iis quæ extra geruntur episcopus a Deo sum constitutus." Eusebius, *Vita Constantini*, lib. iv, cap. xxiv.

[1] "Terret exsiliis et carceribus Ecclesia; credique sibi cogit, quæ exsiliis et carceribus est credita . . . Fugat sacerdotes, quæ fugatis est sacerdotibus propagata . . . Hæc de comparatione traditæ nobis Ecclesiæ, nuncque

This protest is the outcry of a man who had suffered from the intolerance of the civil power, and who had learned by experience how even a Christian state may hamper the liberty of the Church, and hinder the true progress of the Gospel.

To sum up: As late as the middle of the fourth century and even later, all the Fathers and ecclesiastical writers who discuss the question of toleration are opposed to the use of force. To a man they reject absolutely the death penalty and enunciate that principle which was to prevail in the Church down the centuries, *i.e. Ecclesia abhorret a sanguine* [1] (the Church has a horror of bloodshed); and they declare faith must be absolutely free, and conscience a domain wherein violence must never enter. [2]

The stern laws of the Old Testament have been abolished by the New.

deperditæ, res ipsa quæ in oculis omnium est atque ore clamavit." *Liber contra Auxentium*, cap. iv. Written in 365.

[1] "Christianus ne fiat propria voluntate miles, nisi coactus a duce. Habeat gladium, caveat tamen ne criminis sanguinis effusi fiat reus." *Canons of Hippolytus*, in the third or fourth century, no 74–75; Duchesne, *Les origines du culte chrétien*, 2ᵉ ed., p. 309. "Ita neque militare justo licebit," says Lactantius, "neque accusare quemquam crimine capitali, quia nihil distat utrumne ferro an verbo potius occidas; quoniam occisio ipsa prohibetur." *Divin. Institut.*, lib. vi, cap. xx. Cf. the passages quoted from Tertullian, *De Idolatria*, and from Origen, *Contra Celsum*.

[2] "Non est religionis cogere religionem . . . ; sponte, non vi." Tertullian, *loc. cit.* "Non est opus vi et injuria, quia religio cogi non potest." Lactantius, *Divin. Institut.*, lib. v, cap. xx.

CHAPTER II

SECOND PERIOD

From Valentinian I to Theodosius II

The Church and the Criminal Code of the Christian Emperors against Heresy

Constantine considered himself a bishop in externals. His Christian successors inherited this title, and acted in accordance with it. One of them, Theodosius II, voiced their mind when he said that "the first duty of the imperial majesty was to protect the true religion, whose worship was intimately connected with the prosperity of human undertakings."[1]

This concept of the State implied the vigorous prosecution of heresy. We therefore see the Christian emperors severely punishing all those who denied the orthodox faith, or rather their own faith, which they considered rightly or wrongly (sometimes wrongly) the faith of the Church.

---

[1] "Præcipuam imperatoriæ majestatis curam esse perspicimus veræ religionis indaginem, cujus si cultum tenere potuerimus iter prosperitatis humanis aperimus inceptis." Theodosii II, *Novellæ*, tit. iii. (438).

From the reign of Valentinian I, and especially from the reign of Theodosius I, the laws against heretics continued to increase with surprising regularity. We can count as many as sixty-eight enacted in fifty-seven years.[1] They punished every form of heresy, whether it merely differed from the orthodox faith in some minor detail,[2] or whether it resulted in a social upheaval. The penalties differed in severity;[3] *i.e.* exile, confiscation, the inability to transmit property.[4] There were different degrees of exile; from Rome, from the cities, from the Empire.[5] The legislators seemed to think that some sects would die out completely, if they were limited solely to country places. But the severer penalties, like the death penalty, were reserved for those heretics who were disturbers of the public peace, *v.g.* the Manicheans and the Donatists.

[1] On this legislation, cf. Riffel *Geschichtliche Darstellung der Verhaltnisses zwischen Kirche und Staat, von der Gründung der Christenthum bis auf Justinian I*, Mainz, 1836, pp. 656–679; Loening, *Geschichte des deutschen Kirchenrechts*, Strassburg, 1878, vol. i, pp. 95–102; Tanon, *Histoire des tribunaux de l'Inquisition en France*, pp. 127–133.

[2] "Hæreticorum vocabulo continentur et latis adversus eos sanctionibus debent succumbere, qui *vel levi argumento* a judicio catholicæ religionis et tramite detecti fuerint deviare." Law of Arcadius, 395; *Cod. Theodos.*, xvi, v. 28.

[3] "Non omnes eadem austeritate plectendi sunt." Law of 428, *ibid.*, xvi, v. 65.

[4] For instance, the laws of 371, of 381, of 384, of 389, *ibid.*, xvi, v. 3, 7, 13, 18, etc.

[5] The Manicheans banished from Rome, *ibid.*, 67; banished *ab ipso aspectu urbium diversarum*, *ibid.*, 64; banished *ex omni quidem orbe terrarum*, *ibid.*, n. 18 (law of 389).

[6] "Encratites . . . cum Saccoforis sive Hydroparastatis . . . summo supplicio et inexpiabili pœna jubemus affligi." Law of 382, *ibid.*, 9. These were Manichean sects.

The Manicheans, with their dualistic theories, and their condemnation of marriage and its consequences, were regarded as enemies of the State; a law of 428 treated them as criminals "who had reached the highest degree of rascality." [1]

The Donatists, who in Africa had incited the mob of Circumcelliones to destroy the Catholic churches, had thrown that part of the Empire into the utmost disorder. The State could not regard with indifference such an armed revolution. Several laws were passed, putting the Donatists on a par with the Manicheans,[2] and in one instance both were declared guilty of the terrible crime of treason.[3] But the death penalty was chiefly confined to certain sects of the Manicheans.[4] This law did not affect private opinions (except in the case of the Encratites, the Saccophori, and the Hydroparastatæ), but only those who openly practiced this heretical cult.[5] The State did not claim the right of entering the secret recesses of a man's conscience. This law is all the more worthy of remark, inasmuch as Diocletian had legislated more severely against the Manicheans in his Edict of

---

[1] *Ibid.*, 65.

[2] Laws of 407, *ibid.*, 40, 41, 43; law of 428, *ibid.*, 65.

[3] "In mortem quoque inquisitio tendit, nam si in criminibus majestatis licet memoriam accusare defuncti, non immerito et hic debet subire judicium." Law of 407 (*ibid.*, 40), which we will see revived in the Middle Ages.

[4] Law of 382, *ibid.*, 9.

[5] Laws of 410 and 415, *ibid.*, 51 and 56.

287: "We thus decree," he writes Julianus,[1] "against these men, whose doctrines and whose magical arts you have made known to us: the leaders are to be burned with their books; their followers are to be put to death, or sent to the mines." In comparison with such a decree, the legislation of the Christian Emperors was rather moderate.[2]

It is somewhat difficult to ascertain how far these laws were enforced by the various Emperors. Besides we are only concerned with the spirit which inspired them. The State considered itself the protector of the Church, and in this capacity placed its sword at the service of the orthodox faith. It is our purpose to find out what the churchman of the day thought of this attitude of the State.

The religious troubles caused chiefly by three heresies, Manicheism, Donatism, and Priscillianism, gave them ample opportunity of expressing their opinions.

.   .   .   .

The Manicheans, driven from Rome and Milan, took refuge in Africa. It must be admitted that many of them by their depravity merited the full severity of the law. The initiated, or the *elect*, as they were called, gave themselves up to unspeakable crimes. A number of them on being arrested at Carthage confessed immoral

---

[1] Boeking, *Corpus Juris antejustiniani*, vol. i, p. 374.

[2] Justinian, however, made the laws against the Manicheans more severe. His code decreed the death penalty against every Manichean without exception. Cod. Just., book i, tit. v, law ii (487 or 510), *ibid.*, law 12 (527). Cf. Julien Havet, *L'hérésie et le bras séculier au moyen âge*, in his *Œuvres*, Paris, 1896, ii, 121, n. 3.

practices that would not bear repetition, and this de-
bauchery was not peculiar to a few wicked followers,
but was merely the carrying out of the Manichean ritual,
which other heretics likewise admitted.[1]

The Church in Africa was not at all severe in its general
treatment of the sect. St. Augustine, especially, never
called upon the civil power to suppress it. For he could
not forget that he himself had for nine years (373–382),
belonged to this sect, whose doctrines and practices he
now denounced. He writes the Manicheans: "Let those
who have never known the troubles of a mind in search
of the truth proceed against you with vigor. It is impossible for me to do so, for I for years was cruelly tossed
about by your false doctrines, which I advocated and
defended to the best of my ability. I ought to bear
with you now, as men bore with me when I blindly accepted your doctrines."[2] All he did was to hold public
conferences with their leaders, whose arguments he had
no difficulty in refuting.[3]

The conversions obtained in this way were rather
numerous, even if all were not equally sincere. All con-

[1] Augustine, *De hæresibus*, Hæres, 46.

[2] "Illi in vos sæviant qui nesciunt cum quo labore verum inveniatur et
quam difficile caveantur errores . . . Ego autem, qui diu multumque jactatus
. . . omnia illa figmenta . . . et temere credidi et instanter quibus potui
persuasi . . . , sævire in vos non possum," etc. *Contra epistolam Manichæi
quam vocant Fundamenti*, n. 2 et 3.

[3] On St. Augustine's relations with the Manicheans, consult the numerous
works which he devoted to this sect. Cf. Dom Leclerc, *L'Afrique Chrétienne*,
Paris, 1904, vol. ii, pp. 113–122.

verts from the sect were required, like their successors the Cathari of the Middle Ages, to denounce their brethren by name, under the threat of being refused the pardon which their formal retraction merited.[1] This denunciation was what we would call to-day "a service for the public good." We, however, know of no case in which the Church made use of this information to punish the one who had been denounced.

.   .   .   .

Donatism (from Donatus, the Bishop of Casæ Nigræ in Numidia) for a time caused more trouble to the Church than Manicheism.[2] It was more of a schism than a heresy. The election to the see of Carthage of the deacon Cæcilian, who was accused of having handed over the Scriptures to the Roman officials during the persecution of Diocletian, was the occasion of the schism. Donatus and his followers wished this nomination annulled, while their opponents defended its validity. Accordingly, two councils were held to decide the question, one at Rome (313), the other at Arles (314). Both decided against the Donatists; they at once appealed to the Emperor, who confirmed the decrees of the two councils (316). The schismatics in their anger rose in rebellion, and a

---

[1] Cases are cited in the *Admonitio* of St. Augustine, at the beginning of the treatise: *De actis cum Felice Manichæo*, P. L., vol. xlii, col. 510; cf. *Ep.* ccxxxvi.

[2] Dom Leclerc, *L'Afrique Chrétienne*, Paris, 1904, vol. i, ch. iv; vol. ii, ch. vi.

number of them known as Circumcelliones went about stirring the people to revolt. But neither Constantine nor his successors were inclined to allow armed rebellion to go unchallenged. The Donatists were punished to the full extent of the law. They had been the first, re-marks St. Augustine, to invoke the aid of the secular arm. "They met with the same fate as the accusers of Daniel; the lions turned against them." [1]

We need not linger over the details of this conflict, in which crimes were committed on both sides.[2] The Donatists, bitterly prosecuted by the State, declared its action cruel and unjust. St. Optatus thus answers them: "Will you tell me that it is not lawful to defend the rights of God by the death penalty? . . . If killing is an evil, the guilty ones are themselves the cause of it." [3] "It is impossible," you say, "for the State to inflict the death penalty in the name of God." — But was it not in God's name, that Moses,[4] Phinees,[5] and Elias [6] put to death the worshipers of the golden calf, and the apostates of the Old Law?—"These times are altogether different," you reply; "the New Law must not be confounded with the Old.

---

[1] *Ep.* clxxxv, n. 7.

[2] F. Martroye, *Une tentative de révolution sociale en Afrique; Donatistes et Circoncellions* (Revue des Quest. Hist., Oct. 1904, Jan. 1905).

[3] "Quasi in vindictam Dei nullus mereatur occidi . . . Si occidi malum est, mali sui ipsi sunt causa." *De schismate Donatistarum,* lib. iii, cap. vi.

[4] Exod. xxxii. 28.

[5] Numb. xxv. 7–9.

[6] 3 K. 18–40.

Did not Christ forbid St. Peter to use the sword?"[1]   Yes, undoubtedly, but Christ came to suffer, not to defend himself.[2]   The lot of Christians is different from that of Christ.

It is in virtue, therefore, of the Old Law that St. Optatus defends the State's interference in religious questions, and its infliction of the death penalty upon heretics.   This is evidently a different teaching from the doctrine of toleration held by the Fathers of the preceding age.   But the other bishops of Africa did not share his views.

In his dealings with the Donatists, St. Augustine was at first absolutely tolerant, as he had been with the Manicheans.   He thought he could rely upon their good faith, and conquer their prejudices by an honest discussion. "We have no intention," he writes to a Donatist bishop, "of forcing men to enter our communion against their will. I am desirous that the State cease its bitter persecution, but you in turn ought to cease terrorizing us by your band of Circumcelliones. . . . Let us discuss our differences from the standpoint of reason and the sacred Scriptures."[3]

In one of his works, now lost, *Contra partem Donati*, he maintains that it is wrong for the State to force schismatics to come back to the Church.[4]   At the most, he

---

[1] John xviii. 11.

[2] *De Schismate Don.*, cap. vii.

[3] "Ut omnes intelligant non hoc esse propositi mei ut inviti homines ad cujusquam communionem cogantur.   Cesset a nostris partibus terror temporalium potestatum; cesset etiam a vestris partibus terror congregatorum Circumcellionum," etc.   *Ep.* xxiii, n. 7.

[4] "Sunt duo libri mei quorum titulus est *Contra partem Donati.*   In

was ready to admit the justice of the law of Theodosius, which imposed a fine of ten gold pieces upon those schismatics who had committed open acts of violence. But no man was to be punished by the State for private heretical opinions.[1]

The imperial laws were carried out in some cities of North Africa, because many of St. Augustine's colleagues did not share his views. Many Donatists were brought back to the fold by these vigorous measures. St. Augustine, seeing that in some cases the use of force proved more beneficial than his policy of absolute toleration, changed his views, and formulated his theory of moderate persecution: *temperata severitas*.[2]

Heretics and schismatics, he maintained, were to be regarded as sheep who had gone astray. It is the shepherd's duty to run after them, and bring them back to the fold by using, if occasion require it, the whip and the goad.[3] There is no need of using cruel tortures like the rack, the iron pincers, or sending them to the stake; for flogging is sufficient. Besides this mode of

quorum primo libro dixi, non mihi placere ullius secularis potestatis impetu schismaticos ad communionem violenter arctari." *Retract.*, lib. ii, cap. v.

We wonder how this text escaped the Abbé Martin, who in his *Saint Augustin*, Paris, 1901, p. 373, maintains that the Bishop of Hippo "always denied the principle of toleration."

[1] "Non esse petendum ab imperatoribus ut ipsam hæresim juberent omnino non esse, pænam constituendo eis qui in ea esse voluerint." *Ep.* clxxxv, n. 25.

[2] *Ep.* xciii, n. 10.

[3] "Pertinet ad diligentiam pastoralem . . . inventas ad ovile dominicum, si resistere voluerint, flagellorum terroribus vel etiam doloribus revocare." *Ep.* clxxxv, n. 23.

punishment is not at all cruel, for it is used by school-masters, parents, and even by bishops while presiding as judges in their tribunals.[1]

In his opinion the severest penalty that ought to be inflicted upon the Donatists is exile for their bishops and priests, and fines for their followers. He strongly denounced the death penalty as contrary to Christian charity.[2]

Both the imperial officers and the Donatists themselves objected to this theory.

The officers of the Emperor wished to apply the law in all its rigor, and to sentence the schismatics to death, when they deemed it proper. St. Augustine adjures them, in the name of "Christian and Catholic meekness"[3] not to go to this extreme, no matter how great the crimes of the Donatists had been. "You have penalties enough," he writes, "exile, for instance, without torturing their bodies or putting them to death."[4]

---

[1] "Non extendente eculeo, non sulcantibus ungulis non urentibus flammis, sed virgarum verberibus . . . Qui modus coercitionis a magistris artium liberalium et ab ipsis parentibus, sæpe etiam in judiciis solet ab episcopis adhiberi." *Ep.* cxxxiii, n. 2. Augustine here recommends the tribune Marcellinus to treat his prisoners with the same kindness.

[2] "Non tamen supplicio capitali propter servandam etiam circa indignos mansuetudinem christianam, sed pecuniis damnis propositis et in episcopos vel ministros eorum exsilio constituto." *Ep.* clxxxv, n. 26. "Et magis mansuetudo servatur ut coercitione exsiliorum atque damnorum admoneantur." *Ep.* xciii, n. 10.

[3] "Mansuetudo christiana." *Ep.* clxxxv, n. 26. "Propter catholicam mansuetudinem commendandam." *Ep.* cxxxix, n. 2.

[4] "Sed hoc magis sufficere volumus, ut vivi et nulla corporis parte truncati," etc. *Ep.* cxxxiii, n. 1.

3

And when the proconsul Apringius quoted St. Paul to justify the use of the sword, St. Augustine replied: "The apostle has well said, 'for he beareth not the sword in vain.'[1] But we must carefully distinguish between temporal and spiritual affairs."[2] "Because it is just to inflict the death penalty for crimes against the common law, it does not follow that it is right to put heretics and schismatics to death." "Punish the guilty ones, but do not put them to death." "For," he writes another proconsul, "if you decide upon putting them to death, you will thereby prevent our denouncing them before your tribunal. They will then rise up against us with greater boldness. And if you tell us that we must either denounce them or risk death at their hands, we will not hesitate a moment, but will choose death ourselves."[3]

Despite these impassioned appeals for mercy, some Donatists were put to death. This prompted the schismatics everywhere to deny that the State had any right to inflict the death penalty or any other penalty upon them.[4]

[1] Rom. xiii. 4.

[2] "Sed alia causa est Provinciæ, alia est Ecclesiæ. Illius terribiliter gerenda est administratio, hujus clementer commendanda est mansuetudo." *Ep.* cxxxiv, n. 3.

[3] "Proinde si occidendos in his sceleribus homines putaveritis, deterrebitis nos ne per operam nostram ad vestrum judicium aliquid tale perveniat: quo comperto illi in nostram perniciem licentiore audacia grassabuntur, necessitate nobis impacta et indicta ut etiam occidi ab eis eligamus, quam eos occidendos vestris judiciis ingeramus." *Ep.* c, n. 2; cf. *Ep.* cxxxix, n. 2.

[4] "Non ad Imperatorum potestatem hæc coercenda vel punienda pertinere ebdere." *Contra Epistolam Parmeniani*, lib. i, cap. xvi.

St. Augustine at once undertook to defend the rights of the State. He declared that the death penalty, which on principle he disapproved, might in some instances be lawfully inflicted. Did not the crimes of some of these rebellious schismatics merit the most extreme penalty of the law? "They kill the souls of men, and the State merely tortures their bodies; they cause eternal death, and then complain when the State makes them suffer temporal death." [1]

But this is only an argument *ad hominem*. St. Augustine means to says that, even if the Donatists were put to death, they had no reason to complain. He does not admit, in fact, that they had been cruelly treated. The victims they allege are false martyrs or suicides.[2] He denounces those Catholics who, outside of cases of self-defense, had murdered their opponents.[3]

The State also has the perfect right to impose the lesser penalties of flogging, fines, and exile. "For he (the prince) beareth not the sword in vain," says the Apostle. "For he is God's minister; an avenger to execute wrath upon him that doeth evil." [4] It is not true to claim that St. Paul

---

[1] "Videte qualia faciunt et qualia patiuntur! Occidunt animas, affliguntur in corpore; sempiternas mortes faciunt et temporales se perpeti conqueruntur." *In Joann. Tractat.* xi, cap. xv.

[2] *Ibid.*

[3] "Postremo, etiamsi aliqui nostrorum non christiana moderatione ista faciunt, displicet nobis." *Ep.* lxxxvii, n. 8.

[4] *Rom.* xiii, 4; Augustine, *Contra litteras Petiliani,* lib. ii, cap. lxxxiii-lxxxiv; *Contra Epist. Parmeniani,* lib. i, cap. xvi.

here meant merely the spiritual sword of excommunication.[1] The context proves clearly that he was speaking of the material sword. Schism and heresy are crimes which, like poisoning, are punishable by the State.[2] Princes must render an account to God for the way they govern. It is natural that they should desire the peace of the Church their mother, who gave them spiritual life.[3]

The State, therefore, has the right to suppress heresy, because the public tranquillity is disturbed by religious dissensions.[4] Her intervention also works for the good of individuals. For, on the one hand, there are some sincere but timid souls who are prevented by their environment from abandoning their schism; they are encouraged to return to the fold by the civil power, which frees them from a most humiliating bondage.[5]

On the other hand, there are many schismatics in good

---

[1] "Gladius, vindicta spiritualis quæ excommunicationem operatur." *Contra Epist. Parmeniani, ibid.*

[2] *Ibid.* St. Augustine remarks that the Donatists themselves admitted that the State punished poisoners: "Cur in veneficos vigorem legum exerceri juste fateantur?" His reasoning would prove more than he intended, for poisoners were punishable by death.

[3] "Et quomodo redderent rationem de imperio suo Deo? . . . quia pertinet hoc ad reges sæculi christianos, ut temporibus suis pacatam velint matrem suam Ecclesiam, unde spiritaliter nati sunt." *In Joann. Tractatus* xi, cap. xiv.

[4] "Nostri adversus illicitas et privatas vestrorum violentias . . . a potestatibus ordinatis tuitionem petunt, non qua vos persequantur, sed qua se defendant." *Ep.* lxxxii, n. 8.

[5] *Ep.* clxxxv, n. 13.

faith who would never attain the truth unless they were forced to enter into themselves and examine their false position. The civil power admonishes such souls to abandon their errors; it does not punish them for any crime.[1] The Church's rebellious children are not forced to believe, but are induced by a salutary fear to listen to the true doctrine.[2]

Conversions obtained in this way are none the less sincere. Undoubtedly absolute toleration is best in theory, but in practice a certain amount of coercion is more helpful to souls. We must judge both methods by their fruits.

In a word, St. Augustine was at first, by temperament, an advocate of absolute toleration, but later on experience led him to prefer a mitigated form of coercion. When his opponents objected — using words similar to those of St. Hilary and the early Fathers — that "the true Church suffered persecution, but did not persecute,"[3] he quoted Sara's persecution of

[1] "De vobis autem corripiendis et coercendis habita ratio est, quo potius *admoneremini* ab errore discedere, quam pro scelere *puniremini*." *Ep.* xciii, n. 10.

[2] "Timor pænarum . . . saltem intra claustra cogitationis coercet malam cupiditatem." *Contra litteras Petiliani*, lib. ii, cap. lxxxiii. "Melius est (quis dubitaverit?) ad Deum colendum doctrina homines duci quam pænæ timore vel dolore compelli . . . Sed multis profuit prius timore vel dolore cogi ut postea possent doceri." *Ep.* clxxxv, n. 21. "Terrori utili doctrina salutaris adjungitur." *Ep.* xciii, n. 4.

[3] "Illam vere esse Ecclesiam quæ persecutionem patitur, non quæ facit." *Ep.* clxxxv, n. 10.

Agar.[1] He was wrong to quote the Old Testament as
his authority. But we ought at least be thankful that he
did not cite other instances more incompatible with the
charity of the Gospel. His instinctive Christian horror
of the death penalty kept him from making this mistake.

.   .   .   .

Priscillianism brought out clearly the views current in
the fourth century regarding the punishment due to
heresy. Very little was known of Priscillian until lately;
and despite the publication of several of his works in
1889, he still remains an enigmatical personality.[2] His
erudition and critical spirit were, however, so remarkable,
that an historian of weight declares that henceforth we
must rank him with St. Jerome.[3] But his writings were,
in all probability, far from orthodox. We can easily
find in them traces of Gnosticism and Manicheism. He
was accused of Manicheism although he anathematized
Manes. He was likewise accused of magic. He denied
the charge, and declared that every magician deserved
death,[4] according to Exodus: "Wizards thou shalt not

[1] *Ibid.*, n. 11.

[2] On Priscillian and his work, cf. *Priscilliani quod superest*, ed. G. Schepps,
1889, in the *Corpus scriptorum latinorum*, published by the Academy of Vienna,
vol. xviii; Aimé Puéch, in the *Journal des savants*, Feb., April, and May,
1891; Dom Leclerc, *L'Espagne Chrétienne*, Paris, 1906, ch. iii (the author
follows Puéch step by step, and often copies him word for word); Friedrich
Paret, *Priscillianus*, Würzburg, 1891; Kuenstle, *Antipriscilliana*, Frieburg,
1905.

[3] Puéch, p. 121. Cf. Leclerc, p. 164.

[4] Schepps, *op. cit.*, p. 24.

suffer to live." [1]   He little dreamt when he wrote these
words that he was pronouncing his own death sentence.
Although condemned by the council of Saragossa (380),
he nevertheless became bishop of Abila.   Later on he
went to Rome to plead his cause before Pope Damasus,
but was refused a hearing.   He next turned to St. Ambrose, who likewise would not hearken to his defense.[2]
In 385 a council was assembled at Bordeaux to consider
his case anew.   He at once appealed to the Emperor,
"so as not to be judged by the bishops," as Sulpicius
Severus tells us,[3] a fatal mistake which cost him his
life.

He was then conducted to the Emperor at Treves,
where he was tried before a secular court, bishops Idacius
and Ithacius appearing as his accusers.   St. Martin, who
was in Treves at the time, was scandalized that a purely
ecclesiastical matter should be tried before a secular
judge.   His biographer, Sulpicius Severus, tells us [4] "that
he kept urging Ithacius to withdraw his accusation."   He
also entreated Maximus not to shed the blood of these
unfortunates, for the bishops could meet the difficulty

[1] Exod. xxii. 18.

[2] Schepps, op. cit., p. 41.   Priscillian wrote an apology to the Pope entitled *Liber ad Damasum*, *ibid*., p. 39.   Cf. Sulp. Sev. *Chronicon*. ii, P. L.,
vol. xx, col. 155–159; *Dialogi*, iii, 11–23, *ibid*., col. 217–219.

[3] Chronicon, *loc. cit.*   It is worthy of remark that Priscillian in his *Liber
ad Damasum* declared that *in causa fidei* he preferred to be judged by the
Bishops rather than by the civil magistrates.

[4] Sulp. Sev., *loc. cit.*

by driving the heretics from the churches. He asserted that to make the State judge in a matter of doctrine was a cruel, unheard-of violation of the divine law.

As long as St. Martin remained in Treves, the trial was put off, and before he left the city he made Maximus promise not to shed the blood of Priscillian and his companions. But soon after St. Martin's departure, the Emperor, instigated by the relentless bishops Rufus and Magnus, forgot his promise of mercy, and entrusted the case to the prefect Evodius, a cruel and hard-hearted official. Priscillian appeared before him twice, *and was convicted of the crime of magic.* He was made to confess under torture that he had given himself up to magical arts, and that he had prayed naked before women in midnight assemblies. Evodius declared him guilty, and placed him under guard until the evidence had been presented to the Emperor. After reading the records of the trial, Maximus declared that Priscillian and his companions deserved death. Ithacius, perceiving how unpopular he would make himself with his fellow-bishops, if he continued to play the part of prosecutor in a capital case, withdrew. A new trial was therefore ordered. This subterfuge of the Bishop did not change matters at all, because by this time the case had been practically settled. Patricius, the imperial treasurer, presided at the second trial. On his findings, Priscillian and some of his followers were condemned to death. Others of the sect were exiled.

This deplorable trial is often brought forward as an argument against the Church. It is important, therefore, for us to ascertain its precise character, and to discover who was to blame for it.

The real cause of Priscillian's condemnation was the accusation of heresy made by a Catholic bishop. Technically, he was tried in the secular courts for the crime of magic, but the State could not condemn him to death on any other charge, once Ithacius had ceased to appear against him.

It is right, therefore, to attribute Priscillian's death to the action of an individual bishop, but it is altogether unjust to hold the Church responsible.[1]

In this way contemporary writers viewed the matter. The Christians of the fourth century were all but unanimous, says an historian,[2] in denouncing the penalty inflicted in this famous trial. Sulpicius Severus, despite his horror of the Priscillianists, repeats over and over again that their condemnation was a deplorable example;[3] he even stigmatizes it as a crime. St. Ambrose speaks

---

[1] Bernays, *Ueber die Chronik des Sulp. Sev.*, Berlin, 1861, p. 13, was the first to point out that Priscillian was condemned not for heresy, but for the crime of magic. This is the commonly received view to-day. Cf. E. Loening, *Geschichte des deutschen Kirchenrechts*, vol. i, p. 97, n. 3. Aimé Puéch and Dom Leclerc, *loc. cit.*

[2] Puéch, *loc. cit.*, p. 250.

[3] We have also a letter of the Emperor Maximus to Pope Siricius on the trial, in which he says: "Hujusmodi non modo facta turpia, verum etiam fœda dictu proloqui sine rubore non possumus." Migne, P. L., vol. xiii, col. 592 sq.

just as strongly.[1]   We know how vehemently St. Martin
disapproved of the attitude of Ithaciüs and the Emperor
Maximus; he refused for a long time to hold communion
with the bishops who had in any way taken part in the
condemnation of Priscillian.[2]   Even in Spain, where public opinion was so divided, Ithacius was everywhere
denounced.   At first some defended him on the plea of
the public good, and on account of the high authority of
those who judged the case.   But after a time he became
so generally hated that, despite his excuse that he merely
followed the advice of others, he was driven from his
bishopric.[3]   This outburst of popular indignation proves
conclusively, that if the Church did call upon the aid of
the secular arm in religious questions, she did not author-
ize it to use the sword against heretics.[4]

The blood of Priscillian was the seed of Priscillianism.
But his disciples certainly went further than their master;
they became thorough-going Manicheans.   This explains
St. Jerome's[5] and St. Augustine's[6] strong denunciations
of the Spanish heresy.   The gross errors of the Priscillian-

[1] Cf. Gams, *Kirchengeschichte von Spanien*, vol. ii, p. 382.

[2] Sulpicius Severus, *Dialogi*, iii, 11–13.

[3] Sulp. Sev., *Chronicon, loc. cit.*

[4] In a discourse delivered at Rome in 389, the pagan panegyrist, Pacatus,
expresses his horror for those episcopal executioners, "who were present at
the tortures of the accused, and feasted their eyes and ears with their
groans and sufferings."   *Panegyrisi veteres*, ed. Baerhens, Leipzig, 1874,
p. 217.

[5] *De Viris illustribus*, 121–123.

[6] *De hæresibus*, cap. 70.

ists in the fifth century attracted in 447 the attention
of Pope St. Leo. He reproaches them for breaking the
bonds of marriage, rejecting all idea of chastity, and con-
travening all rights, human and divine. He evidently
held Priscillian responsible for all these teachings. That
is why he rejoices in the fact that "the secular princes,
horrified at this sacrilegious folly, executed the author
of these errors with several of his followers." He even
declares that this action of the State is helpful to the
Church. He writes: "The Church, in the spirit of Christ,
ought to denounce heretics, but should never put them
to death; still the severe laws of Christian princes redound
to her good, for some heretics through fear of punishment are won back to the true faith." [1] St. Leo in this
passage is rather severe. While he does not yet require
the death penalty for heresy, he accepts it in the name
of the public good. It is greatly to be feared that the
churchmen of the future will go a great deal further.

The Church is endeavoring to state her position accu-

[1] "Merito patres nostri sub quorum temporibus hæresis hæc nefanda
prorupit, per totum mundum instanter egere ut impius furor ab universa
Ecclesia pelleretur. Quando etiam mundi principes ita hanc sacrilegam
amentiam detestati sunt, ut auctorem ejus cum plerisque discipulis legum
publicarum ense prosternerent. Videbant enim omnem curam honestatis
auferri, omnem conjugiorum copulam solvi, simulque divinum jus humanum-
que subverti, si hujusmodi hominibus usquam vivere cum tali professione
licuisset. Profuit ista districtio ecclesiasticæ lenitati, quæ etsi sacerdotali
contenta judicio, cruentas refugit ultiones, severis tamen christianorum
principum constitutionibus adjuvatur, dum ad spiritale nonnunquam recur-
runt remedium, qui timent corporale supplicium." *Ep.* xv, *ad Turribium*,
P. L., vol. liv, col. 679–680.

rately on the suppression of heresy. She declares that
nothing will justify her shedding of human blood. This
is evident from the conduct and writings of St. Augustine,
St. Martin, St. Ambrose, St. Leo (*cruentas refugit ultiones*),
and Ithacius himself. But to what extent should she
accept the aid of the civil power, when it undertakes to
defend her teachings by force?

Some writers, like St. Optatus of Mileve, and Priscillian, later on the victim of his own teaching, believed
that the Christian state ought to use the sword against
heretics guilty of crimes against the public welfare; and
strangely enough, they quote the Old Testament as their
authority. Without giving his approval to this theory,
St. Leo the Great did not condemn the practical applica-
tion of it in the case of the Priscillianists. The Church,
according to him, while assuming no responsibility for
them, reaped the benefit of the rigorous measures taken
by the State.

But most of the Bishops absolutely condemned the
infliction of the death penalty for heresy, even if the heresy
was incidentally the cause of social disturbances. Such
was the view of St. Augustine,[1] St. Martin, St. Ambrose,
many Spanish bishops, and a bishop of Gaul named
Theognitus;[2] in a word, of all who disapproved of the con-

---

[1] Corrigi eos volumus, non necari; nec disciplinam circa eos negligi volumus,
nec suppliciis quibus digni sunt exerceri.   *Ep.* c, n. 1.

[2] Cf. Sulpicius Severus, *Dialogi*, iii, 12, *loc. cit.*, col. 218.

demnation of Priscillian. As a rule, they protested in the name of Christian charity; they voiced the new spirit of the Gospel of Christ. At the other extremity of the Catholic world, St. John Chrysostom re-echoes their teaching. "To put a heretic to death," he says, "is an unpardonable crime." [1]

But in view of the advantage to the Church, either from the maintenance of the public peace, or from the conversion of individuals, the State may employ a certain amount of force against heretics.

"God forbids us to put them to death," continues St. Chrysostom, "just as he forbade the servants to gather up the cockle," [2] because he regards their conversion as possible; but he does not forbid us doing all in our power to prevent their public meetings, and their preaching of false doctrine.[3] St. Augustine adds that they may be punished by fine and exile.

---

[1] St. John Chrysostom remarks that the Savior forbade the servants to gather up the cockle in the field of the householder, and adds:

Τοῦτο δὲ ἔλεγε, κωλύων πολέμους γίνεσθαι καὶ αἵματα καὶ σφάγας. Οὐ γὰρ δεῖ ʼἀναρεῖν αἱρετικον ἐπεὶ πόλεμος ἄσπονδος εἰς τὴν οἰκουμένην ἔμελλεν εἰσάγεσθαι. *Homilia* xlvi, *in Matthæum*, cap. i.

[2] *Ibid.*, cap. ii.

[3] "Cæterum intra Ecclesiam potestates necessariæ non essent nisi ut quod non prævalet sacerdos efficere per doctrinæ sermonem, potestas hoc imperet per disciplinæ terrorem (cf. the *diligentia disciplinæ* of St. Augustine, *Retractat.*, lib. ii, cap. v). Sic per regnum terrenum cæleste regnum proficit, ut qui intra Ecclesiam positi contra fidem et disciplinam quam Ecclesiæ humilitas exercere non prævalet, cervicibus superborum potestas principalis imponat et ut venerationem mereatur virtute potestatis impertiat . . . Cognoscant principes sæculi Deo debere se rationem reddere propter Ecclesiam

To this extent the churchmen of the day accepted the aid of the secular arm. Nor were they content with merely accepting it. They declared that the State had not only the right to help the Church in suppressing heresy, but that she was in duty bound to do so. In the seventh century, St. Isidore of Seville discusses this question in practically the same terms as St. Augustine.[1]

quam a Christo tuendam suscipiunt (cf. Augustine, *In Joann. Tractat.* xi, cap. xiv). Nam sive augeatur pax et disciplina Ecclesiæ per fideles principes, sive solvatur, ille ab eis rationem exiget, qui eorum potestati suam Ecclesiam credidit." *Sententiarum*, lib. iii, cap. l, n. 4–6, P. L., vol. lxxxiii, col. 723.

[1] We think it important to give Lea's résumé of this period. It will show how a writer, although trying to be impartial, may distort the facts: "It was only sixty-two years after the slaughter of Priscillian and his followers had excited so much horror, that Leo I, when the heresy seemed to be reviving, in 447, not only justified the act, but declared that *if the followers of heresy so damnable were allowed to live*, there would be an end to human and divine law. The final step had been taken, and *the Church was definitely pledged to the suppression of heresy at whatever cost.* It is impossible not to attribute to ecclesiastical influence the successive Edicts by which, from the time of Theodosius the Great, persistence in heresy was punished by death. A powerful impulse to this development is to be found in the responsibility which grew upon the Church from its connection with the State. When it could influence the monarch and procure from him Edicts condemning heretics to exile, to the mines, *and even to death*, it felt that God had put into its hands powers to be exercised and not to be neglected" (vol. i, p. 215). If we read carefully the words of St. Leo (p. 27, note 1), we shall see that the Emperors are responsible for the words that Lea ascribes to the Pope. It is hard to understand how he can assert that the imperial Edicts decreeing the death penalty are due to ecclesiastical influence, when we notice that nearly all the churchmen of the day protested against such a penalty.

CHAPTER III

THIRD PERIOD.

FROM 1100 TO 1250

THE REVIVAL OF THE MANICHEAN HERESIES IN THE MIDDLE AGES

FROM the sixth to the eleventh century, heretics, with the exception of certain Manichean sects, were hardly ever persecuted.[1] In the sixth century, for instance, the Arians lived side by side with the Catholics, under the protection of the State, in a great many Italian cities, especially in Ravenna and Pavia.[2]

During the Carlovingian period, we come across a few heretics, but they gave little trouble.

The *Adoptianism* of Elipandus, Archbishop of Toledo, and Felix, Bishop of Urgel, was abandoned by its authors,

---

[1] In 556, Manicheans were put to death at Ravenna, in accordance with the laws of Justinian. *Agnelli liber pontificalis ecclesiæ Ravennatis*, cap. lxxix, in *Monum. Germaniæ, Rerum Langobard. Scriptores*, p. 331.

[2] "Hujus temporibus pene per omnes civitates regni ejus (Rotharici) duo episcopi erant, unus catholicus et alter arianus. In civitate Ticinensi usque nunc ostenditur ubi arianus episcopus apud basilican Sancti Eusebii residens baptisterium habuit, cum tamen ecclesiæ catholicæ alius episcopus resideret." Pauli diacon., *Histor. Langobard.*, lib. iv, cap. xlii, *Mon. Germ., Rer. Langobard. SS.*, p. 134. We may still visit at Ravenna the Arian and Catholic baptisteries of the sixth century. Cf. Gregorii Magni *Dialogi*, iii, cap. xxix, *Mon. Germ., ibid.*, pp. 534–535.

after it had been condemned by Pope Adrian I, and several provincial councils.[1]

A more important heresy arose in the ninth century. Godescalcus, a monk of Orbais, in the diocese of Soissons, taught that Jesus Christ did not die for all men. His errors on predestination were condemned as heretical by the council of Mainz (848) and Quierzy (849); and he himself was sentenced to be flogged and then imprisoned for life in the monastery of Hautvilliers.[2] But this punishment of flogging was a purely ecclesiastical penalty. Archbishop Hincmar in ordering it declared that he was acting in accordance with the rule of St. Benedict, and a canon of the Council of Agde.[3]

The imprisonment to which Godescalcus was subjected was likewise a monastic punishment. Practically, it did not imply much more than the confinement strictly required by the rules of his convent. It is interesting to note that imprisonment for crime is of purely ecclesias-

[1] Einhard: *Annales*, ann. 792, in the *Mon. Germ. SS.*, vol. i, p. 179.

[2] "In nostra parochia . . . monasteriali custodiæ mancipatus est." Hincmar's letter to Pope Nicholas I, *Hincmari Opera*, ed. Sirmond, Paris, 1645, vol. ii, p. 262.

[3] "Verberum vel corporis castigatione . . . coercendus, says Hincmar, secundum regulam sancti Benedicti." *De non trina deitate*, cap. xviii, in *Hincmari Opera*, vol. i, p. 552. The rule of St. Benedict provided for the *acrior correctio, id est ut verberum vindicta in eum* (monachum) *procedat*, cap. xxviii; cf. *Concilium Agathense*, ann. 506, cap. xxviii: "In monachis quoque par sententiæ forma servetur: quos si verborum increpatio non emendaverit, etiam *verberibus* statuimus coerceri." Recall what St. Augustine said of the use of flogging in the episcopal tribunals of his time.

tical origin. The Roman law knew nothing of it. It was at first a penalty peculiar to monks and clerics, although later on laymen also were subjected to it.

About the year 1000, the Manicheans under various names came from Bulgaria, and spread over western Europe.[1] We meet them about this time in Italy, Spain, France, and Germany. Public sentiment soon became bitter against them, and they became the victims of a general, though intermittent, persecution. Orléans, Arras, Cambrai, Châlons, Goslai, Liège, Soissons, Ravenna, Monteforte, Asti, and Toulouse became the field of their propaganda, and often the place of their execution. Several heretics like Peter of Bruys, Henry of Lausanne, Arnold of Brescia, and Éon de l'Étoile (Eudo de Stella), likewise troubled the Church, who to stop their bold propaganda used force herself, or permitted the State or the people to use it.

It was at Orléans in 1022 that Catholics for the first time during this period treated heretics with cruelty. An historian of the time assures us that this cruelty was due to both king and people: *regis jussu et universæ plebis consensu.*[2] King Robert, dreading the disastrous effects of heresy upon his kingdom, and the consequent

---

[1] Cf. C. Schmidt, *Histoire et doctrine de la secte des Cathares*, vol. i, pp. 16–54, 82.

[2] Raoul Glaber, *Hist.*, lib. iii, cap. viii, *Hist. des Gaules*, vol. x, p. 38. For other authorities consult Julien Havet, *L'hérésie et le bras séculier au moyen âge*, in his *Œuvres*, Paris, 1896, vol. ii, pp. 128–130.

4

loss of souls,[1] sent thirteen of the principal clerics and laymen of the town to the stake.[2] It has been pointed out that this penalty was something unheard-of at the time. "Robert was therefore the originator of the punishment which he decreed."[3] It might be said, however, that this penalty originated with the people, and that the king merely followed out the popular will.

For, as an old chronicler tells us, this execution at Orléans was not an isolated fact; in other places the populace hunted out heretics, and burned them outside the city walls.[4]

Several years later, the heretics who swarmed into the diocese of Châlons attracted the attention of the Bishop of the city, who was puzzled how to deal with them. He consulted Wazo, the Bishop of Liège, who tells us that the French were "infuriated" against heretics.[5] These words would seem to prove that the heretics of the day were prosecuted more vigorously than the documents

---

[1] "Quoniam et ruinam patriæ revera et animarum metuebat interitum." Raoul Glaber, *loc. cit.*

[2] *Ep.* Johannis monachi Floriacensis, in the *Hist. des Gaules*, vol. x, p. 498.

[3] Julien Havet, *op. cit.*, pp. 128–129.

It is not probable that the King was inspired by the laws of the empire against the Manicheans.

[4] *Cartulaire de l'abbaye de Saint-Père de Chartres*, ed. Guérard, vol. i, p. 108 and seq.; cf. *Hist. des Gaules*, vol. x, p. 539.

[5] "Præcipitem Francigenarum rabiem." Anselmi, *Gesta episcop. Leodiensium*, cap. lxiii, *Mon. Germaniæ SS.*, vol. vii, p. 228.

we possess go to show. It is probable that the Bishop of Châlons detested the "fury" of the persecutors. We will see later on the answer that Wazo sent him.

During the Christmas holidays of 1051 and 1052, a number of Manicheans or Cathari, as they were called, were executed at Goslar, after they had refused to renounce their errors. Instead of being burned, as in France, "they were hanged."

These heretics were executed by the orders of Henry III, and in his presence. But the chronicler of the event remarks that every one applauded the Emperor's action, because he had prevented the spread of the leprosy of heresy, and thus saved many souls.[1]

Twenty-five years later, in 1076 or 1077, a Catharan of the district of Cambrai appeared before the Bishop of Cambrai and his clerics, and was condemned as a heretic. The Bishop's officers and the crowd at once seized him, led him outside the city's gates, and while he knelt and calmly prayed, they burned him at the stake.[2]

A little while before this the Archbishop of Ravenna accused a man named Vilgard of heresy, but what the

---

[1] "Imperator . . . quosdam hæreticos . . . consensu cunctorum, ne hæretica scabies latius serpens plures inficeret, in patibulo suspendi jussit." HERIMAN, Aug. *Chronicon*, ann. 1052, *Mon. Germ. SS.*, vol. v, p. 130. Cf. LAMBERTI, *Annales*, 1053, *ibid.*, p. 155.

[2] Chronicon S. Andreæ Camerac., iii, 3, in the *Mon. Germ. SS.*, vol. vii, p. 540.

We have a letter of Gregory VII in which he denounces the irregular character of this execution. *Ibid.*, p. 540, n. 31.

result of the trial was, we cannot discover. But we do know that during this period other persons were prosecuted for heresy, and that they were beheaded or sent to the stake.[1]

At Monteforte near Asti, the Cathari had, about 1034, an important settlement. The Marquis Mainfroi, his brother the Bishop of Asti, and several noblemen of the city, united to attack the castrum; they captured a number of heretics, and on their refusing to return to the orthodox faith, they sent them to the stake.[2]

Other followers of the sect were arrested by the officers of Eriberto, the Archbishop of Milan, who endeavored to win them back to the Catholic faith. Instead of being converted, they tried to spread their heresy throughout the city. The civil magistrates, realizing their corrupting influence, had a stake erected in the public square with a cross in front of it; and in spite of the Archbishop's protest, they required the heretics either to reverence the cross they had blasphemed, or to enter the flaming pile. Some were converted, but the majority of them, covering their faces with their hands, threw themselves into the flames, and were soon burned to ashes.[3]

---

[1] Raoul Glaber, *Hist.*, lib. ii, cap. xii, *Hist. des Gaules*, vol. x, p. 23.

[2] Raoul Glaber, *ibid.*, lib. iv, cap. ii, *Hist. des Gaules*, vol. x, p. 45.

[3] "Quod cum civitatis hujus majores laici comperissent, rogo mirabili accenso, cruce Domini ab altere parte erecta, Heriberto nolente, illis omnibus eductis," etc. LANDULPHE, *Historia Mediolan.*, lib. ii, cap. xxvii, in the *Mon. Germaniæ SS.*, vol. viii, pp. 65–66.

Few details have come down to us concerning the fate of the Manicheans arrested at this time in Sardinia and in Spain; *exterminati sunt,* says a chronicler.[1]

The Cathari of Toulouse were also arrested, and executed: *et ipsi destructi.*[2] A few years later, in 1114, the Bishop of Soissons arrested a number of heretics, and cast them into prison until he could make up his mind how to deal with them. While he was absent at Beauvais, asking the advice of his fellow-bishops assembled there in council, the populace, fearing the weakness of the clergy, attacked the prison, dragged forth the heretics, and burned them at the stake.[3] Guibert de Nogent does not blame them in the least. He simply calls attention to "the just zeal" shown on this occasion by "the people of God," to stop the spread of heresy.

In 1144 the Bishop of Liège, Adalbero II, compelled a number of Cathari to confess their heresy; "he hoped," he said, "with the grace of God to lead them to repent." But the populace, less kindly-hearted, rushed upon them,

---

[1] "Exterminati sunt," says Raoul Glaber, *Hist.,* lib. ii, cap. xii, *Hist. des Gaules,* vol. x, p. 23.

Exterminati may mean *banished* as well as *put to death.* The context, however, seems to refer to the death penalty.

[2] Adhémar de Chabannes, *Chron.,* lib. iii, cap. lix, in the *Mon. Germ. SS.,* vol. iv, p. 143.

[3] "Interea perreximus ad Belvacense concilium consulturi episcopos quid facto opus esset. Sed fidelis interim populus, *clericalem verens mollitiem* (notice these words on "the weakness of the clergy") concurrit ad ergastulum, rapit, et subjecto eis extra urbem igne pariter concremavit." Guibert de Nogent, *De vita sua,* lib. i, cap. xv, *Hist. des Gaules,* vol. xii, p. 366.

and proceeded to burn them at the stake; the Bishop had the greatest difficulty to save the majority of them. He then wrote to Pope Lucius II asking him what was the proper penalty for heresy.[1] We do not know what answer he received.

About the same time, a similar dispute arose between the Archbishop and the people of Cologne regarding two or three heretics who had been arrested and condemned. The clergy asked them to return to the church. But the people, "moved by an excess of zeal," says an historian of the time, seized them, and despite the Archbishop and his clerics led them to the stake. "And marvelous to relate," continues the chronicler, "they suffered their tortures at the stake, not only with patience, but with joy."[2]

One of the most famous heretics of the twelfth century was Peter of Bruys. His hostility toward the clergy helped his propaganda in Gascony. To show his contempt for the Catholic religion, he burned a great number of crosses one Good Friday, and roasted meat in the

---

[1] "Hos turba turbulenta raptos incendio tradere deputavit; sed nos, Dei favente misericordia, pene omnes ab instanti supplicio, de ipsis meliora sperantes, vix tamen eripuimus," etc. Letter of the church of Liège to Pope Lucius II, in MARTÈNE, *Amplissima collectio*, vol. i, col. 776–777.

[2] "Cum per triduum essent admoniti et resipiscere noluissent, rapti sunt *a populis nimio zelo permotis, nobis* (the Archbishop and his tribunal) *tamen invitis*, et in ignem positi atque cremati." Letter of Evervin, provost of Steinfeld to St. Bernard, cap. ii, in *Bernardi Opera*, MIGNE, P. L., vol. clxxxii, col. 677.

flames. This angered the people against him. He was seized and burned at St. Giles about the year 1126.[1]

Henry of Lausanne was his most illustrious disciple. We have told the story of his life elsewhere.[2] St. Bernard opposed him vigorously, and succeeded in driving him from the chief cities of Toulouse and the Albigeois, where he carried on his harmful propaganda. He was arrested a short time afterwards (1145 or 1146), and sentenced to life-imprisonment either in one of the prisons of the Archbishop, or in some monastery of Toulouse.

Arnold of Brescia busied himself more with questions of discipline than with dogma; the only reforms he advocated were social reforms.[3] He taught that the clergy should not hold temporal possessions, and he endeavored to drive the papacy from Rome. In this conflict, which involved the property of ecclesiastics and the temporal power of the Church, he was, although successful for a time, finally vanquished.[4] St. Bernard invoked the aid of the secular arm to rid France of him. Later on Pope

[1] "Sed post rogum Petri de Bruys, quo apud S. Ægidium zelus fidelium flammas dominicæ crucis ab eo succensas eum cremando, ultus est." Peter the Venerable, Letter to the Archbishops of Arles and Embrum, etc., in the *Hist. des Gaules*, vol. xv, p. 640.

[2] *Vie de saint Bernard*, 1st edit., Paris, 1895, vol. ii, pp. 218–233.

[3] For details concerning Arnold of Brescia, cf. Vacandard, *Vie de Saint Bernard*, vol. ii, pp. 235–258, 465–469.

[4] "Dicebat nec clericos proprietatem, nec episcopos regalia, nec monachos possessiones habentes aliqua ratione salvari posse; cuncta hæc principis esse, ab ejusque beneficentia in usum tantum laicorum cedere oportere." Otto Frising., *Gesta Friderici*, lib. ii, cap. xx. Cf. *Historia Pontificalis*, in the *Mon. Germ. SS.*, vol. xx, p. 538.

Eugenius III excommunicated him.   He was executed
during the pontificate of Adrian IV, in 1155.   He was arrested in the city of Rome after a riot which was quelled
by the Emperor Frederic, now the ally of the Pope, and
condemned to be strangled by the prefect of the city.
His body was then burned, and his ashes thrown into the
Tiber, "for fear," says a writer of the time, "the people
would gather them up, and honor them as the ashes of a
martyr." [1]

In 1148, the Council of Reims judged the case of the
famous Éon de l'Étoile (Eudo de Stella).   This strange
individual had acquired a reputation for sanctity while
living a hermit's life.   One day, struck by the words of the
liturgy, *Per Eum qui venturus est judicare vivos et mortuos*,
he conceived the idea that he was the Son of God.   He
made some converts among the lowest classes, who, not
content with denying the faith, soon began to pillage the
churches.   Éon was arrested for causing these disturbances, and was brought before Pope Eugenius III, then
presiding over the Council of Reims.   He was judged
insane, and in all kindness was placed under the charge
of Suger, the Abbot of St. Denis.   He was confined to a
monastery, where he died soon after.[2]

[1] Boso, *Vita Hadriani*, in Watterich, *Romanorum pontificum Vitæ*, vol. ii,
pp. 326 et 330; Otto Frising., *Gesta Friderici*, II, 21 and 23; Vincent de Prague,
in Watterich, vol. ii, p. 349, note; Geroch Reichersberg, *De Investigatione
Antichristi*, lib. i, cap. xlii; cf. p. 50, note.

[2] *Continuatio Gemblacensis*, ad ann. 1146; *Continuatio Præmonstratensis*,

Strangely enough, some of his disciples persisted in believing in him; "they preferred to die rather than renounce their belief," says an historian of the time. They were handed over to the secular arm, and perished at the stake.[1] In decreeing this penalty, the civil power was undoubtedly influenced by the example of Robert the Pious.

It is easy to determine the responsibility of the Church, *i.e.* her bishops and priests, in this series of executions (1020 to 1150). At Orléans, the populace and the king put the heretics to death; the historians of the time tell us plainly that the clergy merely declared the orthodox doctrine. It was the same at Goslar. At Asti, the Bishop's name appears with the names of the other nobles who had the Cathari executed, but it seems certain that he exercised no special authority in the case. At Milan, the civil magistrates themselves, against the Archbishop's protest, gave the heretics the choice between reverencing the cross, and the stake.

At Soissons, the populace, feeling certain that the clergy would not resort to extreme measures, profited by the Bishop's absence to burn the heretics they detested. At

---

ad annum 1148, in the *Mon. Germ. SS.*, vol. vi, pp. 452–454; Robert Du Mont, *Chronicon*, ad ann. 1148, ed. Delisle, vol. i, p. 248; William of Newbridge, *Chron.*, lib. i, cap. xix; Otto Frising, *Gesta Frederici*, lib. i, cap. liv–lv. Cf. Schmidt, *Histoire des Cathares*, vol. i, p. 49.

[1] "Curiæ prius et postea ignibus traditi ardere potius quam ad vitam corrigi maluerunt." William of Newbridge, i, xix.

Liège, the Bishop managed to save a few heretics from the violence of the angry mob. At Cologne, the Archbishop was not so successful; the people rose in their anger and burned the heretics before they could be tried. Peter of Bruys, and the Manichean at Cambrai were both put to death by the people. Arnold of Brescia, deserted by fortune, fell a victim to his political adversaries; the prefect of Rome was responsible for his execution.[1]

In a word, in all these executions, the Church either kept aloof, or plainly manifested her disapproval.

During this period, we know of only one bishop, Théodwin of Liège, who called upon the secular arm to punish heretics.[2] This is all the more remarkable because his predecessor Wazo and his successor, Adalbero II, both

[1] The case of Arnold, however, is not so clear. The *Annales Augustani minores* (*Mon. Germ. SS.*, vol. x, p. 8) declare that the Pope hanged the rebel. Another anonymous writer (cf. Tanon, *Hist. des tribunaux de l'Ing. en France*, p. 456, n. 2) says, with more probability, that Adrian merely degraded him. According to Otto of Freisingen (*Mon. Germ. SS.*, vol. xx, p. 404), Arnold *principis examini reservatus est, ad ultimum a præfecto Urbis ligno adactus.* Finally, Geroch de Reichersberg tells us (*De investigatione Antichristi*, lib. i, cap. xlii, ed. Scheibelberger, 1875, pp. 88–89) that Arnold was taken from the ecclesiastical prison and put to death by the servants of the Roman prefect. In any case, politics rather than religion was the cause of his death.

[2] In 1050, two years after the death of Wazo, he wrote to the king of France, asking him to assemble a council to judge confessed heretics: "Quamquam hujusmodi homines nequaquam oporteat audiri; neque tam est pro illis concilium celebrandum quam de illorum supplicio exquirendum." *Hist. des Gaules*, vol. xi, p. 498. Do these words imply the death penalty? It seems not, for in that case he would not have said: *de supplicio exquirendum.*

protested in word and deed against the cruelty of both sovereign and people.

Wazo, his biographer tells us, strongly condemned the execution of heretics at Goslar, and had he been there would have acted as St. Martin of Tours in the case of Priscillian.[1] His reply to the letter of the Bishop of Châlons reveals his inmost thoughts on the subject. "To use the sword of the civil authority," he says, "against the Manicheans,[2] is contrary to the spirit of the Church, and the teaching of her divine founder. The Savior ordered us to let the cockle grow with the good grain until the harvest time, lest in uprooting the cockle we uproot also the wheat with it.[3] Moreover, continues Wazo, those who are cockle to-day may be converted to-morrow, and be garnered in as wheat at the harvest time. Therefore they should be allowed to live. The only penalty we should use against them is excommunication."[4]

The Bishop of Liège, quoting this parable of Christ which St. Chrysostom had quoted before him, interprets it in a more liberal fashion than the Bishop of Constantinople. For he not only condemns the death penalty, but all recourse to the secular arm.

Peter Cantor, one of the best minds of northern France

[1] *Vita Vasonis*, cap xxv et xxvi, Migne, P. L., vol. cxlii, col. 753.

[2] "An terrenæ potestatis gladio in eos sit animadvertendum necne." *Ibid.*, col. 752.

[3] Matt. xiii. 29–30.

[4] *Vita Vasonis, loc. cit.*, col. 753.

in the twelfth century, also protested against the infliction of the death penalty for heresy, "Whether," he says,
"the Cathari are proved guilty of heresy, or whether they
freely admit their guilt, they ought not to be put to death,
unless they attack the Church in armed rebellion." For
the Apostle said: "A man that is a heretic, after the
first and second admonition, avoid"; he did not say:
"Kill him." "Imprison heretics if you will, but do not
put them to death."[1]

Geroch of Reichersberg, a famous German of the same
period, a disciple and friend of St. Bernard, speaks in a
similar strain of the execution of Arnold of Brescia. He
was most anxious that the Church, and especially the
Roman curia, should not be held responsible for his death.
"The priesthood," he says, "ought to refrain from the
shedding of blood." There is no doubt whatever that
this heretic taught a wicked doctrine, but banishment,
imprisonment, or some similar penalty would have been
ample punishment for his wrong-doing, without sentencing
him to death.[2]

St. Bernard had also asked that Arnold be banished.
The execution of heretics at Cologne gave him a chance

[1] "Ait enim Apostolus: Hæreticum hominem post trinam admonitionem
devita (Tit. iii, 10). Non ait: occide . . . Recludendi ergo sunt, non occidendi." *Verbum abbreviatum*, cap. lxxviii, Migne, P. L., vol. ccv, col. 231.

[2] "Quem ego vellem pro tali doctrina sua quamvis prava vel exsilio vel
carcere aut alia pœna *præter mortem* punitum esse, vel saltem taliter occisum
ut Romana Ecclesia seu curia ejus necis quæstione careat." *De investigatione Antichristi*, lib. i, cap. xlii, ed. Scheibelberger, 1875, pp. 88–89.

to state his views on the suppression of heresy. The courage with which these fanatics met death rather disconcerted Evervin, the provost of Steinfeld, who wrote the Abbot of Clairvaux for an explanation.[1]

"Their courage," he replies, "arose from mere stubbornness; the devil inspired them with this constancy you speak of, just as he prompted Judas to hang himself. These heretics are not real but counterfeit martyrs. (*perfidiæ martyres*). But while I may approve the zeal of the people for the faith, I cannot at all approve their excessive cruelty; for faith is a matter of persuasion, not of force: *fides suadenda est, non imponenda.*" [2]

On principle, the Abbot of Clairvaux blames the bishops and even the secular princes, who through indifference or less worthy reasons fail to hunt for the foxes who are ravaging the vineyard of the Savior. But once the guilty ones have been discovered, he declares that only kindness should be used to win them back. "Let us capture them by arguments and not by force." [3] *i.e.* let us first refute their errors, and if possible bring them back into the fold of the Catholic Church.

If they stubbornly refuse to be converted, let the bishop excommunicate them, to prevent their doing further

---

[1] Evervin's letter in Migne, P. L., vol. clxxxii, col. 676 and seq.

[2] *In Cantica*, Sermo lxiv, n. 12.

[3] "Capiantur, non armis, sed argumentis." *In Cantica*, Sermo lxiv, n. 8. Lactantius had likewise said: "Verbis melius quam verberibus res agenda est." *Divin. Institut.*, lib. v, cap. xx.

injury; if occasion require it, let the civil power arrest them and put them in prison. Imprisonment is a severe enough penalty, because it prevents their dangerous propaganda: [1] *aut corrigendi sunt, ne pereant; aut, ne perimant, coercendi.*[2] St. Bernard was always faithful to his own teaching, as we learn from his mission in Languedoc.[3]

Having ascertained the views of individual churchmen, we now turn to the councils of the period, and find them voicing the self-same teaching. In 1049, the council held at Reims by Pope Leo IX declared all heretics excommunicated, but said nothing of any temporal penalty, nor did it empower the secular princes to aid in the suppression of heresy.[4]

The Council of Toulouse in 1119, presided over by Calixtus II, and the General Council of the Lateran, in 1139, were a little more severe; they not only issued a solemn bull of excommunication against heretics, but ordered the civil power to prosecute them: *per potestates exteras coerceri præcipimus.*[5] This order was, undoubtedly

[1] "Subversores invictis rationibus convincantur, ut vel emendentur ipsi, si fieri potest; vel, si non, perdant auctoritatem facultatemque alios subvertendi." *De Consideratione*, lib. iii, cap. i, n. 3.

[2] *Ibid.;* cf. *Ep.* 241 and 242. For more details, cf. Vacandard *Vie de Saint Bernard*, vol. ii, pp. 211–216, 461–462.

[3] Cf. Vacandard, *op. cit.*, vol. ii, pp. 217–234. Read his letter to his secretary Geoffroy, *Bernardi Vita*, lib. vi, pars 3, Migne, P. L., vol. clxxxv, col. 410–416.

[4] Cf. Labbe, *Concilia*, vol. ix, col. 1042.

[5] Council of Toulouse, can. 3, Labbe, vol. x, col. 857; Council of Lateran, can. 23, *ibid.*, col. 1008.

an answer to St. Bernard's request of Louis VII to banish Arnold from his kingdom. The only penalty referred to by both these councils was imprisonment.

The Council of Reims in 1148, presided over by Eugenius III, did not even speak of this penalty, but simply forbade secular princes to give support or asylum to heretics.[1] We know, moreover, that at this council Éon de l'Étoile was merely sentenced to the seclusion of a monastery.

In fact, the executions of heretics which occurred during the eleventh and twelfth centuries were due to the impulse of the moment. As an historian has remarked: "These heretics were not punished for a crime against the law; for there was no legal crime of heresy and no penalty prescribed. But the men of the day adopted what they considered a measure of public safety, to put an end to a public danger."[2]

Far from encouraging the people and the princes in their attitude, the Church through her bishops, teachers, and councils continued to declare that she had a horror of bloodshed: *A domo sacerdotis sanguinis questio remota sit*, writes Geroch of Reichersberg.[3] Peter Cantor also

---

[1] Can. 18, Labbe, *Concilia*, vol. x, col. 1113.

[2] Julien Havet, *L'hérésie et le bras séculier au moyen âge*, in his *Œuvres*, vol. ii, p. 134. Still certain canonists, like Anselm of Lucca and the author of the *Panormia*, declare about this time that the death penalty may be inflicted upon heretics (cf. Tanon, *op. cit.*, pp. 453, 454), at least upon Manicheans. But these writers had no practical influence outside the *schola*.

[3] *De investigatione Antichristi*, lib. i, cap. xlii, *loc. cit.*, pp. 88–89.

insists on the same idea. "Even if they are proved guilty by the judgment of God," he writes, "the Cathari ought not to be sentenced to death, because this sentence is in a way ecclesiastical, being made always in the presence of a priest. If then they are executed, the priest is responsible for their death, for he by whose authority a thing is done is reponsible therefor: *quia illud ab eo fit, cujus auctoritate fit.*" [1]

Was excommunication to be the only penalty for heresy? Yes, answered Wazo, Leo IX, and the Council of Reims in the middle of the eleventh century. But later on the growth of the evil induced the churchmen of the time to call upon the aid of the civil power. They thought that the Church's excommunication required a temporal sanction. They therefore called upon the princes to banish heretics from their dominions, and to imprison those who refused to be converted. Such was the theory of the twelfth century.

We must not forget, however, that the penalty of imprisonment, which was at first a monastic punishment, had two objects in view: to prevent heretics from spreading their doctrines, and to give them an opportunity of atoning for their sins. In the minds of the ecclesiastical judges, it possessed a penitential, almost a sacra-

---

[1] He was discussing the consequences of a "judgment of God," or ordeal, *Verbum abbreviatum*, cap. lxxviii, Migne, P. L., vol. ccv, col. 231.

mental character. In a period when all Europe was Catholic, it could well supplant exile and banishment, which were the severest civil penalties after the death penalty.

CHAPTER IV

FOURTH PERIOD

From Gratian to Innocent III

The Influence of the Canon Law, and the Revival of the Roman Law

THE development of the Canon law and the revival of the Roman law could not but exercise a great influence upon the minds of princes and churchmen with regard to the suppression of heresy; in fact they were the cause of a legislation of persecution, which was adopted by every country of Christendom.

In the beginning of this period, which we date from Gratian,[1] the prosecution of heresy was still carried on, in a more or less irregular and arbitrary fashion, according to the caprice of the reigning sovereign, or the hasty violence of the populace. But from this time forward we shall see it carried on in the name of both the canon and the civil law: *secundum canonicas et legitimas sanctiones*, as a Council of Avignon puts it.[2]

[1] The Decree of Gratian was written about 1140. Cf. Paul Fournier, *Les origines du Décret de Gratien* in the *Revue d'histoire et de littérature religieuses*, vol. iii, 1898, p. 280.

[2] This council was held in 1209, d'Achery, *Spicilegium*, in-fol., vol. i, p. 704, col. 1.

In Germany and France, especially in northern France, the usual punishment was the stake. We need not say much of England, for heresy seems to have made but one visit there in 1166.[1] In 1160, a German prince, whose name is unknown, had several Cathari beheaded.[2] Others were burned at Cologne in 1163.[3] The execution of the heretics condemned at Vezelai by the Abbot of Vezelai and several bishops forms quite a dramatic picture.

When the heretics had been condemned, the Abbot, addressing the crowd, said: "My brethren, what punishment should be inflicted upon those who refuse to be converted?" All replied: "Burn them." "Burn them." Their wishes were carried out. Two abjured their heresy,

[1] William of Newbridge (*Rerum anglic*, lib. ii, cap. xiii) relates that in 1166 thirty heretics appeared in England, and that the Bishops to stop their propaganda *eos corporali disciplinæ subdendos catholico principi tradiderunt.* King Henry II had them branded on the forehead with a red-hot iron, and publicly flogged; he then banished them, forbidding any one to lodge or succor them. As this happened in the winter time, they were frozen to death. "This pious severity," adds the chronicler, "not only freed England from the pest of heresy, but, by the fear it inspired, kept heretics from ever entering the kingdom." Cf. Raoul de Diceto, *Imagines historiorum*, ed. Stubbs, vol. i, p. 318. It has been questioned whether this penalty of branding with a red-hot iron was not inspired by the canon which Martène attributes to the Council of Reims in 1157 (*Amplissima collectio*, vol. vii, col. 74), and which decrees that obstinate heretics *ferro calido frontem et facies signati pellantur.* But the authencity of this conciliar decree has been denied by an eminent critic, Julien Havet, *op. cit.*, in his *Œuvres*, vol. ii, p. 137. That is why we do not attach much importance to it. Besides, no civil or canon law has been discovered which decrees such a penalty.

[2] Aubri de Trois Fontaines, *Chron.*, ad. ann. 1160, *Mon. German. SS.* vol. xxiii, p. 845.

[3] *Annales Colon. maximi*, ad ann. 1163, *Mon. German. SS.*, vol. vi, p. 778.

and were pardoned, the other seven perished at the stake.[1]

Philip, Count of Flanders, was particularly cruel in prosecuting heretics.[2] He had an able auxiliary also in the Archbishop of Reims, Guillaume aux Blanches-Mains. The chronicle of Anchin tells us that they sent to the stake a great many nobles and people, clerics, knights, peasants, young girls, married women, and widows, whose property they confiscated and shared between them.[3] This occurred in 1183. Some years before, Archbishop Guillaume and his council had sent two heretical women to the stake.[4]

Hugh, Bishop of Auxerre (1183–1206), prosecuted the neo-Manicheans with equal severity; he confiscated the

[1] "Adducti sunt in medium maximæ multitudinis quæ totum claustrum occupabat, stante Guichardo Lugdunensi archiepiscopo et Bernardo Nivernensium episcopo, magistro quoque Galterio Landunensi episcopo, cum Guillelmo Vizeliacensi abbate . . . Abbas dixit omnibus qui aderant: Quid ergo, fratres, vobis videtur faciendum de his qui adhuc in sua perseverant obstinatione? Responderunt omnes: Comburantur! comburantur!" etc. Hugo Pictav., *Historia Vezeliacensis monasterii*, lib. iv, ad finem, *Hist. des Gaules*, vol. xii, pp. 343–344.

[2] "Illo in tempore ubique exquirebantur et perimebantur (hæretici), sed maxime a Philippo comite Flandrensium, qui justa crudelitate eos immisericorditer puniebat." Raoul de Coggeshall, in *Rerum Britann. medii ævi Scriptores*, ed. Stevenson, p. 122.

[3] "Tunc decretalis sententia ab archiepiscopo et comite prefixa est ut deprehensi incendio traderentur, substantiæ vero eorum sacerdoti et principi resignarentur." Sigeberti *Continuatio Aquicinctina*, ad. ann. 1183, in the *Mon. Germ. SS.*, vol. vi, p. 421.

[4] "Quæ, cum salutaribus monitis nulla ratione acquievissent . . . , communi concilio decretum est ut flammis concremarentur." Raoul de Coggeshall, *loc. cit.; Hist. des Gaules*, vol. xviii, p. 92.

property of some, banished others, and sent several to the stake.[1]

The reign of Philip Augustus was marked by many executions.[2] Eight Cathari were sent to the stake at Troyes in 1200,[3] one at Nevers in 1201,[4] and several others at Braisne-sur-Vesle in 1204.[5] A most famous case was the condemnation of the followers of the heretic, Amaury de Beynes. "Priests, clerics, men and women belonging to the sect, were brought before a council at Paris; they were condemned and handed over to the secular court of King Philip." The king was absent at the time. On his return he had them all burned outside the walls of the city.[6]

In 1163 a council of Tours enacted a decree fixing the

---

[1] Robert d'Auxerre, *Chron.*, ad. ann. 1205, in the *Hist. des Gaules*, vol. xviii, p. 273.

[2] Quos Popelicanos vulgari nomine dicunt

. . . .

Convincebantur et mittebantur in ignem,

says Guillaume le Breton, *Philippeis*, lib. i, verses 407–410.

[3] Aubri de Trois-Fontaines, ad. ann. 1200, in the *Mon. Germ. SS.*, vol. xxiii, p. 878.

[4] Cf. *Hist. des Gaules*, vol. xviii, pp. 264 and 729.

[5] *Chron. anonymi Laudunensis canonici*, in the *Hist. des Gaules*, vol. xviii, p. 713.

[6] "Traditi fuerunt curiæ Philippi regis, qui tanquam rex Christianissimus et catholicus, vocatis apparitoribus, fecit omnes cremari, et cremati sunt extra portam, in loco qui nuncupatur Campellus," etc. *Hist. des Gaules*, vol. xvii, pp. 83–84. The women were spared. Cf. Cæsarius of Heisterbach, *Dist.* v, cap. xxii, who tells us that the king was absent when the heretics were condemned. For other references, cf. Julien Havet, *op. cit.*, p. 142, note.

punishment of heresy. Of course it had in view chiefly the Cathari of Toulouse and Gascony: "If these wretches are captured," it says, "the Catholic princes are to imprison them and confiscate their property."[1]

This canon was applied probably for the first time at Toulouse in 1178. The Bishop began proceedings against several heretics, among them a rich noble named Pierre Mauran, who was summoned before his tribunal, and condemned to make a pilgrimage to the Holy Land. His property was confiscated, although later on when he professed repentance it was restored to him, on condition that he dismantle the towers of his castles, and pay the Count of Toulouse a fine of five hundred pounds of silver.[2]

In the meantime the Cathari increased with alarming rapidity throughout this region. Count Raymond V (1148–1194), wishing to strike terror into them, enacted a law which decreed the confiscation of their property and death. The people of Toulouse quoted this law later on in a letter to King Pedro of Aragon to justify their sending heretics to the stake,[3] and when the followers of

---

[1] "Illi vero, si deprehensi fuerint, per catholicos principes *custodiæ mancipati*, omnium bonorum amissione mulctentur." Can. 4, Labbe, *Concilia*, vol. x, col. 1419; *Hist. des Gaules*, vol. xiv, p. 431.

[2] For the details of this case, cf. A letter of Henry, Abbot of Clairvaux, Migne, P. L., vol. cciv, p. 235 and seq.

[3] "Scientes preterito processu longi temporis dominum comitem patrem moderni temporis comitis ab universo Tolose populo accepisse in mandatis *instrumento inde composito*, quod si quis hereticus inventus esset in Tolosana urbe vel suburbio, cum receptatore suo pariter *ad supplicium traderetur*, *publicatis possessionibus utriusque; unde multos combussimus*, et adhuc cum

Simon de Montfort arrived in southern France, in
1209, they followed the example of Count Raymond
by sending heretics to the stake everywhere they
went.[1]

The authenticity of this law has been questioned, on
account of its unheard-of severity.[2]   But Pedro II, King
of Aragon and Count of Barcelona, enacted a law in 1197
which was just as terrible.   He banished the Waldenses
and all other heretics from his dominions, ordering them
to depart before Passion Sunday of the following year
(March 23, 1198).   After that day, every heretic found
in the kingdom or the county was to be sent to the stake,
and his property confiscated.[3]   It is worthy of remark
that in the king's mind the stake was merely a subsidiary
penalty.

In enacting this severe law, Pedro of Aragon declared

invenimus idem facere non cessamus."   Letter written in 1211 by the city
of Toulouse to King Pedro of Aragon, in Teulet, *Layettes du trésor des Chartes*,
vol. i, p. 368.

[1] On this expedition, cf. Achille Luchaire, *op. cit.*, ch. iv. and v; Tanon,
op. cit., pp. 28, 29.

[2] Julien Havet, *op. cit.*, p. 153, note.   The reasons he gives for doubting
it are far from convincing.   He starts with the idea that Raymond V, all his
life, favored the heretics.   Luchaire holds the opposite view (*op. cit.*, p. 46.
Cf. Tanon, *op. cit.*, p. 447).

[3] "Valdenses . . . et omnes alios hæreticos . . . ab omni regno et potes-
tativo nostro tanquam inimicos crucis Christi christianæque fidei violatores
et nostros regnique nostri publicos hostes exire et fugere districte et irremeabiliter
præcipimus . . . Et si post tempus præfixum (Dominicam Passionis Domini)
aliqui in tota terra nostra eos invenerint, duobus partibus rerum suarum
confiscatis, tertia sit inventoris; corpora eorum ignibus crementur."   De
Marca, *Marca Hispanica*, col. 1384.

that he was moved by zeal for the public welfare,[1] and "had simply obeyed the canons of the Holy Roman Church."[2] With the exception of the death penalty by the stake, his reference to the canon law is perfectly accurate. Pope Alexander III, who had been present at the Council of Tours in 1163, renewed, at the Lateran Council in 1179, the decrees already enacted against the heretics of central France. He considered the Cathari, the Brabançons, etc., disturbers of the public welfare, and therefore called upon the princes to protect by force of arms their Christian subjects against the outrages of these heretics. The princes were to imprison all heretics and confiscate their property.[3] The Pope granted indulgences to all who carried on this pious work.

In 1184, Pope Lucius III, in union with the emperor Frederic Barbarossa, adopted at Verona still more vigorous measures. Heretics were to be excommunicated, and then handed over to the secular arm, which was to

[1] Notice the italicized words in the preceding note.

[2] "Sacrosanctæ Romanæ Ecclesiæ canonibus obtemperantes, qui hæreticos a consortio Dei et sanctæ Ecclesiæ et catholicorum omnium exclusos ubique damnandos ac persequendos censuerunt." *Loc. cit.*

[3] The princes are invited "ut tantis cladibus se viriliter opponant et contra eos (hæreticos) armis populum Christianum tueantur. Confiscentur eorum bona et liberum sit principibus hujusmodi homines subjicere servituti." Can. 27, Labbe, *Concilia*, vol. x, col. 1522. The Council of Montpellier in 1195 presided over by the legate of Pope Celestine III renewed this decree in nearly the same terms: "Constituit ut bona hujusmodi pestilentium hominum publicentur et ipsi nihilominus servituti subdantur." Labbe, *Concilia*, vol. x, col. 1796. The word *servitus* (*subjicere servituti* and *servituti subdantur*) used by both councils means imprisonment (Julien Havet, *op. cit.*,

inflict upon them the punishment they deserved (*animadversio debita*).[1] The Emperor decreed the imperial ban against them.[2]

This imperial ban was, as Ficker has pointed out, a very severe penalty in Italy; for it comprised banishment, the confiscation of the property, and the destruction of the houses of the condemned, public infamy, the inability to hold public office, etc.[3] This is beyond question the penalty the King of Aragon alluded to in his

p. 154). It is equivalent to the *custodiæ mancipati* of the Council of Tours in 1163. As Alexander III presided over both councils (Tours and Lateran) it is most probable they decreed the same penalty.

[1] "Si clericus est (hæreticus), vel cujuslibet religionis obumbratione fuscatus, totius ecclesiastici ordinis prerogativa nudetur, et sic omni officio et beneficio spoliatus *secularis relinquatur arbitrio potestatis animadversione debita puniendus*, nisi continuo post deprehensionem erroris ad fidei catholicæ unitatem sponte recurrere et errorem suum ad arbitrium episcopi regionis publice consenserit abjurare, et satisfactionem congruam exhibere. Laicus autem nisi, prout dictum est, abjurata hæresi et satisfactione exhibita confestim ad fidem confugeret orthodoxam, *secularis judicis arbitrio relinquatur, debitam recepturus pro qualitate facinoris ultionem*," etc. Canon 27, inserted in the Decretals of Gregory IX, lib᾽ v, tit. vii, De hereticis, cap. ix.

[2] "Papa eos excommunicavit, imperator vero tam res quam personas ipsorum *imperiali banno* subjecit," says the *Continuatio Zwetlensis altera*, ad ann. 1184, in the *Mon. Germ. SS.*, vol. ix, p. 542. The council had used the words *animadversione puniendi*. *Animadversio* in the Roman law signified the death penalty. Cf. The edict of Valerian in 258: *In continenti animadvertentur*. The imperial formula of condemnation seems to have been: *Gladio animadverti placet*. Cf. Paul Allard, *Dix leçons sur le martyre*, Paris, 1906, p. 269, n. 1. But in the Middle Ages *animadversio* comprised different penalties. We notice, for example, that Frederic Barbarossa, in accordance with the mind of the church, decreed no greater punishment than banishment.

[3] Ficker, *Die gesetzliche Einführung der Todesstrafe für Ketzerei*, in the *Mittheilungen des Instituts für oesterreichische Geschichtsforschung*, vol. i (1880), pp. 187, 188, 194, 195.

enactment. The penalty of the stake which he added, although in conformity with the Roman law, was an innovation.[1]

The pontificate of Innocent III, which began in 1198, marks a pause in the development of the Church's penal legislation against heresy. Despite his prodigious activity, this Pope never dreamt of enacting new laws, but did his best to enforce the laws then in vogue, and to stimulate the zeal of both princes and magistrates in the suppression of heresy.[2]

Hardly had he ascended the pontifical throne when he sent legates to southern France, and wrote urgent letters full of apostolic zeal to the Archbishops of Auch and Aix, the Bishop of Narbonne, and the King of France. These letters, as well as his instructions to the legates, are similar in tone: "Use against heretics the spiritual sword of excommunication, and if this does not prove effective, use the material sword. The civil laws decree banishment and confiscation; see that they are carried out."[3]

---

[1] Tanon has proved, however (*op. cit.*, pp. 433 and seq.), that the canonists had already revived the legislation of the first Christian Emperors against heresy.

[2] Julien Havet, *op. cit.*, p. 155.

[3] "Ecclesiasticæ districionis exercendo rigorem, et etiam, si necesse fuerit, per principes et populum eosdem (hæreticos) facias *virtute materialis gladii* coerceri." Letter of April 1, 1198, to the Archbishop of Auch, Innocent, *Ep.* i, 81. "Nobilibus viris principibus, comitibus et universis baronibus et magnatibus in vestra provincia constitutis præcipiendo mandamus et in remissionem injungimus peccatorum, ut . . . postquam per

At this time the Cathari were living not only in the cities of Languedoc and Provence, but some had even entered the papal States, *v.g.* at Orvieto and Viterbo. The Pope himself went to these cities to combat the evil,[1] and at once saw the necessity of enacting special laws against them. They may be read in his letters of March 25, 1199, and September 22, 1207, which form a special code for the use of the princes and the podestà. Heretics were to be branded with infamy; they were forbid-

dictum fratrem Rainerium fuerint excommunicationis sententia innodati, *eorum bona confiscent et de terra sua proscribant;* et, si post interdictum ejus in terra ipsorum præsumpserint commorari, *gravius animadvertant in eos,* sicut decet principes christianos." Letter to the Archbishop of Aix, April 21, 1198, *Ep.* 194. The words *gravius animadvertant* seem to imply the death penalty, but perhaps the Pope merely meant imprisonment. For in all his laws, Innocent III never once decreed the death penalty. Nearly all historians are agreed on this point, as we will show later on.

" Mandamus ut vos fratres . . . spiritualem gladium exeratis; laici vero bona eorum (hæreticorum) confiscent et eos ejiciant de terra sua." Letter of May 13, 1198, to the legate Gui, *Ep.* i, 165. "Satanæ in interitum carnis traditas nuntietis et expositas personas eorum et judicio seculari, et bona confiscationi tradita," etc. Letter of May 31, 1204, to his legates, *Ep.* vii, 71. Cf. letter of January 29, 1204, to the Bishop of Narbonne, *Ep.* vi, 243; letter to the King of France, *Ep.* vii, 212, etc. The letters of Innocent III are to be found in Migne, P. L., vol. ccxiv–ccxvi.

[1] At Orvieto, where the Bishop had punished the heretics most severely after a riot, Innocent III appointed a podestà Piero Parenzo to enforce the laws and canons against obdurate heretics: "ut pænam exciperet *legibus et canonibus* constitutam." The podestà "alios alligavit ferreis nexibus compeditos, alios censuit publicis verberibus flagellandos, alios extra civitatem cœgit miserabiliter exulare, alios pæna mulctavit pecuniæ . . . , domus etiam fecit dirui plurimorum." *Vita S. Petri Parentii,* cap. vi, in the *Acta SS.,* maii, vol. v, p. 87. On the work and murder of Parenzo, cf. Luchaire, *Innocent III, Rome et l'Italie,* Paris, 1904, pp. 86–91. For Viterbo, cf. *Gesta Innocentii,* cap. cxxiii, in Migne, P. L., vol. ccxiv, col. clxi; *Ep.* Innocent ii, viii, 85 and 105.

den to be electors, to hold public office, to be members of the city councils, to appear in court or testify, to make a will or to receive an inheritance; if officials all their acts were declared null and void; and finally their property was to be confiscated.

"In the territories subject to our temporal jurisdiction," adds the Pope, ".we declare their property confiscated; in other places we order the podestà and the secular princes to do the same, and we desire and command this law enforced under penalty of ecclesiastical censures." [1]

We are not at all surprised at such drastic measures, when we consider the agreement made by Lucius III with Frederic Barbarossa, at Verona. But we wish to call attention to the reasons that Innocent III adduced to justify his severity, on account of the serious consequences they

[1] "Districtius inhibemus ne quis hæreticos receptare quomodolibet vel defendere aut ipsis favere vel credere quoquomodo præsumat . . . In terris vero temporali nostræ jurisdictioni subjectis, bona eorum statuimus publicari; et in aliis idem fieri præcipimus per potestates at principes seculares, quos ad id exequendum, si forte negligentes extiterint, per censuram ecclesiasticam appellatione postposita compelli volumus et mandamus." Letter of March 25, 1199, to the magistrates and people of Viterbo. *Ep.* ii, 1. "Ad eliminandam omnino de patrimonio beati Petri hæreticorum spurcitiam, servanda in perpetuum lege sancimus ut quicumque hæreticus, et maxime Patarenus, in eo fuerit inventus, protinus capiatur et *tradatur seculari curiæ puniendus secundum legitimas sanctiones.* Bona vero ipsius omnia publicentur; ita ut de ipsis unam partem percipiat qui ceperit illum, alteram curia quæ ipsum punierit, tertia vero deputetur ad constructionem murorum illius terræ ubi fuerit interceptus. Domus autem in qua hæreticus fuerit receptatus funditus destruatur, nec quisquam eam reædificare præsumat, sed fiat sordium receptaculum, quæ fuit latibulum perfidorum." Constitution of September 23, 1207, *Ep.* x, 130.

entailed. "The civil law," says the Pope, "punishes traitors with confiscation of their property and death; it is only out of kindness that the lives of their children are spared. All the more then should we excommunicate and confiscate the property of those who are traitors to the faith of Jesus Christ; for it is an infinitely greater sin to offend the divine majesty than to attack the majesty of the sovereign." [1]

Whether this comparison be justified or not, it is certainly most striking. Later on Frederic II and others will quote it to justify their severity.

The Lateran Council in 1215 made the laws of Innocent III canons of the universal Church; it declared all heretics excommunicated, and delivered them over to the State to receive due punishment. This *animadversio debita* entailed banishment with all its consequences and confiscation. The council also legislated against the abettors of heresy, even if they were princes, and ordered the despoiling of all rulers who neglected to enforce the ecclesiastical law in their domains.[2]

---

[1] "Ut temporalis saltem pæna corripiat quem spiritualis non corripit disciplina. Cum enim *secundum legitimas sanctiones reis læse majestatis punitis capite bona confiscentur eorum*, filiis suis vita solummodo misericordia conservata, quanto magis qui, aberrantes in fide, Domini Dei filium Jesum offendunt, a capite nostro, quod est Christus, ecclesiastica debent districtione præcidi et bonis temporalibus spoliari, *cum longe sit gravius æternam quam temporalem lædere majestatem,*" etc. Letter of March 25, 1199, to the magistrates of Viterbo, *Ep.* ii, 1. This text is inserted in the Decretals, cap. x, *De hæreticis*, lib. v, tit. vii.

[2] "Damnati vero præsentibus *sæcularibus potestatibus* aut eorum baillivis

In practice, Innocent III, although very severe towards obdurate heretics, was extremely kind to the ignorant and heretics in good faith. While he banished the Patarins from Viterbo,[1] and razed their houses to the ground, he at the same time protected, against the tyranny of an archpriest of Verona, a society of mystics, the Humiliati, whose orthodoxy was rather doubtful.[2] When, after the massacre of the Albigenses, Pope Innocent was called upon to apply the canon law in the case of Raymond, Count of Toulouse, and to transfer the patrimony of his father to Simon de Montfort, he was the first to draw back from such injustice.[3] Although a framer of severe laws against heresy, he was ready to grant dispensations, when occasion arose.

We must remember also that the laws he enacted were not at all excessive compared with the strict Roman law, or even with the practice then in vogue in France and Germany. It has been justly said: "The laws and letters of Innocent III never once mention

---

relinquantur animadversione debita puniendi, clericis prius a suis ordinibus degradatis, ita quod bona hujusmodi damnatorum, si laici fuerint, confiscentur; si vero clerici, applicentur ecclesiis a quibus stipendia receperunt," etc. Labbe, *Concilia*, vol. xi, col. 148–150; *Decretales*, cap. xiii, *De hæreticis*, lib. v, tit. vii.

[1] *Gesta Innocentii*, cap. cxxiii, Migne, P. L., vol. ccxiv, col. clxi.

[2] "Even if they seem to be a little unorthodox, absolve them if they are willing to submit, and acknowledge their errors."
Letter to the Bishop of Verona, 1199. *Ep.* ii, 228; cf. Luchaire, *Innocent III, la croisade des Albigeois*, pp. 58–60.

[3] Luchaire, *op. cit.*, p. 168 and seq.

the death-penalty for heresy. He merely decrees against them banishment, and the confiscation of their property. When he speaks of having recourse to the secular arm, he means simply the force required to carry out the laws of banishment enacted by his penal code. This code, which seems so pitiless to us, was in reality at that time a great improvement in the treatment of heretics. For its special laws prevented the frequent outbreaks of popular vengeance, which punished not only confessed heretics, but also mere suspects." [1]

In fact, the development in the methods of suppressing heresy from the eleventh century ends with Innocent III in a code that was far more kindly than the cruel customs in vogue at the time.

The death penalty of the stake was common in France in the twelfth century, and in the beginning of the thir-

---

[1] Luchaire, *op. cit.*, pp. 57, 58. Julien Havet also says: "We must in justice say of Innocent III that, if he did bitterly prosecute heretics, and everywhere put them under the ban, he never demanded the infliction of the death penalty. Ficker has brought this out very clearly." *L'hérésie et le bras séculier*, p. 165, n. 3. For Ficker's view, cf. *op. cit.*, pp. 189–192 (*supra*, p. 68). That men who were merely suspected of heresy were summarily condemned and executed, as Luchaire says, we have seen in several instances. A canon of Langres testifies to this fact in his appeal to Innocent III; "the only reason," he says, "that I did not appear before the Bishop or the papal delegates was the fear of death; because in this country (northern France) the piety of the people is so great that they are always ready to send to the stake, not only avowed heretics, but those merely suspected of heresy." (Cf. Luchaire, *op. cit.*, pp. 65, 66.)

Tanon, on the contrary, maintains (*op. cit.*, pp. 448–450) that Innocent III in certain instances did require the infliction of the death penalty upon heretics. Only one of the passages that he adduces is at all doubtful, viz., the

teenth. Most of the executions were due to the passions of the mob, although the Roman law was in part responsible. Anselm of Lucca and the author of the *Panormia* (Ivo of Chartres?) had copied word for word the fifth law of the title *De Hæreticis* of the Justinian code, under the rubric: *De edicto imperatorum in dampnationem hæreticorum.*[1] This law which decreed the death penalty against the Manicheans seemed strictly applicable to the Cathari, who were regarded at the time as the direct heirs of Manicheism.[2] Gratian, in his Decree, maintained the views of St. Augustine on the penalties of heresy, viz., fine and banishment.[3] But some of his commentators, especially Rufinus, Johannes Teutonicus, and an anonymous writer whose work is inserted in Huguccio's great *Summa* of the decree, declared that impenitent heretics might and even ought to be put to death.[4]

These different works appeared before the Lateran

Gravius animadvertant in eos in the Letter of April 21, 1198 (*Ep.* i, 94). Even supposing that this did mean the death penalty, it would not, properly speaking, be the punishment of heresy, but of disobedience to the laws enacted against heresy. But in fact no one can prove that it does not mean life-imprisonment; cf. *Supra*, p. 59, n. 2. In any case, Tanon's view does not agree with what we know of the conduct and writings of Innocent III.

[1] Tanon, *op. cit.*, pp. 453–454.

[2] Tanon, p. 9, n. 1.

[3] Decretum, 2 Pars, Causa xxiii, quest. 4, 6, 7.

[4] Rufinus, in his commentary on Causa 23, quest. 5, proves that "he who has the power of the sword," has the right to execute great criminals, and in Causa 24 he applies this principle to heretics: "Quomodo igitur qui manifeste

Council of 1215.[1] They are a good indication of the
mind of the time. We may well ask whether the Archbishop of Reims, the Count of Flanders, Philip Augustus,
Raymond of Toulouse, and Pedro of Aragon, who authorized the use of the stake for heretics, did not think they
were following the example of the first Christian emperors. We must, however, admit that there is no direct
allusion to the early imperial legislation either in their
acts or their writings. Probably they were more influenced by the customs of the time than by the written
law.

As a matter of fact, Gratian, who with St. Augustine
mentioned only fine and banishment as the penalites for
heresy, was followed for some time. We learn from
Benencasa's *Summa* of the Decree that heretics were

in hæresim labuntur, nec resipiscere volunt, puniendi sunt, in superiori causa
monstratum est." Cf. Tanon, *op. cit.*, pp. 455, 456 and notes. This thesis
is proved at great length. Johannes Teutonicus is more brief in his commentary on ch. 39, quest. 4, of the Decree: *Vides ergo quod hæretici sunt occidendi, primo tamen admonendi.* The anonymous writer, whose commentary
is found in Huguccio's *Summa* of the Decree, teaches the same doctrine on
ch. 39, causa 23, quest. 4: *Quando vult temporales mortes*, id est pænas. Vel
proprie distinguere quod primo debent admoneri et deinde, si pertinaciter
resistere voluerint et incorrigibiles extiterint, poterunt morte affici. He
quotes in favor of his thesis the law *Arcani* against the Manicheans. And
on ch. 41, *Non invenitur*, he adds: "Innuit quod pro sola hæresi non sint
morte puniendi. Solve ut prius. Quando enim sunt incorrigibiles, ultimo
supplicio feruntur, aliter non." Bibliothèque Nationale, Ms. 15379, fol. 49.
Cf. Tanon, *op. cit.*, pp. 456, 457 and notes.

[1] The collection of Anselm of Lucca is prior to 1080. The *Panormia* was
written about the beginning of the twelfth century; the Decree about 1140;
the three commentaries were written a little before 1215. Cf. Tanon, *op. cit.*,
pp. 453–458.

6

punished not by death, but by banishment and confiscation of their property.[1]

The Councils of Tours and Lateran also decreed confiscation, but for banishment they substituted imprisonment, a penalty unknown to the Roman law. The Council of Lateran appealed to the authority of St. Leo the Great, to compel Christian princes to prosecute heresy.[2]

From the time of Lucius III, owing to the influence of the lawyers, the two penalties of banishment and confiscation prevailed. Innocent III extended them to the universal Church.[3]

This was undoubtedly a severer penal legislation

[1] Biblioth. Nation., Ms. 3892, *Summa* of Benencasa: 41, cap. 23, q. 4, *Non invenitur:* Vincentius quæsivit ab Augustino ubi inveniatur exemplum quod ecclesia petierit auxilium a regibus terræ contra inimicos, respondit: Non in Evangelio nec in Apostolo istud exemplum reperitur. Tamen unum exemplum Nabuchodonosor regis, in quo utrumque tempus figuratur, et primitivæ Ecclesiæ in qua justi ab impiis cogebantur ad malum, et Ecclesiæ quæ nunc est, in qua hæretici coguntur a Christianis, *non ad mortem*, sed ad exilium vel dampnum rerum temporalium.

[2] Canon 27, Labbe, *Concilia*, vol. x, col. 1522; Leonis, *Epist.* xv, ad Turribium, Migne, *Pat. lat.*, vol. liv, col. 679–680.

[3] The legate Milo persuaded the consuls of Montpellier to swear, August 1, 1209: "Ipsos (hæreticos) persequemur secundum legitimas sanctiones, et eorum bona omnia pro posse nostro infiscabimus," etc. D'Achery, *Spicilegium*, 1723, in-fol., vol. i, pp, 706, 707. A little later, the Council of Avignon, presided over by the two legates of Innocent III, proposed the oath of the Consuls of Montpellier as a model for the civil authorities of Provence: "ut eos (hæreticos) puniant secundum canonicas et legitimas sanctiones, nihilominus bona ipsorum omnia confiscantes." D'Achery, *Spicilegium*, vol. i, p. 704, col. 1.

We have already mentioned the laws of Innocent (1198) for southern France, and certain cities of Italy (pp. 58–60). We have another letter, January 5, 1199, to the Bishop of Syracuse, recommending him: "excommunicatos

than that of the preceding age. But on the other hand it was an effective barrier against the infliction of the death penalty, which had become so common in many parts of Christendom.

Besides, during this period, the church used vigorous measures only against obdurate heretics, who were also disturbers of the public peace.[1] They alone were handed over to the secular arm; if they abjured their heresy, they were at once pardoned, provided they freely accepted the penance imposed upon them.[2] This kind

(hæreticos) publice nuntiari facias et bona eorum a principibus publicari." *Ep.* i, 509. On December 12, 1206, he exhorted the podestà, consuls, and Council of Faënza: "*quoslibet pravitatis hæreticæ sectatores satagatis a civitate vestra depellere,*" as Prato and Florence had done; *Ep.* ix, 204; cf. Letter of March 10, 1206, *Ep.* ix, 18: "A civitate vestra penitus excludatis et sub *perpetuo banno* consistant nec recipiantur de cætero vel etiam tolerentur in civitate manere nisi ad mandatum Ecclesiæ revertantur, bona eorum . . . confiscentur *secundum legitimas sanctiones* et etiam publicentur." The *bannum perpetuum* and the *legitimæ sanctiones* refer to the old Teutonic law and the Roman law. The Pope even wrote to Hungary (Letter of October 11, 1200, *Ep.* iii, 3), where his laws were observed (cf. *Ep.* v, 110, and Thomæ archdeaconi *Hist. Salonitana* in Schwandner, *Rerum, Hungaric. SS.*, 1746, vol. iii, p. 568). Finally, we have the promise made to the Pope by the emperor Otto IV, March 22, 1209: "Super eradicando autem hæretice pravitatis errore auxilium dabimus et operam efficacem." *Mon. Germ.*, Leges, vol. ii, p. 217. This promise was renewed in the same terms by Frederic II, July 12, 1213, *ibid.*, p. 224.

[1] Innocent III merely condemned to prison in a monastery the heretical abbot of Nevers: "Et quoniam metuendum est ne in laquem desperationis incidens et ad perfidorum hæreticorum insaniam ex toto conversus eorum prævaricationibus contaminet gregem intactum, retrudi eum in districto monasterio faciatis et ibi ad agendam pœnitentiam sub arcta custodia detineri." Letter of June 19, 1199, to a cardinal and a Bishop of Paris. *Ep.* ii, 99.

[2] Cf. Canon 27 of the Lateran Council (1179), which we have quoted

treatment, it was true, was not to last. It, however, deserves special notice, for the honor of those who preached and practiced it.

above, and which is inserted in the Decretals of Gregory ix, cap. ix, *De hæreticis*, lib. v, tit. vii.

CHAPTER V

THE CATHARAN OR ALBIGENSIAN HERESY — ITS ANTI-CATHOLIC AND ANTI-SOCIAL CHARACTER

WHILE Popes Alexander III, Lucius III, and Innocent III, were adopting such vigorous measures, the Catharan heresy by its rapid increase caused widespread alarm throughout Christendom. Let us endeavor to obtain some insight into its character, before we describe the Inquisition, which was destined to destroy it.

The dominant heresy of the period was the Albigensian or Catharan heresy;[1] it was related to Oriental Manicheism[2] through the Paulicians and the Bogomiles, who professed a dualistic theory on the origin of the world.

In the tenth century, the empress Theodora, who detested the Paulicians, had one hundred thousand of

[1] The heretics called themselves "*Cathari*," or "*the Pure.*" They wished thereby to denote especially their horror of all sexual relations, says the monk Egbert: *Sermones contra Catharos*, in Migne, P. L., cxcv, col. 13. Their opponents took delight in ridiculing this name. Cf. the anonymous author of *Errores haereticorum* (of the fourteenth century), quoted by Döllinger: "Kathari dicuntur a charto (cato), cujus posteriora osculantur, in cujus specie eis Lucifer apparet," etc. Beiträge, vol. ii (Dokumente), p. 293.

[2] On the origin of the Manichean heresy, cf. Duchesne, *Histoire ancienne de l'Eglise*, pp. 555, 556.

them massacred;[1] the emperor, Alexis Comnenus (about 1118), persecuted the Bogomiles in like manner.[2] Many, therefore, of both sects went to western Europe, where they finally settled, and began to spread.[3]

As early as 1167, they held a council at St. Felix de Caraman, near Toulouse, under the presidency of one of their leaders, Pope or perhaps only Bishop Niketas (Niquinta) of Constantinople. Other bishops of the sect were present: Mark, who had charge of all the churches of Lombardy, Tuscany, and the Marches of Treviso; Robert de Sperone, who governed a church in the north, and Sicard Cellerier, Bishop of the Church of Albi. They appointed Bernard Raymond, Bishop of Toulouse, Guiraud Mercier, Bishop of Carcassonne, and Raymond of Casalis, Bishop of Val d'Aran, in the diocese of Comminges.[4] Such an organization certainly indicates the extraordinary development of the heresy about the middle of the twelfth century.[5]

About the year 1200 its progress was still more alarm-

---

[1] On the Paulicians, and this massacre, cf. Döllinger, *Beiträge*, vol. i, pp. 1–34.

[2] On the *Bogomiles* (The Friends of God) cf. Vernet, in the *Dictionnaire de Théologie Catholique*, Paris, Letouzey et Ané, vol. ii, col. 927–930.

[3] On their route, cf. Döllinger, *ibid.*, pp. 51–75, Vernet, *ibid.*, vol. ii, col. 1998 and seq.

[4] *Hist. des Gaules*, vol. xiv, pp. 448, 449.

[5] In 1178, the legate Peter of St. Chrysogono was opposed by the Catharan Bishops of Toulouse and Val. d'Aran. At Toulouse he held a public conference with them, after giving them a safe-conduct. Vaissette, *Histoire du Languedoc*, vol. xi, p. 82.

ing. Bonacursus, a Catharan bishop converted to Catholicism, writes about 1190: "Behold the cities, towns and homes filled with these false prophets." [1] Cæsarius, of Heisterbach, tells us that a few years later there were Cathari in about one thousand cities,[2] especially in Lombardy and Languedoc.

There were at least seven to eight hundred of "the Perfected" in Languedoc alone; and to obtain approximately the total number of the sect, we must multiply this number by twenty or even more.[3]

Of course, perfect unity did not exist among the Cathari. The different names by which they were known clearly indicate certain differences of doctrine among them. Some, like the Cathari of Alba and Desenzano,[4] taught with the Paulicians an absolute dualism, affirming that all things created came from two principles, the one essentially good, and the other essentially bad. Two other groups, the Concorrezenses and the Bagolenses,[5] like the ancient Gnostics held a modified form of dualism; they pretended that the evil spirit had so marred the Creator's work, that matter had become the instrument of evil in the world. Still they agreed with the

[1] *Manifestatio hæresis Catharorum*, in Migne, P. L., vol. cciv, col. 778.

[2] *Dialogi*, Antwerp, 1604, p. 289.

[3] This is Döllinger's estimate, *Beiträge*, vol. i, pp. 212, 213.

[4] Alba was a city of Piedmont; Desenzano was a small city southwest of Lac de Garde, where the Cathari were numerous.

[5] Concorezzo was a district of Lombardy, Bagnolo was the name of many cities in Italy; cf. Vernet, *op. cit.*, col. 1993, 1994.

pronounced dualists in nearly all their doctrines and observances; their few theoretical differences were scarcely appreciable in practice.[1]

Still contemporary writers called them by different names. In Italy they were confounded with the orthodox Patarins and Arnaldists of Milan; which explains the frequent use of the word *Patareni* in the constitutions of Frederic II, and other documents.

The Arnaldists or Arnoldists and the Speronistæ, were the disciples of Arnold of Brescia, and the heretical bishop Sperone. Although the chief center of the Cathari in France was Toulouse and not Albi, they were called *Albigeois* (Albigenses), and *Tisserands* (Texerants), because many were weavers by trade; *Arians*, because of their denial of Christ's divinity: *Paulicians*, which was corrupted into *Poplicani, Publicani, Piphes* and *Piples* (Flanders); *Bulgarians* (*Bulgari*), from their origin, which became in the mouths of the people of *Bugari, Bulgri*, and *Bugres*.[2] In fact about 1200, nearly all the heretics of western Europe were considered Cathari.[3]

[1] On the Catharan doctrines, cf. Döllinger, *Beiträge*, vol. i, pp. 132–200; vol. ii (*Dokumente*), pp. 52, 85, 273, 279, 293, 297, 301, 311, 321, 324, 326, 374, 612, 617, 620; Vernet, *op. cit.*, vol. ii, col. 1993 and seq.

[2] For the different names, cf. Döllinger, *Beiträge*, vol. i, pp. 127–132, Lea, *op. cit.*, vol. i, p. 114, note. *Bougre* later on designated any heretic.

[3] The Waldenses differed considerably from the Cathari, although in some things they agreed. For their teachings, cf. Döllinger, *Beiträge*, vol. ii (*Dokumente*), pp. 92, 251, 304, 328, 331, 344, 346, 351, 365, 367. In many documents (cf. the *Processus Inquisitionis*, Appendix A) they were mistaken one for the other.

Catharism was chiefly a negative heresy; it denied the doctrines, hierarchy and worship of the Catholic Church, as well as the essential rights of the State.

These neo-Manicheans denied that the Roman Church represented the Church of Christ. The Popes were not the successors of St. Peter, but rather the successors of Constantine.[1] St. Peter never came to Rome. The relics which were venerated in the Constantinian basilica, were the bones of some one who died in the third century; they were not relics of the Prince of the Apostles.[2] Constantine unfortunately sanctioned this fraud, by conferring upon the Roman pontiff an immense domain, together with the prestige that accompanies temporal authority.[3] How could anyone recognize under the insignia, the purple mantle, and the crown of the successors of St. Sylvester, a disciple of Jesus Christ? Christ had no place where to lay his head, whereas the Popes lived in a palace! Christ rebuked worldly dominion, while the Popes claimed it! What had the Roman curia with its thirst for riches and honors in common with the gospel of Christ? What were these archbishops, primates,

[1] Moneta (a Dominican Inquisitor about 1250), *Adversus Catharos et Valdenses*, ed. Ricchini, 1743, p. 409. St. Dominic died in Moneta's bed at Bologna, Aug. 6, 1231. Cf. Tanon, *op. cit.*, p. 42.

[2] Moneta, *ibid.*, p. 410.

[3] The Middle Ages believed firmly in the donation of Constantine. It was, however, questioned by Wetzel, a disciple of Arnold of Brescia in 1152, in a letter to Frederic Barbarossa, Martène and Durand, *Veterum scriptorum . . . amplissima collectio*, Paris, 1724, vol. ii, col. 554-557.

cardinals, archdeacons, monks, canons, Dominicans, and Friars Minor but the Pharisees of old! The priests placed heavy burdens upon the faithful people, and they themselves did not touch them with the tips of their fingers; they received tithes from the fields and flocks; they ran after the heritage of widows; all practices which Christ condemned in the Pharisees.[1]

And yet withal they dared persecute humble souls who, by their pure life, tried to realize the perfect ideal proposed by Christ! These persecutors were not the true disciples of Jesus. The Roman Church was the woman of the Apocalypse,[2] drunk with the blood of the Saints, and the Pope was Antichrist.[3]

The sacraments of the Church were a mere figment of the imagination. The Cathari made one sacrament out of Baptism, Confirmation, Penance and Eucharist, which they called the *Consolamentum;* they denied the real presence of Jesus Christ in the Eucharist, and they repudiated marriage.[4]

Baptism of water was to them an empty ceremony,[5] as valueless as the baptism of John. Christ had undoubtedly said: "Unless a man be born again of water and the Holy Ghost, he cannot enter into the Kingdom

---

[1] Moneta, *op. cit.*, pp. 390–396.
[2] Apoc. vii, 3, 18.
[3] Moneta, *op. cit.*, p. 397.
[4] Cf. Döllinger, *Beiträge*, vol. ii (*Dokumente*), pp. 294, 297.
[5] Döllinger *ibid.*, pp. 5, 29, 68, 155, 197, 297.

of God."[1]   But the acts of the Apostles proved that baptism was a mere ceremony, for they declared that the Samaritans, although baptized, had not thereby received the Holy Spirit, by whom alone the soul is purified from sin.[2]

The Catholic Church also erred greatly in teaching infant baptism. As their faculties were undeveloped, infants could not receive the Holy Spirit. The Cathari — at least till the middle of the thirteenth century — did not confer the *Consolamentum* upon newly born infants. According to them, the Church could only abandon these little ones to their unhappy destiny.[3]   If they died, they were either forever lost, or, as others taught, condemned to undergo successive incarnations, until they received the *Consolamentum,* which classed them with "the Perfected."

It was preposterous to imagine that Christ wished to change bread and wine into his body in the Eucharist. The Cathari considered transubstantiation as the worst of abominations, since matter, in every form, was the work of the Evil Spirit. They interpreted the gospel texts in a figurative sense: "This is My Body," they said, simply means: "This represents My Body," thus anticipating the teaching of Carlstadt and Zwingli.[4]   They all

[1] John iii. 5.
[2] Act i. 5; viii. 14–17   Moneta, *op. cit.*, p. 290.
[3] Moneta, *op. cit.*, p. 394.   Döllinger, *op. cit.*, vol. i, p. 193; vol. ii (*Dokumente*), pp. 217, 240, 246.
[4] Moneta, *op. cit.*, p. 295; Alanus, *Adversus hæreticos et Waldenses*, ed.

agreed in denouncing Catholics for daring to claim that they really partook of the Body of Christ, as if Christ could enter a man's stomach, to say nothing worse;[1] or as if Christ would expose himself to be devoured by rats and mice.[2]

The Cathari, denying the real presence of Jesus Christ in the Eucharist, rejected the sacrifice of the Mass. God, according to them, repudiated all sacrifices. Did he not teach us through his prophet Osee: "I desire mercy and not sacrifice."[3]

The Lord's supper which the apostles ate so often was something altogether different from the Roman Mass. They knew nothing of sacerdotal vestments, stone altars with shining candelabra, incense, hymns, and chantings. They did not worship in an immense building called a church — a word which should be applied exclusively to the assembly of the saints.[4]

The Cathari, in their hatred of Catholic piety, railed in the most abusive language against the veneration of images, and especially of the cross. The images and statues

Masson, p. 142; Döllinger, *Beiträge*, vol. ii (*Dokumente*), pp. 23, 156, 198, 322.

[1] "Quod mittitur in latrinam ventris et per turpissimum locum, quæ non possent fieri, si esset ibi Deus." Döllinger, *op. cit.*, vol. ii, p. 5.

[2] *Ibid.*, p. 27. Cf. Moneta, *op. cit.*, p. 300; Gregory of Florence, Bishop of Fano, about 1240, *Disputatio inter Catholicum et Paterinum*, in Martène and Durand, *Thesaurus novus anecdotorum*, vol. v, p. 1729.

[3] Osee, vi, 6; Moneta, *op. cit.*, p. 300. *Disputatio inter Catholicum et Paterinum*, p. 1730.

[4] Cf. Döllinger, *op. cit.*, vol. ii (*Dokumente*), pp. 23, 40, 56, 156, 377.

of the saints were to them nothing but idols,[1] which ought to be destroyed. The cross on which Jesus died should be hated rather than reverenced. Some of them, moreover, denied that Jesus had been really crucified; they held that a demon died, or feigned to die in his stead.[2] Even those who believed in the reality of the Savior's crucifixion made this very belief a reason for condemning the veneration of the cross. What man is there, they said, who could see a loved one, for example a father, die upon a cross, and not feel ever after a deep hatred of this instrument of torture?[3] The cross, therefore, should not be reverenced, but despised, insulted and spat upon.[4] One of them even said: "I would gladly hew the cross to pieces with an axe, and throw it into the fire to make the pot boil."[5]

Not only were the Cathari hostile to the Church and her divine worship, but they were also in open revolt against the State, and its rights.

The feudal society rested entirely upon the oath of fealty (*jusjurandum*), which was the bond of its strength and solidity.

According to the Cathari, Christ taught that it was

[1] Döllinger, *ibid.*, vol. ii, pp. 26, 56, 176, 323.

[2] Moneta, *op. cit.*, p. 461; *Disputatio inter Catholicum et Paterinum*, p. 1748.

[3] Döllinger, vol. ii (*Dokumente*), pp. 6, 29, 73, 223.

[4] "Immo homo debebat spuere contra eam et facere omnem vilitatem," etc. Döllinger, *ibid.*, pp. 26; cf. p. 21.

[5] Döllinger, *ibid.*, pp. 168, 169.

sinful to take an oath, and that the speech of every Christian should be yes, yes; no, no. [1] Nothing, therefore, could induce them to take an oath.[2]

The authority of the State, even when Christian, appeared to them, in certain respects, very doubtful. Had not Christ questioned Peter, saying: "What is thy opinion, Simon? The kings of the earth, of whom do they receive tribute or custom? of their own children, or of strangers?" Peter replied: "Of strangers." Jesus said to him: "Then are the children free (of every obligation)." [3]

The Cathari quoted these words to justify their refusal of allegiance to princes. Were they not disciples of Christ, whom the truth had made free? [4] Some of them not only disputed the lawfulness of taxation, but went so far as to condone stealing, provided the thief had done no injury to "Believers." [5]

---

[1] Matt. v, 37; James v, 12.

[2] Döllinger, *Beiträge*, vol. ii (*Dokumente*), pp. 15, 83, 167, 323; Moneta, *op. cit.*, p. 470; Doat, xxii, p. 90; Bernard Gui, *Practica inquisitionis*, p. 239.

[3] Matt. xvii. 24, 25.

[4] Döllinger, *Beiträge*, vol. ii (*Dokumente*), pp. 69, 75; cf. vol. i, p. 183.

[5] Contrary to the Catholic teaching, the Cathari absolved those who stole from "non-believers," without obliging them to make restitution. "Audivit ab Jacobo Auterii et ab aliis quod credentes propter hoc erant audaces ad faciendum malum aliis hominibus et ad inferendum damnum eis, quia confidebant, quod in morte reciperentur et sic absolverentur per eas ab omnibus peccatis et salvarentur, et non audivit ab hæreticis, nec credentibus, quod hæretici inducerent aliquem credentem quem hæreticare volebant quod restitueret alicui illa quæ male abstulerat vel lucratus fuerat ab eo; credit tamen, quod hæretici inducerent credentes, quod si aliquid injuste habuerant

Some of the Cathari admitted the authority of the State, but denied its right to inflict capital punishment. "It is not God's will," said Pierre Garsias, "that human justice condemn any one to death; [1] and when one of the Cathari became consul of Toulouse, he wrote to remind him of this absolute law. [2] But the *Summa contra hæreticos* asserts: "all the Catharan sects taught that the public prosecution of crime was unjust, and that no man had a right to administer justice"; [3] a teaching which denied the State's right to punish.

The Cathari interpreted literally the words of Christ to Peter: "All that take the sword shall perish with the sword," [4] and applied the commandment *Non occides* absolutely. "In no instance," they said, "has one the right to kill another"; [5] neither the internal welfare of a country, nor its external interests can justify murder. War is never lawful. The soldier defending his country is just as much a murderer as the most common criminal.

---

ab aliis credentibus, quod illud redderent, sed (non) credit, quod inducerent eos ad reddendum quod injuste habuerant a non credentibus Tamen hoc communiter hæretici tenebant, quod sive earum credentes redderent illud quod male acquisiverant sive non, solummodo quod reciperentur per hæreticos, quod absoluti essent ab omnibus peccatis et salvarentur." Döllinger, *ibid.*, vol. ii, pp. 248, 249; cf. pp. 245, 246.

[1] Doat, vol. xxii, p. 89.

[2] *Ibid.*, p. 100.

[3] " Quod vindicta non debet fieri; quod justitia non debet fieri per hominem." *Summa contra hæreticos*, ed. Douais, p. 133, Moneta, *op. cit.*, p. 513.

[4] Matt. xxvi. 52.

[5] "Nullo casu occidendum." Doat, xxiii, 100; *Summa contra hæreticos*, p. 133. Cf. Döllinger, *Beiträge*, vol. ii, p. 199.

It was not any special aversion to the crusades, but their horror of war in general, that made the Cathari declare the preachers of the crusades murderers.[1]

These anti-Catholic, anti-patriotic, and anti-social theories were only the negative side of Catharism. Let us now ascertain what they substituted for the Catholic doctrines they denied.

Catharism, as we have already hinted, was a hodge-podge of pagan dualism and gospel teaching, given to the world as a sort of reformed Christianity.

Human souls, spirits fallen from heaven into a material body which is the work of the Evil Spirit, were subject on this earth to a probation, which was ended by Christ, or rather by the Holy Spirit. They were set free by the imposition of hands, the secret of which had been committed to the true Church by the disciples of Jesus.

This Church had its rulers, the Bishops, and its members who are called "the Perfected," "the Consoled," and "the Believers."

We need not dwell upon the episcopate of the Catharan hierarchy. Suffice it to say that the Bishop was always surrounded by three dignitaries, the *Filius Major*, the *Filius Minor*, and the Deacon. The Bishop had charge of the most important religious ceremonies; the imposition of hands for the initiation or *Consolamentum*, the breaking of bread which replaced the Eucharist, and

[1] Doat, xxii, 89; Döllinger, *Beiträge*, vol. ii, pp. 199, 200, 287.

the liturgical prayers such as the recitation of the Lord's Prayer. When he was absent, the *Filius Major,* the *Filius Minor,* or the Deacon took his place. It was seldom, however, that these dignitaries traveled alone; the Bishop was always accompanied by his Deacon, who served as his *socius.*[1]

One joined the Church by promising (the *Convenenza*) to renounce the Catholic faith, and to receive the Catharan initiation (the *Consolamentum*), at least at the hour of death.[2] This was the first step on the road to perfection. Those who agreed to make it were called "the Believers." Their obligations were few. They were not bound to observe the severe Catharan fasts, which we will mention later on. They could live in the world like other mortals, and were even allowed to eat meat and to marry. Their chief duty was "to venerate" "the Perfected," each time they entered their presence. They genuflected, and prostrated themselves three times, saying each time as they rose "Give us your blessing"; the third time they added: "Good Christians, give us God's blessing and yours; pray God that he preserve

---

[1] Cf. Döllinger, *Beiträge,* vol. i, pp. 200–203; vol. ii (*Dokumente*), pp. 194, 266, 278, 292, 295, 324, etc.

[2] "Fecit pactum hæreticis, quod ipsi vocant *la convenensa,* quod peteret hæreticos in infirmitate sua, ut reciperent eum et servarent animam ipsius." *Sententiæ inquisitionis Tolosanæ,* in Limborch, p. 29. "Interrogatus si fecit hæreticis *conventionem,* quod possent eum hæreticare et recipere in fidem et sectam suam in fine, dixit quod sic." Döllinger, *Beiträge,* vol. ii (*Dokumente*), p. 18.

us from an evil death, and bring us to a good end!" The Perfected replied: "Receive God's blessing and ours; may God bless you, preserve you from an evil death, and bring you to a good end." [1]   If these heretics were asked why they made others venerate them in this manner, they replied that the Holy Spirit dwelling within them gave them the right to such homage. [2]   The Believers were always required to pay this extraordinary mark of respect.   In fact it was a *sine qua non* of their being admitted to the *Convenenza*. [3]

The *Convenenza* was not merely an external bond, uniting "the Believers" and "the Perfected," but it was also an earnest of eternal salvation.   It assured the future destiny of "the Believers"; it gave them the right to receive the *consolamentum* on their death-bed. [4]   This remitted all the sins of their life.   Only one thing could deprive them of "this good end"; viz., the absence of one of the Perfected, who alone could lay hands upon them. [5]

---

[1] Döllinger, *ibid.*, p. 4; cf. pp. 18, 19, 25, 30, 39; vol. i, pp. 237, 238.

[2] Döllinger, vol. ii, pp. 4, 376.

[3] Doat, vol. xxxii, fol. 170; cf. Döllinger, *Beiträge*, vol. ii, pp. 27, 145, 182, 183, 187, 236, 249.

[4] "Paciscens cum eis, ut si in articulo mortis esses, licet non haberes usum linguæ nihilominus te in suam sectam reciperent." Doat, *Acta inquisitionis Carcass.*, vol. i, fol. 317; cf. Döllinger, *Beiträge*, vol. i, p. 213; vol. ii, pp. 4, 236.

[5] Ordinarily, "mos hæreticorum existit, quod, ubi duo perfecti hæretici ad hæreticandum aliquem infirmum conveniunt, alter eorum solus et communiter antiquior in hæresi infirmum hæreticet." Döllinger, *Beiträge*, vol. ii, p. 39. But in times of persecution only one of "the Perfected" was required to confer the *consolamentum*.

Those who died without the Catharan *consolamentum* were either eternally lost, or condemned to begin life anew with another chance of becoming one of "the good men." [1] These transmigrations of the soul were rather numerous. The human soul did not always pass directly from the body of a man into the body of another man. It occasionally entered into the bodies of animals, like the ox and the ass. The Cathari were wont to tell the story of "a good Christian," one of "the Perfected," who remembered, in a previous existence as a horse, having lost his shoe in a certain place between two stones, as he was running swiftly under his master's spur. When he became a man he was curious enough to hunt for it, and he found it in the self-same spot. [2] Such humiliating transmigrations were undoubtedly rather rare. A woman named Sybil, "a Believer" and later on one of "the Perfected," remembered having been a queen in a prior existence. [3]

What the *Convenença* promised, the Catharan initiation or *consolamentum* gave; [4] the first made "Believers," and

---

[1] The Cathari commonly taught that there was no hell: *quod infernus nihil est . . . ; quod animæ non damnabuntur.* Cf. *Summa adversus Catharos*, ed. Douais, 132; cf. p. 127. "De corpore in corpus, donec veniret in manus bonorum hominum." Döllinger, *Beiträge*, vol. ii, pp. 36, 174, 175.

[2] Döllinger, *ibid.*, pp. 153, 175.

[3] Döllinger, *ibid.*, p. 24; cf. pp. 31, 36, 153, 174, 191, 207, 216, 235.

[4] The rites of the *Consolamentum* are indicated in a ritual published by Clédat under the title: *Le nouveau Testament traduit au XIIIe siècle en langue provençale, suivi d'un rituel cathare*, Paris, 1888; and in the *Practica inquisitionis hæretice pravitatis* of Bernard Gui, ed. Douais, Paris, 1886.

predisposed souls to sanctity; the second made "the Perfected," and conferred sanctity with all its rights and prerogatives.

The *Consolamentum* required a preparation which we may rightly compare with the catechumenate of the early Christians.[1]

This probation usually lasted one year. It consisted in an honest attempt to lead the life of "the Perfected," and chiefly in keeping their three "lents," abstaining from meat, milk-food and eggs. It was therefore called the time of abstinence (*abstinentia*). One of "the Perfected" was appointed by the Church to report upon the life of the postulant, who daily had to venerate his superior, according to the Catharan rite.[2]

After this probation, came the ceremony of "the delivery" (traditio) of the Lord's Prayer. A number of "the Perfected" were always present. The highest dignitary, the Bishop or "the Ancient," made the candidate a lengthy speech, which has come down to us:

"Understand," he said, "that when you appear before the Church of God you are in the presence of the Father,

[1] Cf. Jean Guiraud, *Le Consolamentum ou initiation cathare*, in *Questions d'histoire et d'archéologie chrétienne*. Paris, 1906, pp. 95–149.

[2] See the case of Guillaume Tardieu in Doat, vol. xxiii, p. 201 and seq. Another case may be found in Ms. 609 (fol. 41) of the library of Toulouse: "Sed dicti heretici noluerunt eam ipsam hereticare donec bene esset instructa fidem et mores hereticorum et fecisset primo tres quadragenas" (the three Catharan lents).

the Son and the Holy Spirit, as the Scriptures prove," etc. Then, having repeated the Lord's Prayer to "the Believer" word for word, and having explained its meaning, he continued: "We deliver to you this holy prayer, that you may receive it from us, from God, and from the Church, that you may have the right to say it all your life, day and night, alone and in company, and that you may never eat or drink without first saying it. If you omit it, you must do penance." The Believer replied: "I receive it from you and from the Church."[1]

After these words came the *Abrenuntiatio.* At the Catholic baptism, the catechumen renounced Satan, with his works and pomps. According to the Catharan ritual, the Catholic Church was Satan.

"The Perfected" said to the Believer: "Friend, if you wish to be one of us, you must renounce all the doctrines of the Church of Rome;" and he replied: "I do renounce them."

— Do you renounce that cross made with chrism upon your breast, head, and shoulders?

— I do renounce it.

— Do you believe that the water of Baptism is efficacious for salvation?

— No, I do not believe it.

— Do you renounce the veil, which the priest placed upon your head, after you were baptized?

[1] Clédat, *Rituel Cathare,* pp. xi-xv.

— I do renounce it.[1]

Again the Bishop addressed "the Believer" to impress upon him the new duties involved in his receiving the Holy Spirit. Those who were present prayed God to pardon the candidate's sins, and then venerated "the Perfected" (the ceremony of the *Parcia*). After the Bishop's prayer, "May God bless thee, make thee a good Christian, and grant thee a good end," the candidate made a solemn promise faithfully to fulfill the duties he had learned during his *probatio*.[2] The words of his promise are to be found in Sacconi: "I promise to devote my life to God and to the gospel, never to lie or swear, never to touch a woman, never to kill an animal, never to eat meat, eggs or milk-food; never to eat anything but fish and vegetables, never to do anything without first saying the Lord's Prayer, never to eat, travel, or pass the night without a *socius*. If I fall into the hands of my enemies or happen to be separated from my *socius*, I promise to spend three days without food or drink. I will never take off my clothes on retiring, nor will I deny my faith even when threatened with death."[3] The ceremony of the *Parcia* was then repeated.

Then, according to the ritual, "the Bishop takes the book (the New Testament), and places it upon the head

[1] Sacconi, *Summa de Catharis*, in Martène and Durand, *Thesaurus novus anecdotorum*, vol. v, p. 1776.

[2] Clédat, *Rituel Cathare*, pp. xvi and xx.

[3] Sacconi, *op. cit.*

of the candidate, while the other "good men" present impose hands upon him, saying: "Holy Father, accept this servant of yours in all righteousness, and send your grace and your Spirit upon him." [1] The Holy Spirit was then supposed to descend, and the ceremony of the *Consolamentum* was finished; "the Believer" had become one of "the Perfected."

However, before the assembly dispersed, "the Perfected" proceeded to carry out two other ceremonies: the vesting and the kiss of peace.

"While their worship was tolerated," writes an historian,[2] "they gave their new brother a black garment; but in times of persecution they did not wear it, for fear of betraying themselves to the officials of the Inquisition. In the thirteenth century, in southern France, they were known by the linen or flaxen belt, which the men wore over their shirts, and the women wore *cordulam cinctam ad carnem nudam subtus mamillas*.[3] They resembled the cord or scapular that the Catholic tertiaries wore to represent the habit of the monastic order to which they belonged. They were therefore called '*haeretici vestiti*,' [4] which became a common term for "the Perfected."

---

[1] *Rituel cathare*, pp. xx and xxv.
[2] Jean Guiraud, *Le consolamentum ou initiation cathare*, loc. cit., p. 134.
[3] Döllinger, *Beiträge*, vol. ii (*Dokumente*), p. 36.
[4] "Hæretici perfecti vulgariter vestiti dicti." Council of Béziers in 1299, in Martène and Durand, *Thesaurus novus anecdotorum*, vol. iv, p. 225. Cf. Döllinger, *Beiträge*, vol. i, p. 205; vol. ii (*Dokumente*), pp. 178, 179, 194, 195.

"The last ceremony was the kiss of peace, which 'the Perfected' gave their new brother, by kissing him twice (on the mouth), *bis in ore ex transverso*. He in turn kissed the one nearest him, who passed on the *pax* to all present. If the recipient was a woman, the minister gave her the *pax* by touching her shoulder with the book of the gospels, and his elbow with hers. She transmitted this symbolic kiss in the same manner to the one next to her, if he was a man. After a last fraternal embrace, they all congratulated the new brother, and the assembly dispersed."[1]

The promises made by this new member of "the Perfected" were not all equally hard to keep. As far as positive duties were concerned, there were but three: the daily recitation of the Lord's Prayer, the breaking of bread, and the *apparellamentum*.

Only "the Perfected" were allowed to recite the Lord's Prayer.[2] The Cathari explained the esoteric character of this prayer by that passage in the Apocalypse which

[1] "Omnes præsentes adoraverunt hæreticos et acceperunt pacem ab hæreticis, scilicet homines osculantes hæreticos bis in ore ex transverso et mulieres acceperunt pacem a libro hæreticorum, deinde osculatæ fuerunt sese ab invicem similiter bis in ore ex transverso," etc.   Döllinger, *ibid.*, vol. ii, p. 41. "Si sint illic mulieres, aliqua illarum recipit pacem de cubito alicujus hæretici." Sacconi, in Martène and Durand, *loc. cit.*, vol. v, p. 1776. "Mulier accepit pacem a libro et humero hæreticorum."   Döllinger, *ibid.*, vol. ii, p. 34; *Rituel cathare*, p. xxi.

[2] "Quod nullus debebat dicere *Pater Noster*, quæ est sancta oratio, nisi esset hæreticus vestitus," etc.   Döllinger, *Beiträge*, vol. ii (*Dokumente*), p. 199; cf. pp. 212, 237, 246.

speaks of the one hundred and forty-four thousand elect who follow the Lamb whithersoever He goeth, and who sing a hymn which only virgins can sing.[1] This hymn was the *Pater Noster*.[2] Married people, therefore, and consequently "the Believers," could not repeat it without profanation. But "the Perfected" were obliged to say it every day, especially before meals.[3]

They blessed the bread without making the sign of the cross.

This "breaking of bread" replaced the Eucharist. They thought in this way to reproduce the Lord's Supper, while they repudiated all the ceremonies of the Catholic mass. "The Believers" partook of this blessed bread when they sat at the table with "the Perfected," and they were wont to carry some of it home to eat from time to time.

Some attributed to it a wonderful sanctifying power, and believed that if at their death none of "the Perfected" were present to administer the *consolamentum*, this "bread of the holy prayer" would itself ensure their

---

[1] *Apoc.* xiv, 1–4.

[2] *Moneta, op. cit.*, p. 328. On the Catharan text of the *Pater Noster*, cf. Döllinger, *Beiträge*, vol. i, p. 229.

[3] "Promisit quod ulterius non esset atque comederet sine socio et sine oratione et quod captus sine socio non comederet per triduum." Doat, *Acta inquisitionis Carcassonæ*, vol. ii, 272. The Perfected had to live with a *socius* who blessed his food, while he in turn had to bless the food of his companion. If he separated from his socius, he had to do without food and drink for three days. This frequently happened when they were arrested and cast into prison.

salvation.[1]   They were therefore very anxious to keep some of it on hand; and we read of "the Believers" of Languedoc having some sent them from Lombardy, when they were no longer able to communicate with their persecuted brethren.[2]

It was usually distributed to all present during the *Apparellamentum.* This was the solemn monthly reunion of all the Cathari, "the Believers " and "the Perfected." [3] All present confessed their sins, no matter how slight, although only a general confession was required. As a rule the Deacon addressed the assembly,[4] which closed with the *Parcia* and the kiss of peace: *osculantes sese invicem ex transverso.*[5]

[1] "Talem panem vocant panem sanctæ orationis et panem fractionis, et *credentes* eorum vocant panem benedictum sive panem signatum." Döllinger, *Beiträge*, vol. ii, p. 4.   "Respondit ei quod dictus panis majorem virtutem centies habebat quam panis qui benedicitur in ecclesia in die dominica, licet non fiat signum crucis super dictum panem nec spargatur aqua benedicta." *Ibid.*, p. 148. "Geralda . . . fecit fieri de pane benedicto per dictum hæreticum propter devotionem et fidem, quam habebat, quod posset salvari in fide dicti hæretici et accepit de dicto pane et comedit et partem reservavit et multis annis conservavit, et aliquando de illo pane comedit." Limborch, *Sententiæ inquisitionis Tolos.*, p. 160. "Dicta Navarra dixit ipsæ Lombardæ quod tantum valebat panis et qui vellet habere bonos homines in obitu et non posset habere eos, eo quod erat panis bonorum hominum." Doat, *Acta inquisit. Carcass.*, vol. v, fol. 188.

[2] Döllinger, *Beiträge*, vol. ii (*Dokumente*), p. 35.

[3] "Servitium hæreticorum quod dicunt *apparellamentum* quod faciunt de mense in mensem." Doat, *op. cit.*, vol. ii, fol. 280.   "*Apparellando* se cum eis de mense in mensem et alia omnia faciendo quæ heretici præcipiunt et faciunt observari," etc.   *Ibid.*, vol. iv, fol. 205.

[4] Sacconi, *loc. cit.*, pp. 1765, 1766; Moneta, *op. cit.*, p. 306; Doat, *Acta Inquisit. Carcass.*, vol. v, fol. 246.   Cf. Döllinger, *Beiträge*, vol. i, pp. 232-235.

[5] Vaissete, *Histoire du Languedoc*, vol. iii, Preuves, p. 387.

There was nothing very hard in this; on the contrary it was the consoling side of their life. But their rigorous laws of fasting and abstinence constituted a most severe form of mortification.

"The Perfected" kept three Lents a year; the first from St. Brice's day (November 13) till Christmas; the second from Quinquagesima Sunday till Easter; the third from Pentecost to the feast of Saints Peter and Paul. They called the first and last weeks of these Lents the strict weeks (*septimana stricta*), because during them they fasted on bread and water every day, whereas the rest of the time they fasted only three days out of the seven. Besides these special penitential seasons they observed the same rigorous fast three days a week all during the year, unless they were sick or were traveling.[1]

These heretics were known everywhere by their fasting and abstinence. "They are good men," it was said, "who live holy lives, fasting three days a week, and never eating meat."[2]

They never ate meat in fact, and this law of abstinence extended, as we have seen, to eggs, cheese, and everything which was the result of animal propagation. They were allowed, however, to eat cold-blooded animals like

[1] Bernard Gui, *Practica inquisitionis*, p. 239.

[2] Douai, *Les manuscrits du château de Merville*, in the *Annales du Midi*, 1890, p. 185.

fish, because of the strange idea they had of their method of propagation.[1]

One of the results, or rather one of the causes of their abstinence from meat was the absolute respect they had for animal life in general. We have seen that they admitted metempsychosis. According to their belief, the body of an ox or an ass might be the dwelling place of a human soul. To kill these animals, therefore, was a crime equivalent to murder. "For that reason," says Bernard Gui, "they never kill an animal or a bird; for they believe that in animals and birds dwell the souls of men, who died without having been received into their sect by the imposition of hands."[2] This was also one of the signs by which they could be known as heretics. We read of them being condemned at Goslar and elsewhere for having refused to kill and eat a chicken.[3]

Their most extraordinary mortification was the law of chastity, as they understood and practiced it. They had a great horror of Christian marriage, and endeavored to defend their views by the Scriptures. Had not Christ

[1] "Numquam comedunt carnes . . . nec caseum nec ova, nec aliquid quod nascitur per viam generationis seu coitus." Bernard Gui, *Practica inquisitionis*, p. 240. Cf. Döllinger, *Beiträge*, vol. ii ((*Dokumente*), pp. 22, 27, 30, 145, 146, 149, 152, 181, 193, 234, 235, 246, 248, 282, 329. Ms. 609 of Toulouse, fol. 2 v°, 36, 39, 41, 46, 65. Cf. Jean Guiraud; *La morale des Albegeois*, in the *Questions d'histoire et d'archéologie chrétienne*, pp. 63–66.

[2] *Practica Inquisitionis*, p. 240.

[3] Cf. Jean Guiraud, *loc. cit.*, pp. 63, 64, 69; Döllinger, *Beiträge*, vol. i, p. 236.

said: "Whosoever should look upon a woman to lust after her, hath already committed adultery with her in his heart";[1] *i.e.* was he not guilty of a crime. "The children of this world marry," he says again, "and are given in marriage; but they that shall be accounted worthy of that world, and of the resurrection of the dead, shall neither be married nor take wives."[2] "It is good," says St. Paul, "for a man not to touch a woman."[3]

The Cathari interpreted these texts literally, and when their opponents cited other texts of Scripture which plainly taught the sacred character of Christian marriage, they at once interpreted them in a spiritual or symbolic sense. The only legitimate marriage in their eyes was the union of the Bishop with the Church, or the union of the soul with the Holy Spirit by the ceremony of the *Consolamentum.*[4]

They condemned absolutely all marital relations. That was the sin of Adam and Eve. Pierre Garsias taught at Toulouse that the forbidden fruit of the Garden of Eden was simply carnal pleasure.[5]

One of the purposes of marriage is the begetting of children. But the propagation of the human species is

---

[1] Matt. v, 28; Döllinger, *Beiträge*, vol. ii (*Dokumente*), p. 56.

[2] Luke xx, 35; Döllinger, *loc. cit.*, p. 91; Moneta, *op. cit.*, 326.

[3] 1 Corinth. vii. 1, 7. Döllinger, *op. cit.*, vol. ii (*Dokumente*), p. 281.

[4] Döllinger, *ibid.*, vol. ii, pp. 29, 54, 55; cf. vol. i, pp. 175-177.

[5] "Quod pomum vetitum primis parentibus nil aliud fuit quam delectatio coitus, et addidit quod ipsum pomum porrexit Adam mulieri." Döllinger, *op. cit.*, vol. ii, p. 34; cf. p. 612, cf. p. 88.

plainly the work of the Evil Spirit. A woman with child is a woman possessed of the devil. "Pray God," said one of "the Perfected" to the wife of a Toulouse lumber merchant, "pray God that he deliver you from the devil within you." [1] The greatest evil that could befall a woman was to die *enceinte;* for being in the state of impurity and in the power of Satan, she could not be saved. We read of the Cathari saying this to Peirona de la Caustra: *quod si decederet prægnans non posset salvari.* [2]

Marriage, because it made such a condition possible, was absolutely condemned. Bernard Gui thus resumes the teaching of the Cathari on this point: "They condemn marriage absolutely; they maintain that it is a perpetual state of sin; they deny that a good God can institute it. They declare the marital relation as great a sin as incest with one's mother, daughter, or sister." [3] And this is by no means a calumnious charge. The language which Bernard Gui attributes to these heretics was used by them on every possible occasion. They were unable to find words strong enough to express their contempt for marriage. "Marriage," they said, "is nothing but licentiousness; marriage is merely prosti-

[1] "Quod rogaret Deum ut liberaret eam de dæmone quam habebat in ventre." Döllinger, *ibid.*, p. 35. "Quod prægnans erat de dæmonio." Ms. 609, of the library of Toulouse, fol. 230.

[2] Doat, vol. xxii, p. 57.

[3] *Practica Inquisitionis*, p. 130.

tution." [1] In their extreme hatred, they even went so far as to prefer open licentiousness to it, saying: "Cohabitation with one's wife is a worse crime than adultery." One might be inclined to think that this was merely an extravagent outburst; but on the contrary, they tried to defend this view by reason. Licentiousness, they argued, was a temporary thing, to which a man gave himself up only in secret; he might in time become ashamed of it, repent and renounce it entirely. The married state on the contrary caused no shame whatever; men never thought of renouncing it, because they did not dream of the wickedness it entailed: *quia magis publice et sine verecundia peccatum fiebat.*[2]

No one, therefore, was admitted to the *consolamentum* unless he had renounced all marital relations. In this case, the woman "gave her husband to God, and to the good men." It often happened, too, that women, moved by the preaching of "the Perfected," condemned their unconverted husbands to an enforced celibacy.[3] This

---

[1] Döllinger, *Beiträge*, vol. ii (*Dokumente*), pp. 40, 156; Ms. 609 of Toulouse, fol. 41 v°, 64.

[2] Döllinger, *ibid.*, vol. ii, p. 23; cf. 156.

[3] "Aladaicis, uxor infirmi, absolvit maritum suum Deo et bonis hominibus." Doat, *Acta inquisit. Carcass.*, vol. ii, fol. 115. "Forneria, mater ipsius testis, fuit hæreticata et recessit a viro suo." *Ibid.*, vol. iv, fol. 204. "Dixit quod ipsa Aladaicis libenter dimitteret virum suum et teneret fidem hæreticorum et recederet cum hæreticis, si placeret eis." Döllinger, *Beiträge*, vol. ii, p. 24. "Dixit (hæreticus) ipsi loquenti si ipse vellet dimittere dictam Ramundam, ipse ex parte Dei absolvebat eum de dicto matrimonio, et sic matrimonium inter eos dictus hæreticus separavit." *Ibid.*, p. 229.

was one of the results of the neo-Manichean teachings.

Moreover, they carried their principles so far as to consider it a crime even to touch a woman.

They forbade a man to sit next to a woman except in case of necessity. "If a woman touches you," said Pierre Autier, "you must fast three days on bread and water; and if you touch a woman, you must fast nine days on the same diet." [1] At the ceremony of the *Consolamentum*, the Bishop who imposed hands on the future sister took great care not to touch her, even with the end of his finger; to avoid doing so, he always covered the postulant with a veil.[2]

But in times of persecution, this over-scrupulous caution was calculated to attract public attention. "The Perfected" (men and women) lived together, pretending that they were married, so that they would not be known as heretics.[3] It was their constant care, however, to avoid the slightest contact. This caused them at times great inconvenience. While traveling, they shared the same bed, the better to avoid suspicion. But they

Cf. Jean Guiraud, *La morale des Albigeois*, in the *Questions d'histoire*, pp. 77–79.

[1] Döllinger, *Beiträge*, vol. ii, p. 243.

[2] "Prius posuerat quemdam pannum linteum album super dictam infirmam," etc. Limborch, *Sententiæ Inquisit. Tolos.*, p. 186; cf. p. 190. A father forbade his daughter to touch him, because he had received the *consolamentum*. *Ibid.*, p. 111.

[3] "Ego non sum hæreticus," said a heretic of Toulouse, "quia uxorem habeo et cum ipsa jaceo et filios habeo," etc. G. Pelhisse, *Chronique*, ed. Douais, p. 94.

slept with their clothes on, and thus managed to follow out the letter of the law: *tamen induti ita quod unus alium in nuda carne non tangebat.*[1]

Many Catholics were fully persuaded that this pretended love of purity was merely a cloak to hide the grossest immorality.[2] But while we may admit that many of "the Perfected" did actually violate their promise of absolute chastity, we must acknowledge that as a general rule they did resist temptation, and preferred death to what they considered impurity.

Many who feared that they might give way in a moment of weakness to the temptations of a corrupt nature sought refuge in suicide,[3] which was called the *Endura.* There were two forms for the sick heretic, suffocation and fasting. The candidate for death was asked whether he desired to be a martyr or a confessor. If he chose to be a martyr, they placed a handkerchief or a pillow over his mouth, until he died of suffocation. If he preferred to be a confessor, he remained without food or drink, until he died of starvation.[4]

---

[1] Döllinger, *Beiträge*, vol. ii, pp. 148, 149.

[2] Döllinger, *ibid.*, pp. 245, 296, 312, 371, 372.

[3] "Tunc imponunt ei quod non debeat amplius comedere carnem nec ova nec caseum, non tangere mulierem . . . , et quod si non posset se abstinere a prædictis, melius est quod moriatur *en la endura*, quam si aliquid prædictorum transgrederetur." Doat, *Acta Inquisit. Carcass.*, vol. xxxii, fol. 170.

[4] "Quando autem in extremo vitæ periculo aliquem recipere volunt, dant ei optionem utrum velit in regno cœlorum esse consors martyrum, vel confessorum. Si elegerit statum martyrum, tunc manutergio ad hoc specialiter deputato . . . strangulant ipsum. Si statum confessorum elegerit, tunc post

The Cathari believed that "the Believers," who asked for the *consolamentum* during sickness, would not keep the laws of their new faith, if they happened to get well. Therefore, to safeguard them against apostasy, they were strongly urged to make their salvation certain by the *endura*. A manuscript of the Register of the Inquisition of Carcassonne, for instance, tells us of a Catharan minister who compelled a sick woman to undergo the *endura*, after he had conferred upon her the Holy Spirit. He forbade any one "to give her the least nourishment . . . and as a matter of fact no food or drink was given her that night or the following day, lest perchance she might be deprived of the benefit of the *consolamentum*." [1]

One of "the Perfected," named Raymond Belhot, congratulated a mother whose daughter he had just "consoled," and ordered her not to give the sick girl anything to eat or drink until he returned, even though she requested it. "If she asks me for it," said the mother, "I will not have the heart to refuse her." "You must refuse her," said "the good man," "or else cause great injury to her soul." From that moment the girl neither ate nor drank; in fact she

---

manus impositionem nihil dant ei ad usum vel ad esum, nisi puram aquam ad bibendum, et ita fame ipsum perimunt." Döllinger, *ibid.*, p. 373 (this passage is taken from the *Summa de Catharis* of Sacconi). Cf. pp. 271, 370.

[1] "Ne dicta infirma perderet bonum quod receperat." Ms. 609 of the library of Toulouse, fol. 134.

did not ask for any nourishment. She died the next Saturday.[1]

About the middle of the thirteenth century, when the Cathari began to give the *consolamentum* to infants, they were often cruel enough to make them undergo the *endura*. "One would think," says an historian of the time, "that the world had gone back to those hateful days when unnatural mothers sacrificed their children to Moloch." [2]

It sometimes happened that the parents of "the consoled" withstood more or less openly the cruelty of "the Perfected."

When this happened, some of "the Perfected" remained in the house of the sick person, to see that their murderous prescriptions were obeyed to the letter. Or if this was impossible, they had "the consoled" taken to the house of some friend, where they could readily carry out their policy of starvation.[3]

But as a general rule the "heretics" submitted to the *endura* of their own free will. Raymond Isaure tells us of a certain Guillaume Sabatier, who began the *endura* in a retired villa, immediately after his initiation; he starved

---

[1] Döllinger, *Beiträge*, vol. ii (*Dokumente*), p. 250.

[2] *Ibid.*, vol. i, p. 222; cf. p. 193.

[3] "Post aliquot dies (after the Catharan initiation) hæretici extraxerunt dictum infirmum de domo sua et portaverunt in domum hæreticorum, et ibi dictus infirmus obiit." Doat, *Acta Inquisit. Carcass.*, vol. ii, fol. 115. This was a frequent case in the Acts of the Inquisition of Carcassonne, says Döllinger, *Beiträge*, vol. i, p. 225, n. 1.

himself to death in seven weeks.[1] A woman named Gentilis died of the *endura* in six or seven days.[2] A woman of Coustaussa, who had separated from her husband, went to Saverdum to receive the *consolamentum*. She at once began the *endura* at Ax, and died after an absolute fast of about twelve weeks.[3] A certain woman named Montaliva submitted to the *endura;* during it "she ate nothing whatever, but drank some water; she died in six weeks."[4] This case gives us some idea of this terrible practice; we see that they were sometimes allowed to drink water, which explains the extraordinary duration of some of these suicidal fasts.[5]

Some of the Cathari committed suicide in other ways. A woman of Toulouse named Guillemette first began to subject herself to the *endura* by frequent blood letting; then she tried to weaken herself more by taking long baths; finally she drank poison, and as death did not come quickly enough, she swallowed pounded glass to per-

---

[1] Döllinger, *ibid.*, vol. ii, p. 19.

[2] *Ibid.*, p. 24.

[3] "Quædam mulier de Constanciano . . . *quæ dimiserat maritum suum* et fugerat ad partes Savartesii, misit se ad *enduram* . . .; duodecim septimanis vel circa, antequam moreretur, stetit in *endura.*" *Ibid.*, p. 25.

[4] Ms. 609, of the library of Toulouse, fol. 28. Cf. Döllinger, *Beiträge*, vol. ii, p. 26. "Posuit se et stetit in *endura* donec fuit mortua, ita quod *nihil comedebat, nec bibebat nisi aquam.*"

[5] Sometimes the heretics undergoing the *endura* put sugar in the water they drank, *aquam cum zucara.* Limborch, *Liber sentent,* fol. 79 B.

forate her intestines.[1] Another woman opened her veins in the bath.[2]

Such methods of suicide were exceptional, although the *endura* itself was common,[3] at least among the Cathari of Languedoc.[4] "Every one," says a trustworthy historian, "who reads the acts of the tribunals of the Inquisition of Toulouse and Carcassonne must admit that the *endura,* voluntary or forced, put to death more victims than the stake of the Inquisition."[5]

Catharism, therefore, was a serious menace to the church, to the state, and to society.

Without being precisely a Christian heresy, its customs, its hierarchy, and above all its rites of initiation — which

---

[1] Ms. 609, of Toulouse, fol. 33.

[2] *Ibid.,* fol. 70. Cf. Tanon, *op. cit.,* pp. 224, 225.

[3] "Hæreticati seu in sanitate seu in ægritudine ex tunc non debebant comedere aliquid vel bibere, sed si non possent abstinere a potu, debebant bibere aquam frigidam, et sic non ex hâc endura erat magnum meritum, et quando moriebantur, eorum anima ibat ad regnum patris. Audivit etiam, quod si hæreticati facerent se minui, quousque totus sanguis de corpore exivisset, bonum opus faciebant, ut sic cito mori possent et cito venire ad gloriam Patris. Et taliter occidere se non reputabant malum vel peccatum, sed bonum et meritum." Döllinger, *Beiträge,* vol. ii (*Dokumente*), p. 248.

[4] Molinier (*L'Endura*, pp. 293, 294) thinks that this practice was peculiar to Languedoc, and only came into vogue at the close of the thirteenth century. In this hypothesis, we must hold not only that Sacconi's *Summa de Catharis* is interpolated (cf. *supra*, p. 116), but also that those guilty of the interpolation were men of Languedoc. This last conjecture is rather improbable.

[5] Döllinger, *Beiträge,* vol. i, p. 226. Cf. cases of *endura* cited by Döllinger, *op. cit.,* vol. ii, pp. 20, 24, 25, 26, 37, 136, 138, 139, 141, 142, 147, 157, 205, 234, 238, 239, 242, 248, 250, 271, 295, 370, 373. Molinier (*L'Endura*, p. 288) himself writes: "Cruel as it was, the *endura* seems always to have accompanied the *consolamentum,* at least with some of the Albigensian ministers."

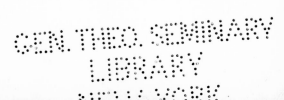

we have purposely explained in detail — gave it all the appearance of one. It was really an imitation and a caricature of Christianity. Some of its practices were borrowed from the primitive Christians, as some historians have proved.[1] That in itself would justify the Church in treating its followers as heretics.

Besides, the Church merely acted in self-defense. The Cathari tried their best to destroy her by attacking her doctrines, her hierarchy, and her apostolic character. If their false teachings had prevailed, disturbing as they did the minds of the people, the Church would have perished.

The princes, who did not concern themselves with these heretics, while they merely denied the teachings of the Church, at last found themselves attacked just as vigorously. The Catharan absolute rejection of the oath of fealty was calculated to break the bond that united subjects to their suzerain lords, and at one blow to destroy the whole edifice of feudalism. And even granting that the feudal system could cease to exist without dragging down in its fall all form of government, how could the State provide for the public welfare, if she did not possess the power to punish criminals, as the Cathari maintained?

But the great unpardonable crime of Catharism was its attempt to destroy the future of humanity by its

[1] Jean Guiraud, *Le consolamentum ou initiation cathare*, in *Questions d'histoire*, p. 145 seq.

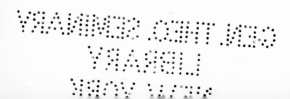

endura, and its abolition of marriage. It taught that the sooner life was destroyed the better. Suicide, instead of being considered a crime, was a means of perfection. To beget children was considered the height of immorality. To become one of "the Perfected," which was the only way of salvation, the husband must leave his wife, and the wife her husband. The family must cease to exist, and all men were urged to form a great religious community, vowed to the most rigorous chastity. If this ideal had been realized, the human race would have disappeared from the earth in a few years. Can any one imagine more immoral and more anti-social teaching?

The Catholic Church has been accused of setting up a similar ideal.[1] This is a gross calumny. For while Catharism made chastity a *sine qua non* of salvation, and denounced marriage as something infamous and criminal, the Church merely counsels virginity to an élite body of men and women in whom she recognizes the marks of a special vocation, according to the teaching of the Savior, "He that can take, let him take it." *Qui potest capere capiat.*[2] She endeavors at the same time to uphold the sacrament of marriage, declaring it a holy state,[3] in which the majority of mankind is to work out its salvation.

There is consequently no parity whatever between the

---

[1] Molinier repeats this accusation (*L'Endura*, p. 282, n. 2).
[2] Matt. xix. 11–12.
[3] Cf. *Summa contra hæreticos*, pp. 96–99.

two societies and their teachings.   In bitterly prosecuting
the Cathari, the Church truly acted for the public good.
The State was bound to aid her by force, unless it wished
to perish herself with all the social order.   This explains
and to a certain degree justifies the combined action of
Church and State in suppressing the Catharan heresy,

CHAPTER VI

FIFTH PERIOD

GREGORY IX AND FREDERIC II

THE ESTABLISHMENT OF THE MONASTIC INQUISITION

THE penal system codified by Innocent III was rather liberally interpreted in France and Italy. In order to make the French law agree with it, an oath was added to the coronation service from the time of Louis IX, whereby the King swore to exterminate, *i.e.*, banish all heretics from his kingdom.[1] We are inclined to interpret in this sense the laws of Louis VIII (1226) and Louis IX (April, 1228), for the south of France. The words referring to the punishment of heretics are a little vague: "Let them be punished," says Louis VIII, with the punishment they deserve." *"Animadversione debita puniantur.* The other penalties specified are infamy and confiscation; in a word, all the consequences of banishment."[2]

[1] Godefroy, *Le cérémonial français*, vol. i, p. 27. We have seen that the Council of Avignon and the town of Montpellier adopted the laws of Innocent III.

[2] "Statuimus quod hæretici qui a catholica fide deviant, quocumque nomine censeantur, postquam fuerint de hæresi per episcopum loci vel per aliam personam ecclesiasticam quæ potestatem habeat (papal legate) condemnati, indilate animadversione debita puniantur," etc. *Ordonnances des roys de France*, vol. xii, pp. 319, 320.

Louis IX re-enacted this law in the following terms: "We decree that our barons and magistrates . . . do their duty in prosecuting heretics." *"De ipsis festinanter faciant quod debebunt."* [1] These words in themselves are not very clear, and, if we were to interpret them by the customs of a few years later,[2] we might think that they referred to the death penalty, even the stake; but comparing them with similar expressions used by Lucius III and Innocent III, we see that they imply merely the penalty of banishment.

However, a canon of the Council of Toulouse in 1229 seems to make the meaning of these words clear, at least for the future. It decreed that all heretics and their abettors are to be brought to the nobles and the magistrates to receive due punishment, *ut animadversione debita puniantur.* But it adds that "heretics, who, *through fear of death* or any other cause, except their own free will, return to the faith, are to be imprisoned by the bishop of the city to do penance, that they may not corrupt

---

[1] "Statuimus et mandamus ut barones terræ . . . solliciti sint et . . . predictos (hæreticos) diligenter investigare studeant et fideliter invenire, et cum eos invenerint, præsentent sine mora . . . personis ecclesiasticis superius memoratis, ut, eis præsentibus, de errore hæresis condemnatis, omni odio, prece et pretio . . . postpositis, de ipsis festinanter faciant quod debebunt." *Ordonnances des roys de France*, vol. i, p. 51; Labbe, *Concilia*, vol. vii, col. 171.

[2] We will mention later on the penalties decreed against heretics in the *Établissements de Saint Louis* and the *Coutumes de Beauvaisis* de Beaumanoir. Julien Havet (*op. cit.*, pp. 169, 170), however, explains the *animadversio debita* of the laws of Louis VIII and Louis IX in accordance with the later documents, *i.e.* the penalty of the stake.

others"; the bishop is to provide for their needs out of the property confiscated.[1] *The fear of death* here seems to imply that the *animadversio debita* meant the death penalty. That would prove the elasticity of the formula. At first it was a legal penalty which custom interpreted to mean banishment and confiscation; later on it meant chiefly the death penalty; and finally it meant solely the penalty of the stake. At any rate, this canon of the Council of Toulouse must be kept in mind; for we will soon see Pope Gregory IX quoting it.

In Italy, Frederic II promulgated on November 22, 1220, an imperial law which, in accordance with the pontifical decree of March 25, 1199, and the Lateran Council of 1215, condemned heretics to every form of banishment, to perpetual infamy, together with the confiscation of their property, and the annulment of all their civil acts and powers. It is evident that the emperor was influenced by Innocent III, for having declared that the children of heretics could not inherit their father's property, he adds a phrase borrowed from the papal decree of 1199, viz., "that to offend the divine majesty

---

[1] "Hæreticos, credentes, fautores et receptatores seu defensores eorum, adhibita cautela · ne fugere possint, archiepiscopo vel episcopo, dominis locorum seu bajulis eorumdem cum omni festinantia studeant intimare, ut *animadversione debita puniantur* . . . Hæretici autem qui *timore mortis* vel alia quacumque causa, *dummodo non sponte*, redierent ad catholicam unitatem, ad agendam pœnitentiam per episcopum loci in muro tali includantur cautela quod facultatem non habeant alios corrumpendi." D'Achery, *Spicilegium*, in-fol., vol. i, p. 711.

was a far greater crime than to offend the majesty of the emperor." [1]

This at once put heresy on a par with treason, and consequently called for a severer punishment than the law actually decreed. We will soon see others draw the logical conclusion from the emperor's comparison, and enact the death penalty for heresy.

The legates of Pope Honorius were empowered to introduce the canonical and imperial legislation into the statutes of the Italian cities, which hitherto had not been at all anxious to take any measures whatever against heretics. They succeeded in Bergamo, Piacenza, and Mantua in 1221; [2] and in Brescia in 1225. [3] In 1226, the emperor himself ordered the podestà of Pavia to banish all heretics from the city limits. [4] About the year 1230, therefore, it was the generally accepted

[1] "Catharos, Paterenos, Leonistas, Speronistas, Arnoldistas, et omnes hæreticos utriusque sexus, quocumque nomine censeantur, perpetua dampnamus infamia, diffidamus atque bannimus, censentes ut bona talium confiscentur nec ad eos revertantur, ita quod filii ad successionem eorum pervenire non possint, cum longe gravius sit æternam quam temporalem offendere majestatem," etc., cap. vi; cf. cap. vii. *Monum. Germaniæ, Leges*, sect. iv, vol. ii, pp. 107–109.

[2] The Latin, Ms. 5152 at the National library of Paris contains the *Acta* of Cardinal Hugolino of 1221, regarding the changes in the statutes of the various Italian cities. In the statutes of Piacenza, for example, he had inserted *de verbo ad verbum statutum ultimi Lateranensis concilii* (1215) *et leges domini imperatoris Frederici super hæreticis expellendis et conservanda ecclesiastica libertate*. For more details, cf. Ficker, *op. cit.*, p. 196, with references.

[3] Cf. Raynaldi, *Annal. Eccles.*, for the year 1225, sect. 47; cf. Ficker, *op. cit.*, pp. 199, 200.

[4] Cf. Ficker, *op. cit.*, p. 430.

law throughout all Italy (recall what we have said above about Faenza, Florence, etc.) to banish all heretics, confiscate their property, and demolish their houses.

Two years had hardly elapsed when, through the joint efforts of Frederic II and Gregory IX, the death penalty of the stake was substituted for banishment;[1] Guala, a Dominican, seems to have been the prime mover in bringing about this change.

Frederic II, influenced by the jurists who were reviving the old Roman law,[2] promulgated a law for Lombardy in 1224, which condemned heretics to the stake, or at least to have their tongues cut out.[3] This penalty of the stake was common — if not legal — in Germany. For instance, we read of the people of Strasburg burning about eighty heretics about the year 1212,[4] and we could

[1] We have seen above (p. 64) that according to both the civil and canon law heretics were subject to the death-penalty throughout the Middle Ages. But the laws of Frederic II induced the Pope to inflict this penalty of the stake.

[2] In 1231, in his law *Inconsutilem tunicam*, the emperor made a direct reference to the old Roman law: *Prout veteribus legibus est indictum.*

[3] "Utriusque juris auctoritate muniti . . . duximus sanciendum: ut *quicumque* per civitatis antistitem vel diœcesis in qua degit, post condignam examinationem *fuerit de hæresi manifeste convictus et hæreticus judicatus*, per potestatem, concilium et catholicos viros civitatis et diœcesis eorumdem, *ad requisitionem antistitis illico capiatur, auctoritate nostra ignis judicio concremandus*, ut vel ultricibus flammis pereat, aut, si miserabili vitæ ad coercitionem aliorum elegerint reservandum, eum linguæ plectro deprivent," etc. A Constitution sent to the Archbishop of Magdeburg, in the *Mon. Germ.*, *Leges*, sect. iv, vol. ii, p. 126.

[4] "Hæretici . . . comprehensi sunt in civitate Argentina. Producti, vero cum negarent hæresim, judicio ferri candentis ad legitimum terminum reser-

easily cite other similar executions.[1]   The emperor, therefore, merely brought the use of the stake from Germany
into Italy.   Indeed it is very doubtful whether this law
was in operation before 1230.[2]

But in that year, Guala, the Dominican, who had become Bishop of Brescia,[3] used his authority to enact
for his episcopal city the most severe laws against
heresy.   The podestà of the city had to swear that he
would prosecute heretics as Manicheans and traitors,
according to both the canon and the civil law, especially
in view of Frederic's law of 1224.[4]   Innocent III's comparison between heretics and traitors, and between the
Cathari and the Manicheans, now bore fruit.   Traitors
deserved the death penalty, while the old Roman
law sent the Manicheans to the stake; accordingly

vantur, quorum numerus fuit octoginta vel amplius de utroque sexu.   Et
pauci quidem ex eis innocentes apparuerunt, reliqui omnes coram ecclesia
convicti per adustionem dampnati sunt et incendio perierunt."   *Annales
Marbacenses*, ad ann. 1215, in the *Mon Germ. SS.*, vol. xvii, p. 174.

[1] Cf. Julien Havet, *op. cit.*, pp. 143, 144.

[2] Cf. on this point Ficker, *op. cit.*, pp. 198, 430, 431.

[3] On Guala, cf. Ficker, *op. cit.*, pp. 199–201.

[4] "Infra decem dies," says the podestà, " eos et eas puniam velut hæreticos
Manicheos et reos criminum lese majestatis secundum leges et jura imperialia
et canonica et specialiter infra scriptam legem Domini Frederici imperatoris
et secundum ejus tenorem."   Then follows the imperial law of 1224.   This
statute of the city of Brescia is found in the *Monumenta historiæ patriæ*,
vol. xvi, pp. 1584, 1644.   On the date, 1130, cf. Ficker, *op. cit.*, p. 199.   We
know that Innocent III, in his law of 1199, was the first to put heresy on a
par with treason, although he did not draw the logical conclusion from this
comparison.   He also compared the Cathari and the Patarins to the Manicheans (*Ep.* x, 54), without saying anything about the death penalty.   Guala
drew the logical conclusion.

Gaula maintained that all heretics deserved the stake.

Pope Gregory IX adopted this stern attitude, probably under the influence of the Bishop of Brescia, with whom he was in frequent correspondence.[1] The imperial law of 1224 was inscribed in 1230 or 1231 upon the papal register, where it figures as number 103 of the fourth year of Gregory's pontificate.[2] The Pope then tried to enforce it, beginning with the city of Rome. He enacted a law in February, 1231, ordering, as the Council of Toulouse had done in 1229, heretics condemned by the Church to be handed over to the secular arm, to receive the punishment they deserved, *animadversio debita*. All who abjured and accepted a fitting penance were to be imprisoned for life, without prejudice to the other penalties for heresy, such as confiscation.[2]

About the same time, Annibale, the Senator of Rome,

---

[1] Cf. Ficker, *op. cit.*, p. 200. Gregory IX was four years Pope before he enacted these new laws.

[2] Dampnati vero per ecclesiam *seculari judicio relinquantur animadversione debita puniendi*, clericis prius a suis ordinibus degradatis. Si qui autem de predictis, postquam fuerint deprehensi, redire voluerint ad agendam condignam pœnitentiam, in perpetuo carcere detrudantur. *Registers* of Gregory IX, n. 539; Raynaldi, *Annales*, ad ann. 1231, sects. 14–15; inserted in the Decretales, cap. xv, *De hæreticis*, lib. v, tit. vii, where, in place of *redire voluerint*, we read *noluerint*. *Voluerint* is the true reading, as we may prove by comparison with the text of the Council of Toulouse (1229), and the imperial law of 1231, in which Frederic II, writes: "Si qui de predictis, postquam fuerint deprehensi, territu mortis *redire voluerint* ad agendam pœnitentiam, in perpetuum carcerem detrudantur." Cap. ii, *Mon. Germ.*, *Leges*, sect. iv, vol. ii, p 196.

established the new jurisprudence of the Church in the eternal city. Every year, on taking office, the Senator was to banish (*diffidare*) all heretics. All who refused to leave the city were, eight days after their condemnation, to receive the punishment they deserved. The penalty, *animadversio debita*, is not specified, as if every one knew what was meant.[1]

Inasmuch as repentant heretics were imprisoned for life, it seems certain that the severer penalty reserved for obstinate heretics must have been the death penalty of the stake, for that was the mode of punishment decreed by the imperial law of 1224, which had just been copied on the registers of the papal chancery. But we are not left to mere conjecture. In February, 1231, a number of Patarins were arrested in Rome; those who refused to abjure were sent to the stake, while those who did abjure were sent to Monte-Cassino and Cava to do

---

[1] "Omnes hæretici in Urbe . . . singulis annis a senatore, quando regiminis sui præstiterit juramentum, perpetuo diffidantur. Item hæreticos qui fuerint in Urbe reperti præsertim per inquisitores datos ab Ecclesia vel alios viros catholicos senator capere teneatur et captos etiam detinere, postquam fuerint per Ecclesiam condempnati, infra octo dies *animadversione debita puniendos.*" Raynaldi, ad ann. 1231, sect. 16–17; Ficker, *op. cit.*, p. 205. These statutes are similar to those of Brescia (1230); the statutes of Bologna (1246) read: "Hæretici et fautores eorum in perpetuo banno ponantur et alias pænas et alias injurias sustineant secundum formam Statutorum Domini papæ Gregorii." Consequently, the podestà had to swear that he would banish all heretics; if they remained in the city, and refused to abjure, they were condemned and burned. Ficker, *op. cit.*, pp. 205, 206. We see that the penalty of the stake was enforced only when the penalty of banishment had proved inefficacious. This reminds us of the law of Pedro, King of Aragon in 1197.

penance.[1] This case tells us instantly how we are to interpret the *animadversio debita* of contemporary documents.

Frederic II exercised an undeniable influence over Gregory IX, and the Pope in turn influenced the emperor. Gregory wrote denouncing the many heretics who swarmed throughout the kingdom of Sicily (the two Sicilies), especially in Naples and Aversa, urging him to prosecute them with vigor. Frederic obeyed.[2] He was then preparing his Sicilian Code, which appeared at Amalfi in August, 1231. The first law, *Inconsutilem tunicam,* was against heretics. The emperor did not have to consult any one about the penalty to be decreed against heresy; he had merely to copy his own law, enacted in Lombardy in 1224. This new law declared heresy a crime against society on a par with treason, and liable to the same penalty. And that the law might not be a dead letter for lack of accusers, the state officials were commanded to prosecute it just as they would any other crime. This

---

[1] "Eodem mense (February), nonnulli Paterenorum in Urbe inventi sunt, quorum alii sunt igne cremati, cum inconvertibiles essent; alii donec pœniteant sunt ad Casinensem ecclesiam et apud Cavas directi." Ryccardus de S. Germano, ad ann. 1231, in the *Mon. Germ. SS.*, vol. xix, p. 363; cf. *Vita Gregorii,* in Muratori, *Rerum italicarum SS.*, vol. iii, p. 578. On March 3d, Gregory sent a number of heretics to the Abbot of La Cava, ordering him to keep them *in arctissima fovea et sub vinculis ferreis.* Cf. Ficker, *op. cit.,* p. 207.

[2] Cf. the reply of Frederic to Gregory IX, February 28, 1231, in Huillard-Bréolles, *Historia diplomatica Frederici II,* vol. iii, p. 268. Ryccardus de S. Germano, *loc. cit.*

was in reality the beginning of the Inquisition. All suspects were to be tried by an ecclesiastical tribunal, and
if, being declared guilty, they refuse to abjure, they were
to be burned in presence of the people.[1]

Once started on the road to severity, Frederic II did
not stop. To aid Gregory IX in suppressing heresy, he
enacted at Ravenna, in 1237, an imperial law condemning
all heretics to death.[2] The kind of death was not indicated. But every one knew that the common German cus-

---

[1] "Statuimus in primis, ut crimen hæreseos et damnatæ sectæ cujuslibet,
quocumque nomine censeantur sectatores (prout veteribus legibus est indictum) inter publica crimina numerentur: immo crimine læsæ majestatis
nostræ debet ab omnibus horribilius judicari, quod in divinæ majestatis
injuriam noscitur attentatum, quamvis judicii potestate alterum alteri non
excellat. Nam sicuti perduellionis crimen personas adimit damnatorum
et bona, et damnat post obitum memoriam defunctorum; sic et in prædicto
crimine, quo Patereni notantur, per omnia volumus observari . . . Per
officiales nostros, sicut et alios malefactores, inquiri ac inquisitione notatos
. . . a viris ecclesiasticis et prælatis examinari jubemus. Per quos si inventi
fuerit a fide catholica saltem in articulo deviare ac . . . in erroris concepta
insania perseverent, præsentis nostræ legis edicto damnatos, mortem pati
. . . decernimus quam affectant: ut vivi in conspectu populi comburantur,
flammarum commissi judicio." *Constitut. Sicil.*, i, 3, in Eymeric, *Directorium
inquisitorum*, Appendix, p. 14.

[2] "Ut hæretici . . . ubicumque per imperium dampnati ab Ecclesia fuerint
et *seculari judicio assignati, animadversione debita* puniantur. Si qui de
predictis, postquam fuerint deprehensi territu mortis redire voluerint ad
agendam pœnitentiam, in perpetuum carcerem detrudantur." The *animadversione debita* is explained further on by a passage taken from the law of
the Senator of Rome: "Præterea quicumque hæretici reperti fuerint in civi-
tatibus, opidis seu aliis locis imperii per inquisitores ab apostolica sede datos
et alios orthodoxæ fidei zelatores, hii qui jurisdictionem ibidem habuerint
ad inquisitorum et aliorum catholicorum virorum insinuationem eos capere
teneantur et captos arctius custodire donec per censuram ecclesiasticam
condempnatos dampnabili morte perimant." *Mon. Germ., Leges*, sect. iv,
vol. ii, p. 196. Then follows a comparison with the *rei lesæ majestatis*.

tom of burning heretics at the stake had now become the law.[1] For by three previous laws, May 14, 1238, June 26, 1238, and February 22, 1239, the emperor had declared that the Sicilian Code and the law of Ravenna were binding upon all his subjects; the law of June 26, 1238, merely promulgated these other laws throughout the kingdom of Arles and Vienne.[2] Henceforth all uncertainty was at an end. The legal punishment for heretics throughout the empire was death at the stake.

Gregory IX did not wait for these laws to be enacted to carry out his intentions.

As early as 1231 he tried to have the cities of Italy and Germany adopt the civil and canonical laws in vogue at Rome against heresy, and he was the first to inaugurate that particular method of prosecution, the permanent tribunal of the Inquisition.

We possess some of the letters which he wrote in June, 1231, urging the bishops and archbishops to further his plans.[3] He did not meet with much success, however,

---

[1] The most ancient book on German customs, the *Sachsenspiegel*, written probably a little before 1235 (cf. *Hansische Geschichtsblätter*, 1876, pp. 102, 103), condemns (ii, 13, sect. 7) heretics to the stake: "Swilch cristen man ungeloubic ist oder mit zcoubere umme gêt oder mit vergifnisse, unde des verwunden wirt, den sal man ûf der hurt burnen." *Sachsenspiegel*, ed. Weiske et Hildebrand, 1877, p. 47.

[2] Cf. these imperial laws in the *Mon. Germ.*, *Leges*, sect. iv, vol. ii, pp. 281–284. Cf. for more details, Ficker, *op. cit.*, p. 223.

[3] For the letters sent to the Bishop of Salsburg, cf. Ficker, *op. cit.*, p. 204. There is also a letter to the Dominicans of Freisach, dated November 27, 1231, published in the *Acta imperii* of Winkelmann, and another to Conrad

although the Dominicans and the Friars Minor did their best to help him. Still some cities like Milan, Verona, Piacenza and Vercelli adopted the measures of persecution which he proposed. At Milan, Peter of Verona, a Dominican, on September 15, 1233, had the laws of the Pope and the Senator of Rome inscribed in the city's statutes.[1] The *animadversio debita* was henceforth interpreted to mean the penalty of the stake. "In this year," writes a chronicler of the time, "the people of Milan began to burn heretics."[2] In the month of July, sixty heretics were sent to the stake at Verona.[3] The podestà of Piacenza sent to the Pope the heretics he had arrested.[4] Vercelli, at the instance of the Franciscan, Henry of Milan, incorporated in 1233 into its statutes the law of the Senator

of Marburg, October 11, 1231, in Kuchenbecker, *Analecta Hassiaca*, vol. iii, p. 73. For further details concerning these documents, cf. Ficker, *op. cit.*, pp. 213, 214.

[1] Corio, *L'istoria di Milano*, ed. Vinegia, 1554, fol. 96; cf. Ficker, *op. cit.*, pp. 210, 211.

[2] "Mediolanenses incipierunt comburere ereticos." *Memoriæ Mediolanenses*, ad ann. 1233, in the *Mon. Germ. SS.*, vol. xviii, p. 402. (The chronicler is ignorant of what happened at Milan in 1034.) The podestà Oldrado de Tresseno of Lodi, who governed Milan in 1233, and who presided over the executions of heretics, recorded the facts in an inscription on his statue, which can still be read on the façade of the *Palazzo della Ragione* in Milan:

> Atria qui grandis solii regalia scandis,
> Præsidis hic memores Oldradi semper honores,
> Civis Laudensis, fidei tutoris et ensis,
> Qui solium struxit, Catharos, ut debuit, uxit.

[3] Cf. Parisius de Cereta, *Mon. Germ. SS.*, vol. xix, p. 8, and Maurisius in Muratori, *Rer. Ital. SS.*, vol. xiii, p. 38.

[4] *Annal. Placent.*, in *Mon. Germ. SS.*, vol. xviii, p. 454.

of Rome and the imperial law of 1224; it, however, omitted in the last named law the clause which decreed the penalty of cutting out the tongue.[1] In Germany, the Dominican, Conrad of Marburg was particularly active, in virtue of his commission from Gregory IX. In accordance with the imperial law, we find him sentencing to the stake a great number of heretics.[2]

It may be admitted, however, that in his excessive zeal he even went beyond the desires of the sovereign pontiff. Gregory IX did not find everywhere so marked an eagerness to carry out his wishes. A number of the cities of Italy for a long time continued to punish obstinate heretics according to the penal code of Innocent III, *i.e.* by banishment and confiscation.[3]

That the penalty of the stake was used at this time in France is proved by the burning of one hundred and eighty-three Bulgarians or Bugres at Mont-Wimer in 1239,[4] and by two important documents, the *Établisse-*

[1] Cf. Corio, *L'istoria di Milano, loc. cit.* For further details regarding upper Italy, cf. Ficker, *op. cit.*, pp. 210, 211.

[2] The papal letter of October 11, 1231, says: "Quatenus prelatis, clero et populo convocatis generalem faciatis predicationem . . . et adjunctis vobis discretis aliquibus ad hæc sollicitius exsequenda, diligenti perquiratis sollicitudine de hæreticis et etiam infamatis, et si quos culpabiles et infamatos inveneritis, nisi examinati velint absolute mandatis Ecclesiæ obedire, procedatis contra eos juxta statuta nostra contra hæreticos noviter promulgata." Kirchenbecker, *Analecta Hassiaca*, vol. iii, p. 73. We will relate further on how Conrad understood his mission of Inquisitor, and how he fulfilled it.

[3] Cf. on this point, Ficker, *op. cit.*, p. 224.

[4] Aubri de Trois-Fontaines, ad ann. 1239, *Mon. Germ. SS.*, vol. xxiii, pp. 944, 945. For other references to this fact, cf. Julien Havet, *op. cit.*,

ments de Saint Louis and the *Coutumes de Beau-vaisis.*

"As soon as the ecclesiastical judge has discovered, after due examination, that the suspect is a heretic, he must hand him over to the secular arm; and the secular judge must send him to the stake." [1] Beaumanoir says the same thing: "In such a case, the secular court must aid the Church; for when the Church condemns any one as a heretic, she is obliged to hand him over to the secular arm to be sent to the stake; for she herself cannot put any one to death." [2]

It is a question whether this legislation is merely the codification of the custom introduced by popular uprisings against heresy and by certain royal decrees, or whether it owes its origin to the law of Frederic II which Gregory IX tried to enforce in France, as he had done in Germany and Italy. This second hypothesis is hardly probable. The tribunals of the Inquisition did not have to import into France the penalty of the stake; they found it already established in both central and northern France.

In fact, Gregory IX urged everywhere the enforcement of the existing laws against heresy, and where none existed he introduced a very severe system of prosecution. He was

p. 171, n. 2. Mont-Wimer or Mont-Aimé is situated in Marne, a commune of Bergères-les-Vertus.

[1] *Établissements de saint Louis*, ch. cxxiii; cf. ch. lxxxv; in the *Ordonnances des roys de France*, vol. i, pp. 211, 175.

[2] *Coutumes de Beauvaisis*, xi, 2; cf. xxx, 11, ed Beugnot, vol. i, pp. 157, 413.

the first, moreover, to establish an extraordinary and permanent tribunal for heresy trials — an institution which afterwards became known as the monastic Inquisition.

.   .   .   .

The prosecution and the punishment of heretics in every diocese was one of the chief duties of the bishops, the natural defenders of orthodoxy. While heresy appeared at occasional intervals, they had little or no difficulty in fulfilling their duty. But when the Cathari and the Patarins had sprung up everywhere, especially in southern Italy and France and northern Spain, the secrecy of their movements made the task of the bishops extremely hard and complicated. Rome soon perceived that they were not very zealous in prosecuting heresy. To put an end to this neglect, Lucius III jointly with the emperor Frederic Barbarossa and the bishops of his court enacted a decretal at Verona in 1184, regulating the *episcopal inquisition.*

All bishops and archbishops were commanded to visit personally once or twice a year, or to empower their archdeacons or other clerics to visit every parish in which heresy was thought to exist. They were to compel two or three trustworthy men, or, if need be, all the inhabitants of the city, to swear that they would denounce every suspect who attended secret assemblies, or whose manner of living differed from that of the ordinary Catholic. After the bishop had questioned all who had been brought before his tribunal, he was empowered to punish them as he deemed fit, unless the accused succeeded in establishing their innocence. All who superstitiously refused to take the required oath (we have seen how the Cathari considered it criminal to take an oath) were to be condemned and punished as heretics, and if they refused to abjure they were handed over to the secular arm.[1] This was an attempt to recall the bishops to a sense of their duty. The Lateran Council of 1215 reenacted the laws of Lucius III; and to ensure their enforcement it decreed that every bishop who neglected his duty should be deposed, and another consecrated in his place.[2] The Council of Narbonne in 1227 likewise ordered the bishops to appoint synodal witnesses (*testes synodales*) in every parish to prosecute heretics.[3] But all these decrees, although properly countersigned and placed in the archives, remained practically a dead letter. In the first place it was very difficult to obtain the synodal witnesses. And again, as a contemporary bishop, Lucas de Tuy, assures us, the bishops for the most part were not at all anxious to prosecute heresy. When reproached for their inaction they replied: "How can we condemn those who are neither convicted nor confessed?" [4]

---

[1] Lucius III, *Ep.* clxxi, Migne, P. L., vol. cci, col. 1297 and seq.

[2] The Bull *Excommunicamus*, Decretals, cap. xiii, in fine, *De hæreticis*, lib. v, tit. vii.

[3] Can. 14, Labbe, *Concilia*, vol. xi, pars i, col. 307, 308.

[4] Lucas Tudensis, *De altera vita fideique controversiis adversus Albigensium*

The Popes, as the rulers of Christendom, tried to make up for the indifference of the bishops by sending their legates to hunt for the Cathari in their most hidden retreats. But they soon realized that this legatine inquisition was ineffective.[1]

"Bishop and legate," writes Lea, "were alike unequal to the task of discovering those who carefully shrouded themselves under the cloak of the most orthodox observance; and when by chance a nest of heretics was brought to light, the learning and skill of the average Ordinary failed to elicit a confession from those who professed the most entire accord with the teachings of Rome. In the absence of overt acts, it was difficult to reach the secret thoughts of the sectary. Trained experts were needed whose sole business it should be to unearth the offenders, and extort a confession of their guilt."[2]

At an opportune moment, therefore, two mendicant orders, the Dominicans and the Franciscans, were instituted to meet the new needs of the Church. Both orders devoted themselves to preaching; the Dominicans were especially learned in the ecclesiastical sciences, i.e. canon law and theology.

"The establishment of these orders," continues Lea, "seemed a providential interposition to supply the Church

errores, cap. xix, in the Bibliotheca Patrum, 4 ed., vol. iv, col. 575–714. Lucas was Bishop of Tuy in Galicia, from 1239 to 1249.

[1] Cf. Lea, op. cit., vol. i, p. 315 and seq.
[2] Cf. Lea, op. cit., vol. i, p. 318.

of Christ with what it most sorely needed. As the necessity grew apparent of special and permanent tribunals, devoted exclusively to the widespread sin of heresy, there was every reason why they should be wholly free from the local jealousies and enmities which might tend to the prejudice of the innocent, or the local favoritism which might connive at the escape of the guilty. If, in addition to this freedom from local partialities, the examiners and judges were men specially trained to the detection and conversion of the heretics; if also, they had by irrevocable vows renounced the world; if they could acquire no wealth, and were dead to the enticement of pleasure, every guarantee seemed to be afforded that their momentous duties would be fulfilled with the strictest justice — that while the purity of the faith would be protected, there would be no unnecessary oppression or cruelty or persecution dictated by private interests and personal revenge. Their unlimited popularity was also a warrant that they would receive far more efficient assistance in their arduous labors than could be expected by the bishops, whose position was generally that of antagonism to their flocks, and to the petty seigneurs and powerful barons whose aid was indispensable.[1]

Gregory IX fully understood the help that the Dominicans and Franciscans could render him as agents of the Inquisition throughout Christendom.[2]

[1] Lea, *op. cit.*, pp. 318, 319.

[2] Of course these religions were to render other services to the church.

It is probable that the Senator of Rome refers to them in his oath in 1231, when he speaks of the *Inquisitores datos ab Ecclesia*.[1] Frederic II, in his law of 1232, also mentions the *Inquisitores ab apostolica sede datos*.[2] The Dominican Albéric traveled through Lombardy in November, 1232, with the title of *Inquisitor hæreticæ pravitatis*.[3] In 1231 a similar commission was entrusted to the Dominicans of Freisach, and to the famous Conrad of Marburg.[4] Finally, to quote but one more instance, Gregory IX, in 1233, wrote an eloquent letter to the bishops of southern France in which he said: "We, seeing you engrossed in the whirlwind of cares, and scarce able to breathe in the pressure of overwhelming anxieties, think it well to divide your burdens, that they may be more easily borne. We have therefore determined to send preaching friars against the heretics of France and the adjoining provinces, and we beg, warn, and exhort you, ordering you as you reverence the Holy See, to receive them kindly, and to treat them well, giving them in this as in all else, favor, counsel, and aid, that they may fulfill their office."[5]

Their duties are outlined in a letter of Gregory IX to

---

[1] Raynaldi, *Annales*, ad ann. 1231, sect. 16, 17; cf. Ficker, *op. cit.*, p. 205.

[2] Cap. iii, in the *Mon. Germ., Leges*, sect. iv, vol. ii, p. 196.

[3] Potthast, *Regesta Roman. Pontif.*, no. 904, 1.

[4] Cf. Ficker, *op. cit.*, p. 213; cf. Potthast, n. 8859, 8860.

[5] Potthast, no. 9143–9152. At the same time, Gregory IX sent a bull "to the Priors and Friars of the Order of Preachers." Cf. Lea, *op. cit.*, p. 329 and seq. Robert le Bougre was appointed inquisitor for northern France. April 19, 1233. Ripoll, *Bullarium*, vol. i, p. 45.

Conrad of Marburg, October 11, 1231: "When you arrive in a city, summon the bishops, clergy, and people, and preach a solemn sermon on faith; then select certain men of good repute to help you in trying the heretics and suspects denounced before your tribunal. All who on examination are found guilty or suspected of heresy must promise to absolutely obey the commands of the Church; if they refuse, you must prosecute them, according to the statutes which we have recently promulgated." [1] We have in these instructions all the procedure of the Inquisition: the time of grace; the call for witnesses and their testimony; the interrogation of the accused; the reconciliation of repentant heretics; the condemnation of obdurate heretics.

Each detail of this procedure calls for a few words of explanation.

The Inquisitor first summoned every heretic of the city to appear before him within a certain fixed time, which as a rule did not exceed thirty days. This period was called "the time of grace" (*tempus gratiæ*).[2] The heretics who abjured during this period were treated with leniency. If secret heretics, they were dismissed with

[1] Kuchenbecker, *Analecta Hassiaca*, vol. iii, p. 73; cf. Ficker, *op. cit.*, p. 213. Similar instructions may be found in the *Processus inquisitionis* (Appendix A).

[2] "Quod et *tempus gratiæ* sive indulgentiæ appellamus." *Processus Inquisitionis*, cf. Appendix A. "Assignato eis termino competenti quod *tempus gratiæ* vocare soletis." Consultation of the Archbishop of Narbonne, at the Council of Béziers in 1246, c. ii. Cf. Tanon, *op. cit.*, p. 330, note 2.

only a slight secret penance; if public heretics, they were exempted from the penalties of death and life-imprisonment, and sentenced either to make a short pilgrimage, or to undergo one of the ordinary canonical penances.[1]

If the heretics failed to come forward of their own accord, they were to be denounced by the Catholic people. At first the number of witnesses required to make an accusation valid was not determined; later on two were declared necessary.[2] In the beginning, the Inquisition could only accept the testimony of men and women of good repute; and the Church for a long time maintained that no one should be admitted as an accuser who was a heretic, was excommunicated, a homicide, a thief, a sorcerer, a diviner, or a bearer of false witness.[3] But her hatred of heresy led her later on to set aside this law, when the faith was

---

[1] "Illis autem qui ad mandatum Ecclesiæ venerint, non imponetur publica pœnitentia, nisi sint publici hæretici . . . cum quibus etiam ita misericordia fiat quod non condempnentur ad mortem, non ad carcerem perpetuum, non ad peregrinationem nimis longam, sed aliæ pœnitentiæ injungantur quas pro qualitate delicti inquisitores viderint imponendas." Consultation of the cardinal Bishop of Albano, in Doat, vol. xxxi, fol. 5. On the acts of this cardinal, who was none other than Pierre de Colmieu, the old Archbishop of Rouen, cf. Tanon, *op. cit.*, pp. 144, 145.

[2] G. Durand, *Speculum judiciorum*, lib. i, parts iv, *De teste*, sect. 11. Gui Foucois (who became Pope under the name of Clement IV) thought that more than two witnesses were helpful, and in some cases absolutely necessary." "Ideoque non crederem tutum ad vocem duorum testium hominem bonæ opinionis damnare, licet videar contra jus dicere." Consultation in Doat, vol. xxxvi, quest. **xv.** Cf. Eymeric, *Directorium*, 3ª pars, *De testium multiplicatione*, p. 445.

[3] Pseudo-Julii, *Ep.* ii, cap. 17; Gratian, *Decretum*, pars 2ª, *Causa* v, quaest. iii, cap. v.

in question. As early as the twelfth century, Gratian had declared that the testimony of infamous and heretical witnesses might be accepted in trials for heresy.[1]

The edicts of Frederic II declared that heretics could not testify in the courts, but this disability was removed when they were called upon to testify against other suspects.[2] In the beginning, the Inquisitors were loath to accept such testimony. But in 1261 Alexander IV assured them that it was lawful to do so.[3] Henceforth the testimony of a heretic was considered valid, although it was always left to the discretion of the Inquisition to reject it at will. This principle was finally incorporated into the canon law, and was enforced by constant practice.[4] All legal exceptions were henceforth declared inoperative except that of moral enmity.[5]

Witnesses for the defence rarely presented themselves. Very seldom do we come across any mention of them.[6]

---

[1] Pars ii, *Causa* ii, quaest. vii, cap. xxii; *Causa* vi, quaest. i, cap. xix.

[2] *Historia diplomatica Frederici II*, vol. iv, pp. 299, 300. Frederic re-enacted at Ravenna, February 22, 1232, the law of 1220 against heretics, with the additional clause: "Adjicimus quod hæreticus convinci per hæreticum possit."

[3] Bull *Consuluit*, of January 23, 1261, in Eymeric, *Directorium inquisitorum*, Appendix, p. 40.

[4] Cap. v, *In fidei favorem*, Sexto v, 2; Eymeric, *Directorium inquisitorum*, p. 105.

[5] Eymeric, *ibid.*, 3ª pars, quaest. lxvii, pp. 606, 607. Pegna, *ibid.*, pp. 607, 609, declares that great cruelty or even insulting words — *v.g.* to call a man *cornutus* or a woman *meretrix* — might come under the head of enmity, and invalidate a man's testimony.

[6] Cf. Lea, *op. cit.*, vol. i, pp. 445, 447.

This is readily understood, for they would almost inevitably have been suspected as accomplices and abettors of heresy. For the same reason, the accused were practically denied the help of counsel. Innocent III had forbidden advocates and scriveners to lend aid or counsel to heretics and their abettors.[1] This prohibition, which in the mind of the Pope was intended only for defiant and acknowledged heretics, was gradually extended to every suspect who was striving to prove his innocence.[2]

Heretics or suspects, therefore, denounced to the Inquisition generally found themselves without counsel before their judges.

They personally had to answer the various charges of the indictment (*capitula*) made against them. It certainly would have been a great help to them, to have known the names of their accusers. But the fear — well-founded it was true [3] — that the accused or their friends would

[1] Decretals, cap. xi, *De hæreticis*, lib. v, tit. vii.

[2] Eymeric, *Directorium inquisitorum*, 3ª pars, quaest. xxxix, p. 565; cf. 446; Lea, *op. cit.*, vol. i, 444. Sometimes, however, the accused was granted counsel, but *juxta juris formam ac stylum et usum officii Inquisitionis;* cf. Vidal, *Le tribunal d'Inquisition*, in the *Annales de Saint-Louis des Français*, vol. ix (1905), p. 299, note. Eymeric himself grants one (*Directorium*, pp. 451–453). But this lawyer was merely to persuade his client to confess his heresy; he was rather the lawyer of the court than of the accused. Vidal, *op. cit.*, pp. 302, 303. Pegna, however, says (in Eymeric, *Directorium* 2ª pars, ch. xi, Comm. 10) that in his time the accused was allowed counsel, if he were only suspected of heresy. Cf. Tanon, *op. cit.*, pp. 400, 401.

[3] Guillem Pelhisse tells us that the Cathari sometimes killed those who had denounced their brethren. "*Persecutores eorum percutiebant, vulnerabant et occidebant,*" *Chronique*, ed. Douais, p. 90. A certain Arnold Dominici, who had denounced seven heretics, was killed at night in his bed by "the

revenge themselves on their accusers, induced the Inquisitors to withhold the names of the witnesses.[1]   The
only way in which the prisoner could invalidate the testimony against him was to name all his mortal enemies.
If his accusers happened to be among them, their testimony was thrown out of court.[2]   But otherwise, he was
obliged to prove the falsity of the accusation against him
— a practically impossible undertaking.   For if two witnesses, considered of good repute by the Inquisitor, agreed
in accusing the prisoner, his fate was at once settled;[3]
whether he confessed or not, he was declared a heretic.

Believers." *Ibid.*, pp. 98, 99.   As early as 1229, the papal legate, after his
investigation in the South, brought back all the testimony with him to Rome,
"ne forte si aliquando inventa fuisset (inquisitio) in terra ista a malevolis,
in mortem testium qui contra tales deposuerant redundaret," and even this did
not prevent the heretics from killing the accusers of their brethren: "nam et
sola suspicione, post recessum ipsius legati, fuere tales aliqui et persecutores
hæreticorum plurimi interfecti."   C. de Puy-Laurens, *Chronique,* cap. 40.
Cf. Lea, *op. cit.,* vol. i, p. 438; Tanon, *op. cit.,* p. 390.

[1] Eymeric, *Directorium,* 3ᵃ pars, q. 72; *An nomina testium et denuntia-
torum sint delatis publicanda,* p. 627.   The law on this point varied from
time to time.   But between the years 1244 and 1254 a manual of the Inquisition (*Processus inquisitionis,* cf. Appendix A) says: "Neque a juris ordine
deviamus nisi quod testium non publicamus nomina propter ordinationem
sedis apostolicæ sub domino Gregorio (IX) provide factam et ab Innocentio
(IV) postmodum innovatam."   Cf. bull of Alexander IV, *Layettes du trésor
des Chartes,* vol. iii, n. 4221.   When Boniface VIII incorporated into the
canon law the rule of withholding the names of witnesses, he expressly said
that they might be produced, if there was no danger in doing so.   Cap. 20,
Sexto v, 2.   Cf. Lea, *op. cit.,* p. 438 and note; Vidal, *Le tribunal d'Inquisition
de Pamiers* in the *Annales de Saint Louis des Français,* vol. ix, pp. 294, 295.

[2] Eymeric, *Directorium,* 3ᵃ pars, *De defensionibus reorum,* p. 446 and seq.

[3] According to the *Processus inquisitionis* the rule was: "Ad nullius condempnationem sine lucidis et apertis probationibus vel confessione propria
processimus."   Appendix A.   Cf. Eymeric, *De duodecimo modo terminando*

After the prisoner had been found guilty, he could choose one of two things; he could abjure his heresy and manifest his repentance by accepting the penance imposed by his judge, or he could obstinately persist either in his denial or profession of heresy, accepting resolutely all the consequences of such an attitude.

If the heretic abjured, he knelt before the Inquisitor as a pentitent before his confessor. He had no reason to fear his judge. For, properly speaking, he did not inflict punishment.

"The mission of the Inquisition," writes Lea, "was to save men's souls; to recall them to the way of salvation, and to assign salutary penance to those who sought it, like a father-confessor with his penitent. Its sentences, therefore, were not like those of an earthly judge, the retaliation of society on the wrong-doer, or deterrent examples to prevent the spread of crime; they were simply imposed for the benefit of the erring soul, to wash away its sin. The Inquisitors themselves habitually speak of their ministrations in this sense."[1]

But "the sin of heresy was too grave to be expiated simply by contrition and amendment."[2] The Inquisitor, therefore, pointed out other means of expiation: "The penances customarily imposed by the Inquisition were

processusm fidei per condempnationem convicti de hæresi et persistentis in negativa, in the *Directorium*, 3ᵃ pars, pp. 521–525.

[1] Lea, *op. cit.*, p. 459.
[2] Lea, *ibid.*, p. 463.

10

comparatively few in number. They consisted, firstly, of pious observances — recitation of prayers, frequenting of churches, the discipline, fasting, pilgrimages, and fines nominally for pious uses, — such as a confessor might impose on his ordinary penitents. These were for offences of trifling import. "Next in grade are the *pœnæ confusibiles*, — the humiliating and degrading penances, of which the most important was the wearing of yellow crosses sewed upon the garments; and finally, the severest punishment among those strictly within the competence of the Holy Office, the *murus* or prison." [1]

If the heretic refused to abjure, his obduracy put an end to the judge's leniency, and withdrew him at once from his jurisdiction.

"The Inquisitor never condemned to death, but merely withdrew the protection of the Church from the hardened and impenitent sinner who afforded no hope of conversion, or from him who showed by relapse that there was no trust to be placed in his pretended repentance." [2]

It was at this juncture that the State intervened. The ecclesiastical judge handed over the heretic to the secular arm,[3] which simply enforced the legal penalty of the stake.

---

[1] Lea, *ibid.*, p. 462. For further details about these penances, *ibid.*, p. 463 and seq.; cf. Ch. Molinier, *L'Inquisition dans le midi de la France au XIIIe et au XIVe siècles*, pp. 358–398.

[2] Lea, *ibid.*, p. 460.

[3] "Quia sacrosancta Romana Ecclesia non habet amplius quod faciat contra te, pro tuis demeritis in hiis scriptis te relinquimus curiæ seculari."

However, the law allowed the heretic to abjure even at the foot of the stake; in that case his sentence was commuted to life imprisonment.[1]

It is hard to conceive of a greater responsibility than that of a mediæval Inquisitor. The life or death of the heretic was practically at his disposal. The Church, therefore, required him to possess in a pre-eminent degree the qualities of an impartial judge. Bernard Gui, the most experienced Inquisitor of his time (1308–1323), thus paints for us the portrait of the ideal Inquisitor: "He should be diligent and fervent in his zeal for religious truth, for the salvation of souls, and for the destruction of heresy. He should always be calm in times of trial and difficulty, and never give way to outbursts of anger or temper. He should be a brave man, ready to face death if necessary, but while never cowardly running from danger, he should never be foolhardy in rushing into it. He should be unmoved by the entreaties or the bribes of those who appear before his tribunal; still he must not harden his heart to the point of refusing to delay or mitigate punishment, as circumstances may require from time to time.

Liber sententiarum inquisitionis Tholosanæ ab anno Ch. 1307 *ad ann.* 1323, in Limborch, *Historia Inquisitionis,* Amsterdam, 1692, p. 91.

[1] "Si qui . . . territu mortis redire voluerint ad agendam pœnitentiam, in perpetuum carcerem detrudantur." Constitution of Frederic (1232) quoted above; cf. the Council of Toulouse (1229) and the text of Gregory IX. For heretics converted at the foot of the stake, cf. Eymeric, *op. cit.,* 3ª pars, *De decimo modo terminandi processum fidei per condemnationem hæretici impœnitentis non relapsi,* p. 515.

In doubtful cases, he should be very careful not to believe too easily what may appear probable, and yet in reality is false; nor on the other hand should he stubbornly refuse to believe what may appear improbable, and yet is frequently true. He should zealously discuss and examine every case, so as to be sure to make a just decision. . . . Let the love of truth and mercy, the special qualities of every good judge, shine in his countenance, and let his sentences never be prompted by avarice or cruelty.[1]

This portrait corresponds to the idea that Gregory IX had of the true Inquisitor. In the instructions which he gave to the terrible Conrad of Marburg, October 21, 1223, he took good care to warn him to be prudent as well as zealous: "Punish if you will," he said, "the wicked and perverse, but see that no innocent person suffers at your hands": *ut puniatur sic temeritas perversorum, quod innocentiæ puritas non lædatur*.[2] Gregory IX cannot be accused of injustice, but he will ever be remembered as the Pope who established the Inquisition as a permanent tribunal, and did his utmost to enforce everywhere the death penalty for heresy.

[1] *Practica Inquisitionis*, pars 6ª, ed. Douais, 1886, pp. 231–233. Eymeric gives a similar portrait of the ideal Inquisitor. *Directorum*, 3ª pars, quæst. 1, *De Conditione Inquisitionis*, p. 534; cf. quæst, xvi, *De conditionibus vicarii inquisitoris*, p. 547. The Inquisitor had to be forty years old: *ibid.*, p. 535. This was fixed by Clement V, *Clementinarum*, lib. v, tit. iii, cap. i–iii.

[2] Quoted by Ficker, *op. cit.*, p. 220.

This Pope was, in certain respects, a very slave to the letter of the law. The protests of St. Augustine and many other early Fathers did not affect him in the least. In the beginning while he was legate, he merely insisted upon the enforcement of the penal code of Innocent III, which did not decree any punishment severer than banishment, but he soon began to regard heresy as a crime similar to treason, and therefore subject to the same penalty, death. Certain ecclesiastics of his court with extremely logical minds, and rulers like Pedro II of Aragon and Frederic II, had reached the same conclusion, even before he did. Finally, in the fourth year of his pontificate, and undoubtedly after mature deliberation, he decided to compel the princes and the podestà to enforce the law condemning heretics to the stake.

He did his utmost to bring this about. He did not forget, however, that the Church could not concern herself in sentences of death. In fact, his law of 1231 decrees that: "Heretics condemned by the church are to be handed over to the secular courts to receive due punishment (*animadversio debita*)." [1] The emperor Frederic II had the same notion of the distinction between the two powers. His law of 1224 points out carefully that heretics convicted by an ecclesiastical trial are to be burned in the name of the civil authority: *auc-*

---

[1] "Dampnati vero per Ecclesiam *seculari judicio relinquantur*, animadversione debita puniendi." *Decretales*, cap. xv, *De Hæreticis*, lib. v, tit. vii.

toritate nostra ignis judicio concremandus.[1]   The imperial
law of 1232 likewise declares that heretics condemned
by the Church are to be brought before a secular tribunal
to receive the punishment they deserve.[2]   This explains
why Gregory IX did not believe that in handing over heretics to the secular arm he participated directly or indirectly
in a death sentence.[3]   The tribunals of the Inquisition

[1] *Mon. Germ.*, *Leges*, sect. iv, vol. ii, p. 126.

[2] "Hæretici . . . ubicumque per imperium dampnati ab Ecclesia fuerint et
seculari judicio assignati, animadversione debita puniantur." *Ibid.*, p. 196.
The Sicilian constitution of 1233 decrees that all who have been declared
impenitent heretics, *præsentis nostræ legis edicto damnatos, mortem pati
decernimus*. In Eymeric, *Directorium*, Appendix, p. 15.

[3] Lea writes (*op. cit.*, vol. i, p. 536, note): " Gregory IX had no scruple in
asserting the duty of the church to shed the blood of heretics." In a brief of
1234 to the Archbishop of Sens, he says: *Nec enim decuit Apostolicam Sedem,
in oculis suis cum Madianita cœunte Judæo, manum suam a sanguine prohibere, ne si secus ageret non custodire populum Israel . . . videretur.* Ripoll,
i, 66. This is certainly a serious charge, but the citation he gives implies
something altogether different. Lea has been deceived himself, and in turn
has misled his readers, by a comparison which he mistook for a doctrinal
document. The context, we think, clearly shows that the Pope was making
a comparison between the Holy See and the Jewish leader Phinees, who had
slain an Israelite and a harlot of Madian, in the very act of their crime (Num.
xxv. 6, 7). That does not imply that the church uses the same weapons.
Even if the comparison is not a very happy one, still we must not exaggerate
its import. We quote the rest of the papal letter, so that our readers may
see that it did not treat of the execution of heretics at all. "Fratribus ordinis
Prædicatorum habentibus zelum Dei et in opere potentibus Apostolica scripta
direximus, ut ad caput hujusmodi reptilium conterendum, vulpes parvulas
capiendas et maxillas eorum, qui Christi Ecclesiam lacerebant, in freno cohi-
bendas et camo, potentes assurgerent, et oves errantes ad ovile suis humeris
reportarent nec non personas infectas scabra rubigine vetustatis lima suæ
prædicationis eraderent, ut mundæ in sanctuarium Domini et cælestem
patriam introirent; nec enim decuit apostolicam sedem, in oculis suis cum
Madianita cœunte Judæo, manum suam a sanguine prohibere (the weapons
used by the Holy See are simply the *Scripta apostolica*, cited above), ne si

which he established in no way modified this concept of ecclesiastical justice. The Papacy, the guardian of orthodoxy for the universal Church, simply found that the Dominicans and the Franciscans were more docile instruments than the episcopate for the suppression of heresy. But whether the Inquisition was under the direction of the bishops or the monks, it could have been conducted on the same lines.

But as a matter of fact, it unfortunately changed completely under the direction of the monks. The change effected by them in the ecclesiastical procedure resulted wholly to the detriment of the accused. The safeguards for their defense were in part done away with. A pretense was made to satisfy the demands of justice by requiring that the Inquisitors be prudent and impartial judges. But this made everything depend upon individuals, whereas the law itself should have been just and impartial. In this respect, the criminal procedure of the Inquisition is markedly inferior to the criminal procedure of the Middle Ages.

secus ageret non custodire populum Israel, nec super grege suo noctis vigilias vigilare, sed dormire seu dormitare potius videretur. Porro nec fuit mandantis intentio, nec scribentis voluntas hoc habuit, ut super aliis Provinciis, præterquam de hæresi infamatis ad eos scripta hujusmodi emanarent . . . Mandamus . . . contra hæreticos hujusmodi studeatis solicite debitum Pastoralis officii exercere, et eos reconciliare Domino . . ." Ripoll, *Bullarium ord. FF. Prædicatorum*, vol. i, p. 66.

CHAPTER VII

SIXTH PERIOD

DEVELOPMENT OF THE INQUISITION

INNOCENT IV AND THE USE OF TORTURE

THE successors of Gregory IX were not long in perceiving certain defects in the system of the Inquisition. They tried their best to remedy them, although their efforts were not always directed with the view of mitigating its rigor. We will indicate briefly their various decrees pertaining to the tribunals, the penalties and the procedure of the Inquisition.

In appointing the Dominicans and the Franciscans to suppress heresy, Gregory IX did not dream of abolishing the episcopal Inquisition. This was still occasionally carried on with its rival, whose procedure it finally adopted. Indeed no tribunal of the Inquisition could operate in a diocese without the permission of the Bishop, whom it was supposed to aid.[1] But it was inevitable that the Inquisitors would in time encroach upon the episcopal authority, and relying upon their

---

[1] Lea, *op. cit.*, vol. i, p. 330 seq.

papal commission proceed to act as independent judges. This abuse frequently attracted the attention of the Popes, who, after some hesitation, finally settled the law on this point.

"If previous orders requiring it" (episcopal concurrence), writes Lea, "had not been treated with contempt, Innocent IV would not have been obliged, in 1254, to reiterate the instructions that no condemnations to death or life imprisonment should be uttered without consulting the Bishops; and in 1255 he enjoined Bishop and Inquisitor to interpret in consultation any obscurities in the laws against heresy, and to administer the lighter penalties of deprivation of office and preferment. This recognition of episcopal jurisdiction was annulled by Alexander IV, who, after some vacillation, in 1257 rendered the Inquisition independent by releasing it from the necessity of consulting with the Bishops even in cases of obstinate and confessed heretics, and this he repeated in 1260. Then there was a reaction. In 1262, Urban IV, in an elaborate code of instructions, formally revived the consultation in all cases involving the death penalty or perpetual imprisonment; and this was repeated by Clement IV in 1265. Either these instructions, however, were revoked in some subsequent enactment, or they soon fell into desuetude, for in 1273, Gregory X, after alluding to the action of Alexander IV in annulling consultation, proceeds to direct that Inquisitors in deciding upon sentences shall proceed in accordance with the counsel of the Bishops or their delegates, so that the episcopal authority might share in decisions of such moment." [1]

This decretal remained henceforth the law. But as the Inquisitors at times seemed to act as if it did not exist, Boniface VIII and Clement IV strengthened it by declaring null and void all grave sentences in which the Bishop had not been consulted.[2] The consultation, however, between the Bishop and Inquisitor could be conducted through delegates.[3] In insisting upon this, the Popes proved that they were anxious to give the sentences of the Inquisition every possible guarantee of perfect justice.

Another way in which the Popes labored to render the sentences of the Inquisition just was the institution of experts. As the questions which arose before the tribunals in matters of heresy were often very complex, "it was soon found requisite to associate with the Inquisitors in the rendering of sentences men versed in the civil and canon law, which had by this time become an intricate study requiring the devotion of a lifetime. Accordingly they were empowered to call in experts to

[1] *Ibid.*, p. 335.   Cf. Tanon, *op. cit.*, pp. 413–416.

[2] *Sexto*, lib. v, tit ii, cap. 17, *Per hoc;* Clementin; lib. v, tit. iii, cap. i, *Multorum querela.*

[3] The Decretal *Multorum querela;* Eymeric, *Directorium*, p. 112.   Often the Bishop and the Inquisitor named the one delegate.

deliberate with them over the evidence, and advise with them on the sentence to be rendered." [1]

The official records of the sentences of the Inquisition frequently mention the presence of these experts, *periti* and *boni viri*.[2] Their number, which varied according to circumstances, was generally large. At a consultation called by the Inquisitors in January, 1329, at the Bishop's palace in Pamiers, there were thirty-five present, nine of whom were jurisconsults; and at another in September, 1329, there were fifty-one present, twenty of whom were civil lawyers.[3]

"At a comparatively early date, the practice was adopted of allowing a number of culprits to accumulate whose fate was determined and announced in a solemn *Sermo* or auto de fé. . . . In the final shape which the assembly of counsellors assumed, we find it summoned to meet on Fridays, the *Sermo* always taking place on Sundays. When the number of criminals was large, there was not much time for deliberation in special cases. The assessors were always to be jurists and Mendicant

---

[1] Lea, *op. cit.*, vol. i, p. 388. Cf. The Bull of Innocent IV, July 11, 1254. *Layettes du Trésor des Chartes*, vol. iii, no. 4111 (cf. 4113). Alexander IV calls them experts, *periti*, in his bull of April 15, 1255, Potthast, *Regesta*, no. 15, 804; Registers edited by De la Roncière, no. 372; Alexander renewed his decree in a bull of April 27, 1260, Coll. Doat, xxx, fol. 204; cf. also Urban IV, Bull of August 2, 1264.

[2] Douais, *La Formule; communicato bonorum virorum consilio des sentences inquisitoriales*, in the *Congrès scientifique international des Catholiques* (section of *Sciences historiques*), Fribourg (Switzerland), 1898, pp. 316–367.

[3] *Ibid.*, p. 323.

Friars, selected by the Inquisitor in such numbers as he saw fit. They were severally sworn on the Gospels to secrecy, and to give good and wise counsel, each one according to his conscience, and to the knowledge vouchsafed him by God. The Inquisitor then read over his summary of each case, sometimes withholding the name of the accused, and they voted the sentence "Penance at the discretion of the Inquisitor" — "that person is to be imprisoned, or abandoned to the secular arm"—while the Gospels lay on the table "so that our judgment might come from the face of God, and our eyes might see justice."[1]

We have here the beginnings of our modern jury. As a rule, the Inquisitors followed the advice of their counsellors, save when they themselves favored a less severe sentence.[2] The labor of these experts was considerable, and often lasted several days. "A brief summary of each case was submitted to them. Eymeric maintained that the whole case ought to be submitted to them; and that was undoubtedly the common practice. But Pegna on the other hand thought it was better to withhold from the assessors the names of both the witnesses and the prisoners. He declares that this was the common practice of the Inquisition, at least as far as the names were

<hr>

[1] Lea, *op. cit.*, vol. i, p. 389; Doat, vol. xxvii, fol. 108. The *Sermones* of the Inquisitor Bernard of Caux were not always held on Sundays (Tanon, *op. cit.*, p. 425).

[2] Douais, *La formule: Communicato bonorum virorum consilio, loc. cit.*, pp. 324, 326.

concerned.[1] This was also the practice of the Inquisitors of southern France, as Bernard Gui tells us. The majority of the counsellors received a brief summary of the case, the names being withheld. Only a very few of them were deemed worthy to read the full text of all the interrogatories." [2]

We can readily see how the *periti* or *boni viri,* who were called upon to decide the guilt or innocence of the accused from evidence considered in the abstract, without any knowledge of the prisoners' names or motives, could easily make mistakes. In fact, they did not have data enough to enable them to decide a concrete case. For tribunals are to judge criminals and not crimes, just as physicians treat sick people and not diseases in the abstract. We know that the same disease calls for different treatment in different individuals; in like manner a crime must be judged with due reference to the mentality of

---

[1] Eymeric, *Directorium,* 3ᵃ pars, quest. 80, Comm. 129, p. 632.

[2] Tanon, *op. cit.,* p. 421. " Ante sermonem vero, captato tempore opportuno, petitur per inquisitores consilium a prædictis (bonis viris), facta prius extractione summaria et compendiosa de culpis, in quo complete tangitur substantia cujuslibet personæ . . . *sine expressione nominis alicujus personæ ad cautelam, ut liberius de pœnitentia pro tali culpa imponenda sine affectione personæ judicent consulentes.* Solidius tamen consilium, si omnia complete exprimerentur, quod faciendum est ubi et quando possunt haberi personæ consulentes quibus non est periculum revelare; esset etiam minus calumpniosum. *Sed tamen non fuit usus inquisitonis ab antiquo,* propter periculum jam prætactum; verumptamen confessiones singulorum prius integraliter explicantur coram doycesano vel ejus vicario, aliquibus peritis paucis et secretariis et juratis." Bernard Gui, Practica, 3ᵃ pars, p. 83. On the communication of the names, cf. a bull of Alexander IV. *Layettes du trésor des Chartes,* vol. iii, no. 4221.

the one who has committed it. The Inquisition did not seem to understand this.[1]

The assembly of experts, therefore, instituted by the Popes did not obtain the good results that were expected. But we must at least in justice admit that the Popes did their utmost to protect the tribunals of the Inquisition from the arbitrary action of individual judges, by requiring the Inquisitors to consult both the *boni viri* and the Bishops.

Over the various penalties of the Inquisition the Popes likewise exercised a supervision, which was always just and at times most kindly.

The greatest penalties which the Inquisition could inflict were life imprisonment, and abandonment of the prisoner to the secular arm. It is only with regard to the first of these penalties that we see the clemency of both Popes and Councils. Anyone who considers the rough manners of this period, must admit that the Church did a great deal to mitigate the excessive cruelty of the mediæval prisons.

The Council of Toulouse, in 1229, decreed that repentant heretics "must be imprisoned, in such a way that they could not corrupt others." [2] It also declared

---

[1] Even in our day the jury is bound to decide on the merits of the case submitted to it, without regarding the consequences of its verdict. The foreman reminds the jurymen in advance that "they will be false to their oath if, in giving their decision, they are biased by the consideration of the punishment their verdict will entail upon the prisoner."

[2] "Ad agendam pœnitentiam . . . in muro tali includantur cautela quod

that the Bishop was to provide for the prisoners' needs out of their confiscated property. Such measures betoken an earnest desire to safeguard the health, and to a certain degree the liberty of the prisoners.   In fact, the documents we possess prove that the condemned sometimes enjoyed a great deal of freedom, and were allowed to receive from their friends an additional supply of food, even when the prison fare was ample.[1]

But in many places the prisoners, even before their trial, were treated with great cruelty. "The papal orders were that they (the prisons) should be constructed of small, dark cells for solitary confinement, only taking care that the *enormis rigor* of the incarceration should not extinguish life." [2]   But this last provision was not always carried out.   Too often the prisoners were confined in narrow cells full of disease, and totally unfit for human habitation.[3]   The Popes, learning this sad state of affairs, tried to remedy it.   Clement V was particularly

---

facultatem non habeant alios corrumpendi."   D'Achery, *Spicilegium*, in-fol. vol. i, p. 711.

[1] Cf. on this point Vidal., *op. cit.*, in *Annales de Saint-Louis des Français*, 1905, pp. 361–368.

[2] Lea, *op. cit.*, vol. i, p. 491.

[3] "In aliis domunculis sunt miseri commorantes in compedibus tam ligneis quam ferreis, nec se movere possunt, sed subtus se egerunt atque mingunt nec jacere possunt nisi resupini in terra frigida; et in hujusmodi tormentis nocte dieque longis temporibus quotidie perseverant.   In aliis vero carcerum locis degentibus, non solum lux et aer subtrahitur, sed et victus excepto pane doloris et aqua, quæ etiam rarissime ministratur."   Document quoted by Vidal, *op. cit.*, 1905, p. 362, note.   Cf. Lea, *op. cit.*, vol. i, pp. 491, 492.

zealous in his attempts at prison reform.[1] That he succeeded in bettering, at least for a time, the lot of these
unfortunates, in whom he interested himself, cannot be
denied.[2]

If the reforms he decreed were not all carried out, the
blame must be laid to the door of those appointed to
enforce them. History frees him from all responsibility.

The part played by the Popes, the Councils, and the
Inquisitors in the infliction of the death penalty does not
appear in so favorable a light. While not directly par-
ticipating in the death sentences, they were still very
eager for the execution of the heretics they abandoned to
the secular arm. This is well attested by both documents and facts.

Lucius III, at the Council of Verona in 1184,
ordered sovereigns to swear, in the presence of their
Bishops, to execute fully and conscientiously the ecclesiastical and civil laws against heresy. If they refused or neglected to do this, they themselves were

---

[1] He ordered that the prisons be kept in good condition, that they be
looked after by both Bishop and Inquisitor, each of whom was to appoint
a jailer who would keep the prison keys, that all provisions sent to the prisoners should be faithfully given them, etc. Cf. Decretal *Multorum querela*
in Eymeric, *Directorium*, p. 112.

[2] His legates Pierre de la Chapelle and Béranger de Frédol visited in
April, 1306, the prisons of Carcasconne and Albi, changed the jailers, removed
the irons from the prisoners, and made others leave the subterraneous cells in
which they had been confined. Doat, vol. xxxiv, fol. 4 and seq; Douais,
Documents, vol. ii, p. 304 seq. Cf. Compayré, *Études historiques sur l'Albigeois*, pp. 240–245.

liable to excommunication and their rebellious cities to interdict.[1]

Innocent IV, in 1252, enacted a law still more severe, insisting on the infliction of the death penalty upon heretics. "When," he says, "heretics condemned by the Bishop, his Vicar, or the Inquisitors, have been abandoned to the secular arm, the podestà or ruler of the city must take charge of them at once, and within five days enforce the laws against them."[2]

This law, or rather the bull *Ad Extirpanda*, which contains it, was to be inscribed in perpetuity in all the local statute books. Any attempt to modify it was a crime, which condemned the offender to perpetual infamy, and a fine enforced by the ban. Moreover, each podestà, at the beginning and end of his term, was required to have this bull read in all places designated by the Bishop and the Inquisitors, and to erase from the statute books all laws to the contrary.[3]

At the same time, Innocent IV issued instructions to

---

[1] "Eis excummunicatione ligandis et terris ipsorum interdicto Ecclesiæ supponendis. Civitas autem quæ his institutis duxerit resistendum vel . . . punire neglexerit . . . , aliarum caræt commercio civitatum," etc. Decretal *Ad abolendam*, in the Decretals, cap, ix, *de Hæreticis*, lib. v, tit. vii. Cf. Sexto, lib. v, tit. ii, c. 2. *Ut Officium;* Council of Arles, 1254, can. iii; Council of Béziers, 1246, can. ix.

[2] "Damnatos de hæresi . . . potestas vel rector . . . eos sibi relictos recipiat statim, vel infra quinque dies ad minus, circa eos constitutiones contra tales editas servaturus." Bull *Ad extirpanda*, May 15, 1252, in Eymeric, *Directorium*, Appendix, p. 8.

[3] *Ibid.*

II

the Inquisitors of upper Italy, urging them to have this bull and the edicts of Frederic II inserted in the statutes of the various cities.[1] And to prevent mistakes being made as to which imperial edicts he wished enforced, he repeated these instructions in 1254, and inserted in one of his bulls the cruel laws of Frederic II, viz.: the edict of Ravenna, *Commissis nobis*, which decreed the death of obdurate heretics; and the Sicilian law, *Inconsutilem tunicam*, which expressly decreed that such heretics be sent to the stake.[2]

These decrees remained the law as long as the Inquisition lasted. The bull *Ad Extirpanda* was, however, slightly modified from time to time. " In 1265, Clement IV again went over it, carefully making some changes, principally in adding the word ' Inquisitors ' in passages where Innocent had only designated the Bishops and Friars, thus showing that the Inquisition had, during the interval, established itself as the recognized instrumentality in the prosecution of heresy, and the next year he repeated Innocent's emphatic order to the Inquisitors to enforce the insertion of his legislation and that of his predecessors upon the statute books everywhere, with the free use of excommunication and interdict." [3]

---

[1] Cf. the bulls *Cum adversus*, *Tunc potissime*, *Ex Commissis nobis*, etc., in Eymeric, *ibid.*, pp. 9–12.

[2] *Ibid.*, pp. 13–15.

[3] Lea, *op. cit.*, vol. i, p. 339; cf. Potthast, *Regesta*, nos. 19348, 19423, 19428, 19433, 19522, 19896, 19905.

A little later, Nicholas IV, who during his short pontificate (1288–1292), greatly favored the Inquisition in its work, re-enacted the bulls of Innocent IV and Clement IV, and ordered the enforcement of the laws of Frederic II, lest perchance they might fall into desuetude.[1]

It is therefore proved beyond question that the Church, in the person of the Popes, used every means at her disposal, especially excommunication, to compel the State to enforce the infliction of the death penalty upon heretics. This excommunication, moreover, was all the more dreaded, because, according to the canons, the one excommunicated, unless absolved from the censure, was regarded as a heretic himself within a year's time, and was liable therefore to the death penalty.[2] The princes of the day, therefore, had no other way of escaping this penalty, except by faithfully carrying out the sentence of the Church.

.   .   .   .

The Church is also responsible for having introduced torture into the proceedings of the Inquisition. This cruel practice was introduced by Innocent IV in 1252.

---

[1] *Registers*, published by Langlois, no. 4253. For the interest Nicholas IV took in the Inquisition, cf. Douais, *Monuments*, vol. i, pp. xxx–xxxi.

[2] Alexander IV decreed this penalty against the contumacious, Sexto, *De Hæreticis*, cap. vii. Boniface VIII extended it to those princes and magistrates who did not enforce the sentences of the Inquisition: quam excommunicationem si per annum animo sustinuerit pertinaci, extunc velut hæreticus condemnetur. Sexto, *De Hæreticis*, cap. xviii in Eymeric,, 2ᵃ pars, p. 110. Cf. *ibid.*, 2ᵃ pars, quest. 47, pp. 360, 361.

Torture had left too terrible an impression upon the minds of the early Christians to permit of their employing it in their own tribunals. The barbarians who founded the commonwealths of Europe, with the exception of the Visigoths, knew nothing of this brutal method of extorting confessions. The only thing of the kind that they allowed was flogging, which, according to St. Augustine, was rather akin to the correction of children by their parents. Gratian, who recommends it in his *Decretum*,[1] lays it down as an "accepted rule of canon law that no confession is to be extorted by torture."[2] Besides, Nicholas I, in his instructions to the Bulgarians, had formally denounced the torturing of prisoners.[3] He advised that the testimony of three persons be required for conviction;

[1] *Causa* v, quæst. v, Illi qui, cap. iv; *Causa* xii, quæst. ii, Fraternitas.

[2] "Confessio ergo in talibus non extorqueri debet, sed potius sponte profiteri. Pessimum est enim de suspicione aut extorta confessione quemquam judicare," etc. *Causa* xv, quaest. vi, cap. i. It has been said that severe flogging might be a most violent form of torture. Tanon (*op. cit.*, pp. 371, 372). But St. Augustine certainly did not mean this.

[3] "Si fur vel latro deprehensus fuerit et negaverit quod ei impingitur, asseritis apud vos quod judex caput ejus verberibus tundat et aliis stimulis ferreis, donec veritatem depromat, ipsius latera pungat: quam rem nec divina lex, nec humana prorsus admittit, cum non invita, sed spontanea debeat esse confessio; nec sit violenter elicienda, sed voluntarie proferenda. Denique, si contigerit vos, etiam illis pænis illatis, nihil de his quæ passo in crimen objiciuntur, penitus invenire, nonne saltem nunc erubescitis et quam impie judicetis agnoscitis? Similiter autem si homo criminatus, talia passus sustinere non valens dixerit se perpetrasse quod non perpetravit; ad quem, rogo, tantæ impietatis magnitudo revolvitur, nisi ad eum qui hunc talia cogit mendaciter confiteri? Quamvis non confiteri noscatur sed loqui hoc ore profert, quod corde non tenet." *Responsa ad Consulta Bulgarorum*, cap. lxxxvi, Labbe, *Concilia*, vol. viii, col. 544.

if these could not be obtained, the prisoner's oath upon the Gospels was to be considered sufficient.

The ecclesiastical tribunals borrowed from Germany another method of proving crime, viz., the ordeals, or judgments of God.

There was the duel, the ordeal of the cross, the ordeal of boiling water, the ordeal of fire, and the ordeal of cold water. They had a great vogue in nearly all the Latin countries, especially in Germany and France. But about the twelfth century they deservedly fell into great disfavor, until at last the Popes, particularly Innocent III, Honorius III, and Gregory IX, legislated them out of existence.[1]

At the very moment the Popes were condemning the ordeals, the revival of the Roman law throughout the West was introducing the customs of antiquity. It was then "that jurists began to feel the need of torture, and accustom themselves to the idea of its introduction. The earliest instances with which I have met," writes Lea, "occur in the Veronese code of 1228, and the Sicilian constitutions of Frederic II in 1231, and in both of these the references to it show how sparingly and hesitatingly it was employed. Even Frederic, in his ruthless edicts, from 1220 to 1239, makes no allusion to it, but in accord-

---

[1] Decretals, lib. v, tit. xxxv, cap. i–iii. Cf. Vacandard, *L'Église et les Ordalies* in *Études de critique et d'histoire*, 3d ed., Paris, 1906, pp. 191–215. On the abuse of ordeals in trials for heresy, cf. Tanon, *op. cit.*, pp. 303–312.

ance with the Verona decree of Lucius III, prescribes the recognized form of canonical purgation for the trial of all suspected heretics." [1]

The use of torture, as Tanon has pointed out, had perhaps never been altogether discontinued. Some ecclesiastical tribunals, at least in Paris, made use of it in extremely grave cases, at the close of the twelfth and the beginning of the thirteenth century.[2] But this was exceptional; in Italy, apparently, it had never been used.

Gregory IX ignored all references to torture made in the Veronese code, and the constitutions of Frederic II. But Innocent IV, feeling undoubtedly that it was a quick and effective method for detecting criminals, authorized the tribunals of the Inquisition to employ it. In his bull *Ad Extirpanda,* he says: "The podestà or ruler (of the city) is hereby ordered to force all captured heretics to confess and accuse their accomplices by torture which will not imperil life or injure limb, just as thieves and robbers are forced to accuse their accomplices and to confess their crimes; for these heretics are true thieves, murderers of souls, and robbers of the sacraments of God." [3] The Pope here tries to defend the use of torture,

---

[1] Lea, *op. cit.*, vol. i, p. 421. Cf. Paul Fournier, *Les officialités au moyen âge*, Paris, 1880, pp. 249, 280; Esmein, *Histoire de la procédure criminelle en France*, Paris, 1882, pp. 19, 77.

[2] Tanon, *op. cit.*, pp. 362-373; *Notice sur le Formulaire de Guillaume de Paris*, 1888, p. 33.

[3] "Teneatur potestas vel rector hæreticos . . . cogere citra membri diminu-

by classing heretics with thieves and murderers. A mere comparison is his only argument.

This law of Innocent IV was renewed and confirmed November 30, 1259, by Alexander IV,[1] and again on November 3, 1265, by Clement IV.[2] The restriction of Innocent III to use torture "which should not imperil life or injure limb" (*Cogere citra membri diminutionem et mortis periculum*), left a great deal to the discretion of the Inquisitors. Besides flogging, the other punishments inflicted upon those who refused to confess the crime of which they were accused were antecedent imprisonment, the rack, the *strappado*, and the burning coals.[3]

When after the first interrogatory the prisoner denied what the Inquisitors believed to be very probable or certain, he was thrown into prison. The *durus carcer et arcta vita*[4] was deemed an excellent method of extorting confessions.

"It was pointed out," says Lea, "that judicious re-

tionem et mortis periculum, tanquam vere latrones et homicidas animarum . . . errores suos expresse fateri." Bull *Ad extirpanda*, in Eymeric, *Directorium*, Appendix, p. 8.

[1] Potthast, *Regesta*, no. 17714.

[2] *Ibid.*, no. 19433.

[3] Vidal (*Le tribunal d'inquisition de Pamiers, loc. cit.*, i, 1905, p. 286) quotes also the torture of the boots, and the torture of water, which were seldom used; the last was peculiar to Spain. Cf. *ibid.*, pp. 284–286.

[4] "Per durum carcerem et vitam arctam est ab eis confessio extorquenda." Document of 1253 or 1254, published by Douais, *Documents*, vol. i, p. lxvii. Cf. Tanon, *op. cit.*, pp. 360–362.

striction of diet not only reduced the body, but weakened the will, and rendered the prisoner less able to resist alternate threats of death and promises of mercy. Starvation, in fact, was reckoned one of the regular and most efficient methods to subdue unwilling witnesses and defendants." [1] This was the usual method employed in Languedoc. "It is the only method," writes Mgr. Douais,[2] "to extort confessions mentioned either in the records of the notary of the Inquisition of Carcassonne [3] or in the sentences of Bernard Gui.[4] It was also the practice of the Inquisitors across the Rhine." [5]

Still the use of torture, especially of the rack and the *strappado,* was not unknown in southern Europe, even before the promulgation of Innocent's bull *Ad Extirpanda.*[6]

The rack was a triangular frame, on which the prisoner

---

[1] Lea, *op. cit.*, vol. i, p. 421.

[2] Douais, *Documents*, vol. i, p. ccxl.

[3] Douais, *Documents*, vol. ii, p. 115 and seq.

[4] *Loc cit.*, pp. 105, 114, 120, 145. Mgr. Douais adds: This is the only method of extorting confession mentioned by Bernard Gui in his *Practica*. This is not accurate. We will see later on that the *Practica* also recommends the use of torture. Mgr. Douais here alludes to the following passage: "Quando aliquis vehementer suspectus . . . persistat in negando . . . non est aliqualiter relaxandus, sed detinendus per annos plurimos, ut vexatio det intellectum." *Practica*, 5ᵃ pars, ed. Douais, p. 302.

[5] "Si autem recuset hoc facere (confiteri), recludatur in carcere et incutiatur ei timor quod testes contra ipsum habeantur, et si per testes convictus fuerit, nulla fiat ei misericordia quin morti tradetur; et sustentetur tenui victu, quia timor talis humiliabit eum," etc. David d'Augsburg, *Tractatus de inquisitione hereticorum*, ed. Preger, Mainz, 1878, p. 43.

[6] Cf. several cases in Languedoc a little before 1243 in Douais, *Documents*, vol. i, p. 240.

was stretched and bound, so that he could not move. Cords were attached to his arms and legs, and then connected with a windlass, which when turned dislocated the joints of the wrists and ankles.

The *strappado* or vertical rack was no less painful. The prisoner with his hands tied behind his back was raised by a rope attached to a pulley and windlass to the top of a gallows, or to the ceiling of the torture chamber; he was then let fall with a jerk to within a few inches of the ground. This was repeated several times. The cruel torturers sometimes tied weights to the victim's feet to increase the shock of the fall.

The punishment of burning, "although a very dangerous punishment," as an Inquisitor informs us, was occasionally used. We read of an official of Poitiers, who, following a Toulousain custom, tortured a sorceress by placing her feet on burning coals (*juxta carbones accensos*).[1] This punishment is described by Marsollier in his *Histoire de l'Inquisition*. First a good fire was started; then the victim was stretched out on the ground, his feet manacled, and turned toward the flame. Grease, fat, or some other combustible substance was rubbed upon them, so that they were horribly burned. From time to time a screen was placed between the victim's feet and the

---

[1] "De concilio quorumdam proborum qui se asserebant vidisse penis examinari hæreticos in partibus Tholosanis, fecisti plantas pedum ejusdem mulieris juxta carbones accensos apponi." Letter of John XXII, July 28, 1319, in Vidal, *op. cit.*, October, 1905, p. 5.

brazier, that the Inquisitor might have an opportunity to resume his interrogatory.

Such methods of torturing the accused were so detestable, that in the beginning the torturer was always a civil official, as we read in the bull of Innocent IV.[1] The canons of the Church, moreover, prohibited all ecclesiastics from taking part in these tortures, so that the Inquisitor who, for whatever reason, accompanied the victim into the torture chamber, was thereby rendered irregular, and could not exercise his office again, until he had obtained the necessary dispensation. The tribunals complained of this cumbrous mode of administration, and declared that it hindered them from properly interrogating the accused. Every effort was made to have the prohibition against clerics being present in the torture chamber removed. Their object was at last obtained indirectly. On April 27, 1260, Alexander IV authorized the Inquisitors and their associates to mutually grant all the needed dispensations for irregularities that might be incurred.[2] This permission was granted a second time by Urban IV, August 4, 1262;[3] it was practically an authorization to assist at the interrogatories at which torture was employed. From this time the Inquisitors did not scruple to appear in person in the torture chamber. The man-

---

[1] "Teneatur podestà vel rector hereticos cogere," etc.   Bull *Ad exirpanda*.

[2] Collection Doat, xxxi, fol. 277, quoted by Douais, *Documents*, vol. i, p. xxv, n. 3.

[3] *Regesta*, no. 18390; Eymeric, *Directorium*, p. 132.

uals of the Inquisition record this practice and approve it.[1]

Torture was not to be employed until the judge had been convinced that gentle means were of no avail.[2] Even in the torture chamber, while the prisoner was being stripped of his garments and was being bound, the Inquisitor kept urging him to confess his guilt. On his refusal, the *vexatio* began with slight tortures. If these proved ineffectual, others were applied with gradually increased severity; at the very beginning the victim was shown all the various instruments of torture, in order that the mere sight of them might terrify him into yielding.[3]

The Inquisitors realized so well that such forced confessions were valueless, that they required the prisoner to confirm them after he had left the torture chamber. The torture was not to exceed a half hour. "Usually," writes Lea, "the procedure appears to be that the torture was continued until the accuser signified his readiness to confess, when he was unbound and carried into another room where his confession was made. If, however,

[1] Eymeric, *Directorium*, 3ª pars, p. 481; Pegna's Commentary, p. 482.

[2] A grave suspicion against the prisoner was required before he could be tortured. "It would be iniquitous, and a violation of both human and divine law to torture anyone, unless there was good evidence against him, *perche in negotio di tanta importanza si puo facilmente commetter errore*," says the Inquisitor Eliseo Masini in his *Sacro Arsenale ovvero prattica dell' Officio della santa Inquisizione*, Bologna, 1665, pp. 154, 155.

[3] Eymeric, *Directorium*, 3ª pars., p. 481, col. 1.

the confession was extracted during the torture, it was read over subsequently to the prisoner, and he was asked if it were true. . . . In any case the record was carefully made that the confession was free and spontaneous, without the pressure of force or fear." [1]

"It is a noteworthy fact, however, that in the fragmentary documents of inquisitorial proceedings which have reached us the references to torture are singularly few. . . . In the six hundred and thirty-six sentences borne upon the register of Toulouse from 1309 to 1323, the only allusion to torture is in the recital of the case of Calvarie, but there are numerous instances in which the information wrung from the convicts who had no hope of escape could scarce have been procured in any other manner. Bernard Gui, who conducted the Inquisition of Toulouse during this period, has too emphatically expressed his sense of the utility of torture on both principals and witnesses for us to doubt his readiness in its employment." [2]

---

[1] Lea, *op. cit.*, vol. i, p. 427. Cf. Eymeric, *Directorium, ibid.*, p. 481 col. 2; Vidal, *op. cit.*, 1905, p. 283. The Abbé Vidal, *op. cit.*, p. 155, quotes an instance of these pretended spontaneous confessions at the tribunal of Pamiers; the records state that a certain Guillem Agassa *prædicta confessus fuit sponte;* whereas a little before we read: "*postquam depositus fuit de tormento.*" Lea also quotes the case of Guillem Salavert, who, in 1303, testified that his confession *esse veram, non factam vi tormentorum*, although he had been actually tortured, *op. cit.*, vol. i. p. 428.

[2] Lea. *op. cit.*, p. 424. "Talis arctari seu restringi poterit in dieta, vel alias in carcere seu vinculis, vel etiam *quæstionari* de consilio peritorum, prout qualitas negotii et personæ conditio exegerit, ut veritas eruatur," says Bernard

Besides, the investigation which Clement V ordered into the iniquities of the Inquisition of Carcassonne proves clearly that the accused were frequently subjected to torture.[1] That we rarely find reference to torture in the records of the Inquisition need not surprise us. For in the beginning, torture was inflicted by civil executioners outside of the tribunal of the Inquisition; and even later on, when the Inquisitors were allowed to take part in it, it was considered merely a means of making the prisoner declare his willingness to confess afterwards. A confession made under torture had no force in law; the second confession only was considered valid. That is why it alone, as a rule, is recorded.

But if the sufferings of the victims of the Inquisition were not deemed worthy of mention in the records, they were none the less real and severe. Imprudent or heartless judges were guilty of grave abuses in the use of torture. Rome, which had authorized it, at last intervened, not, we regret to say, to prohibit it altogether, but at least to reform the abuses which had been called to her attention. One reform of Clement V ordered the Inquisition never

Gui in his *Practica*, p. 284; cf. p. 112, no. 20; p. 138, no. 36. "Possunt etiam tales heretici *per questionum tormenta* citra membri diminutionem et mortis periculum . . . et errores suos expresse fateri et accusare alios hæreticos." *Ibid.*, p. 218. We may well be astonished, therefore, to find Mgr. Douais, the editor of the *Practica*, affirming that "the *Practica* of Bernard Gui is silent on the question of torture." *Documents*, vol. i, p. 238.

[1] Clement V required the consent of the Inquisitor and the local Bishop before a heretic could be tortured, *vel tormentis exponere illis*. Decretal *Multorum querela*, in Eymeric. *Directorium*, 2ª pars, p. 112.

to use torture without the Bishop's consent, if he could be reached within eight days.[1]

"Bernard Gui emphatically remonstrated against this as seriously crippling the efficiency of the Inquisition, and proposed to substitute for it the meaningless phrase that torture should only be used *with mature and careful deliberation*, but his suggestion was not heeded, and the Clementine regulations remained the law of the Church." [2]

The code of the Inquisition was now practically complete, for succeeding Popes made no change of any importance. The data before us prove that the Church forgot her early traditions of toleration, and borrowed from the Roman jurisprudence, revived by the legists, laws and practices which remind one of the cruelty of ancient paganism. But once this criminal code was adopted, she endeavored to mitigate the cruelty with which it was enforced. If this preoccupation is not always visible — and it is not in her condemnation of obdurate heretics —we must at least give her the credit of insisting that torture "should never imperil life or injure limb": *Cogere citra membri diminutionem et mortis periculum.*

We will now ask how the theologians and canonists interpreted this legislation, and how the tribunals of the Inquisition enforced it.

[1] Decretal, *Multorum querela.*

[2] Lea, *op. cit.*, vol. i, p. 424; Bernard Gui, *Practica*, ed. Douais, 4ᵈ pars, p. 188. Bernard Gui did not hesitate to assert (*ibid.*, p. 174) that the bulls of Clement V: *Multorum querela* and *Nolentes* ought to be modified or even repealed so as to give more freedom to the Inquisitors: *indigent ut remedientur, suspendantur aut moderentur in melius, seu potius totaliter.*

CHAPTER VIII

THEOLOGIANS, CANONISTS, AND CASUISTS OF THE INQUISITION

THE gravity of the crime of heresy was early recognized in the Church. Gratian discussed this question in a special chapter of his *Decretum*.[1] Innocent III, Guala the Dominican, and the Emperor Frederic II, as we have seen, looked upon heresy as treason against Almighty God, *i.e.* the most dreadful of crimes.

The theologians and even the civil authorities did not concern themselves much with the evil effects of heresy upon the social order, but viewed it rather as an offense against God. Thus they made no distinction between those teachings which entailed injury on the family and on society, and those which merely denied certain revealed truths. Innocent III, in his constitution of September 23, 1207, legislated particularly against the Patarins, but he took care to point out that no heretic, no matter what the nature of his error might be, should be allowed to escape the full penalty of the law.[2] Fred-

---

[1] *Causa* xxxi, q. vii, cap. 16.

[2] "Servanda in perpetuum lege sancimus ut *quicumque hæreticus, maxime Paterenus* . . . protinus capiatur et tradatur seculari curiæ puniendus secundum legitimas sanctiones," etc. *Ep.* x, 130.

eric II spoke in similar terms in his Constitutions of 1220, 1224, and 1232.[1] This was the current teaching throughout the Middle Ages.[2]

But it is important to know what men then understood by the word heresy. We can ascertain this from the theologians and canonists, especially from St. Raymond of Pennafort and St. Thomas Aquinas. St. Raymond gives four meanings to the word heretic, but from the standpoint of the canon law he says: "A heretic is one who denies the faith."[3] St. Thomas Aquinas is more accurate. He declares that no one is truly a heretic unless he obstinately maintains his error, even after it has been pointed out to him by ecclesiastical authority. This is the teaching of St. Augustine.[4]

[1] "Catharos, Paterenos, Leonistas, Speronistas, Arnoldistas, *et omnes hæreticos utriusque sexus, quocumque nomine censeantur*, perpetua dampnamus infamia," etc. Constitution of November 22, 1220, cap. 6, in *Mon. Germ.*, *Leges*, sect. iv, vol. ii, pp. 107–109. "Ut *quicumque . . . fuerit de hæresi manifeste convictus et hæreticus judicatus . . .* illico capiatur," etc. Constitut. de 1223, *ibid.*, p. 126. "Si inventi fuerint a fide catholica *saltem in articulo deviare . . .* , mortem pati decernimus." Sicilian Constitution, i, 3, in Eymeric, *Direct. Inquisit.*, Appendix, p. 14. This recalls the law of Arcadius of 395. *Cod. Theod.*, xvi, v. 28; cf. *supra* p. 9, n. 2.

[2] Cf. the canonists cited by Tanon, *op. cit.*, pp. 455–458. An anonymous writer, whose commentary is found in Huguccio's Summa of the Decretum, says: "Innuit quod *pro sola hæresi* non sint morte puniendi. Solve ut prius. Quando enim sunt incorrigibiles, ultimo supplicio feriantur; aliter non." Bibl. nation., Ms. 15379, fol. 49.

[3] "Hæreticus 1^0 qui errat a fide," etc. S. Raymundi, *Summa*, lib. i, cap. *De Hæreticis*, sect. i, Roman Edition, 1603, p. 39.

[4] "Hæresis consistit circa ea quæ fidei sunt . . . dissentiendo cum pertinacia ab illis." *Summa*, IIa, IIae, quaest. xi, Conclusio; cf. *ibid.*, ad 3um, quotations from St. Augustine

But by degrees the word, taken at first in a strict sense, acquired a broader meaning. St. Raymond includes schism in the notion of heresy. "The only difference between these two crimes," he writes, "is the difference between genus and species"; every schism ends in heresy. And relying on the authority of St. Jerome, the rigorous canonist goes so far as to declare that schism is even a greater crime than heresy. He proves this by the fact that Core, Dathan, and Abiron,[1] who seceded from the chosen people, were punished by the most terrible of punishments. "From the enormity of the punishment, must we not argue the enormity of the crime?" St. Raymond therefore declares that the same punishment must be inflicted upon the heretic and the schismatic.[2]

"The authors of the treatises on the Inquisition," writes Tanon, "classed as heretics all those who favored heresy, and all excommunicates who did not submit to the church within a certain period. They declared that a man excommunicated for any cause whatever, who did not seek absolution within a year, incurred by this act of rebellion a light suspicion of heresy; that he could then be cited before the Inquisitor to answer not only for the crime which had caused his excommunication, but also for his orthodoxy. If he did not answer this second sum-

---

[1] Num. xvi. 31–33.

[2] "Talis est differentia qualiter inter genus et speciem . . . ; peccatum gravius hæresi . . . , quis enim dubitaverit esse sceleratius commissum quod est gravius vindicatum?" *Loc. cit.*, lib. i, cap. *De schismatics*, pp. 45–47.

mons, he was at once considered excommunicated for heresy, and if he remained under this second excommunication for a year, he was liable to be condemned as a real heretic. The light suspicion caused by his first excommunication became in turn a vehement and then a violent suspicion which, together with his continued contumacy, constituted a full proof of heresy."[1]

The theologians insisted greatly upon respect for ecclesiastical and especially Papal authority. Everything that tended to lessen this authority seemed to them a practical denial of the faith. The canonist Henry of Susa (Hostiensis +1271), went so far as to say that "whoever contradicted or refused to accept the decretals of the Popes was a heretic."[2] Such obedience was looked upon as a culpable disregard of the rights of the papacy, and consequently a form of heresy.[3]

Tanon, *op. cit.*, pp. 235, 236. "Si quis per annum excommunicatus stetit pro contumacia in causa quæ non sit fidei, efficitur suspectus leviter de hæresi, et ut responsurus de fide potest citari. Si renuit comparere, eo facto est excommunicatus, tanquam contumax in causa fidei, et consequenter aggravatur, quia jam fit suspectus de hæresi vehementer . . . Tunc vel infra annum comparet, vel non. Si non, tunc anno elapso est ut hæreticus condemnandus. Transivit enim suspicio levis in vehementem, et vehemens in violentam." Eymeric, *Directorium*, 2^a pars, quest. 47, pp. 360, 361. This theory was not carried out in practice (*op. cit.*, p. 236).

[2] "Hæreticus est, qui decretalibus epistolis contradicit aut eos non recipit." In Baluze-Mansi, *Miscellanea*, vol. ii, p. 275; cf. Döllinger, *La papauté*, Paris, 1904, p. 335, n. 362.

The canonist, Zanchino Ugolini, in his *Tractatus de Hæreticis*, cap. ii, published at Rome in 1568, at the expense of Pius V, includes in his enumeration of heresies neglect to observe the papal decretals, because this constituted an apparent contempt for the power of the Keys. Lea, *op. cit.*, vol. i, p. 229, note.

Superstition was also classed under the heading of heresy. The canonist, Zanchino Ugolini tells us that he was present at the condemnation of an immoral priest, who was punished by the Inquisitors not for his licentiousness, but because he said mass every day in a state of sin, and urged in excuse that he considered himself pardoned by the mere fact of putting on the sacred vestments.[1]

The Jews, as such, were never regarded as heretics. But the usury they so widely practiced evidenced an unorthodox doctrine on thievery, which made them liable to be suspected of heresy. Indeed we find several Popes upbraiding them "for maintaining that usury is not a sin." Some Christians also fell into the same error, and thereby became subject to the Inquisition. Pope Martin V, in his bull of November 6, 1419, authorizes the Inquisitors to prosecute these usurers.[2]

Sorcery and magic were also put on a par with heresy. Pope Alexander IV had decided that divination and sorcery did not fall under the jurisdiction of the Inquisition, unless there was manifest heresy involved.[3] But

---

[1] *Tractat, de Hæret.*, cap. ii; cf. Lea, *ibid.*, p. 400. Sentences of this kind were rather rare; cf. Tanon, *op. cit.*, pp. 249, 250, notes.

[2] "Demum etiam quidam Christiani et Judæi non verentur asserere quod usura non sit peccatum, aut recipere decem pro centum mutuo datis seu quicquam ultra sortem; in his et similibus atque in nonnullis aliis spiritualibus et gravibus præceptis multipliciter excedunt. Nos igitur discretioni tuæ committimus quatenus ad extirpationem omnium hujusmodi pravitatum et errorum vigilanter insistas." Bull *Inter cætera*, sent to the Inquisitor Pons Feugeyron. Cf. Tanon, *cit.*, pp. 243, 245.

[3] Bull of December 9, 1257, in Doat, xxxi, fol. 244–249, analyzed by Douais,

casuists were not wanting to prove that heresy was involved in such cases.[1] The belief in the witches' nightly rides through the air, led by Diana or Herodias of Palestine, was very widespread in the Middle Ages, and was held by some as late as the fifteenth century. The question whether the devil could carry off men and women was warmly debated by the theologians of the time. "A case adduced by Albertus Magnus, in a disputation on the subject before the Bishop of Paris, and recorded by Thomas of Cantimpré, in which the daughter of the Count of Schwalenberg was regularly carried away every night for several hours, gave immense satisfaction to the adherents of the new doctrine, and eventually an ample store of more modern instances was accumulated to confirm Satan in his enlarged privileges."[2] Satan, it seems, imprinted upon his clients an indelible mark, the *stigma diabolicum*.

"In 1458, the Inquisitor Nicholas Jaquerius remarked reasonably enough that even if the affair was an illusion, it was none the less heretical, as the followers of Diana

Documents, vol. i, p. xxv. Cf. Bull, *Quod super Nonnullis*, of January 10, 1260: "Respondetur quod . . . inquisitores ipsi de iis (divinationibus et sortilegiis), nisi manifeste saperent hæresim se nullatenus intromittant." Ripoll., vol. i, p. 388.

[1] For the attitude of the church toward sorcerers, cf. Lea, *op. cit.*, vol. iii, pp. 434–436. When the celebrated canonist, Astesanus of Asti, wrote his *Summa de Casibus Conscientiæ* in 1317, the canons decreed only a penance of forty days for magic.

[2] Lea, *op. cit.*, vol. iii, p. 497; Thomas of Cantimpré. *Bonum Universale*, lib. iii, cap. lv.

and Herodias were necessarily heretics in their waking hours." [1]

About 1250, the Inquisitor Bernard of Como taught categorically that the phenomena of witchcraft, especially the attendance at the witches' Sabbat, were not fanciful but real: "This is proved," he says, "from the fact that the Popes permitted witches to be burned at the stake; they would not have countenanced this, if these persons were not real heretics, and their crimes only imaginary, for the Church only punishes proved crimes." [2] Witchcraft was, therefore, amenable to the tribunals of the Inquisition. [3]

---

[1] Lea, *op. cit.*, pp. 497, 498, with reference to Nicholas Jaquerius, *Flagellum hæreticorum*, cap. vii and xxviii.

[2] "Præterea plurimæ hujus perfidæ sectæ . . . combustæ, quod minime factum fuisset, neque summi pontifices hoc tolerassent, si talia tantummodo phantastice et in somniis contingerent, et tales personæ realiter et veraciter hæreticæ non essent, et in hæresi realiter et manifeste deprehensæ . . . nam ecclesia non punit crimina nisi manifesta et vere deprehensa . . . Per hæc ergo omnia quæ dicta sunt, et per plura alia quæ adduci possent, liquido constat, quod tales strigiæ ad præfatum ludum non in somniis neque phantastice, ut quidam affirmant, sed realiter et corporaliter ac vigilando vadant." *Lucerna Inquisitorum*, Romæ, 1584, p. 144.

[3] In a letter of one of the cardinals of the Holy Office, dated 1643, witchcraft is classed with heresy: "Contra quoscumque hæreticos et a fide christiana apostatas, aut cujusvis damnatæ hæresis sectatores, sortilegia hæresim sapientia, seu de hæresi vel de apostasia a fide suspectos, divinationes et incantationes aliaque diabolica maleficia et prestigia contractantes." Douais, *Documents*, vol. i, p. ccliv. In practice, the heretical tendency of witchcraft was hard to determine. Each judge, therefore, as a rule, pronounced sentence according to his own judgment. In 1451, Nicholas V enlarged the powers of Hugues le Noir, Inquisitor of France, by granting him jurisdiction over divination, even when it did not savor of heresy. (Lea, *op. cit.*, vol. iii, 512, Ripoll, *Bullarium*, vol. iii, p. 301.) In this way astrologers, palmists,

While the casuists thus increased the number of crimes which the Inquisition could prosecute, on the other hand they shortened the judicial procedure then in vogue.

Following the Roman law, the Inquisition at first recognized three forms of action in criminal cases — *accusatio, denuntiatio* and *inquisitio*. In the *accusatio*, the accuser formally inscribed himself as able to prove his accusation; if he failed to do so, he had to undergo the penalty which the prisoner would have incurred (*pœna talionis*).[1] "From the very beginning, he was placed in the same position as the one he accused, even to the extent of sharing his imprisonment."[2] The *denuntiatio* did not in any way bind the accuser; he merely handed in his testimony, and then ceased prosecuting the case; the judge at once proceeded to take action against the accused. In the *inquisitio*, there was no one either to accuse or denounce the criminal; the judge cited the suspected criminal before him and proceeded to try him. This was the most common method of procedure; from it the Inquisition received its name.[3]

and diviners all became subject to the Inquisition. Cf. Bull of Sixtus V, *Cœli et terræ*, January 5, 1586, on astrologers. (Eymeric, *Directorum*, Pegna's *Bullarium*, p. 142.)

[1] "Et hoc quidem generaliter verum est, quod nullus auditur accusans sine libelli inscriptione, in quo obliget se ad pænam talionis." Tancrède, *Ordo judiciorum*, lib. ii, cap. Qualiter, Lyons ed., 1547, p. 91. For the practice and exceptions cf. Tanon, *op. cit.*, p. 260, n. 4.

[2] Tancrède, *ibid.*, cf. Tanon, *op. cit.*, p. 259.

[3] On these three forms of action, cf. Eymeric, *Directorium*, 3[a] pars, p. 413

The Inquisitorial procedure was therefore inspired by the Roman law. But in practice the *accusatio,* which gave the prisoner a chance to meet the charges against him, was soon abandoned. In fact the Inquisitors were always most anxious to set it aside. Urban IV enacted a decree, July 28, 1262, whereby they were allowed to proceed *simpliciter et de plano, absque advocatorum strepitu et figura.*[1] Bernard Gui insisted on this in his *Practica.*[2] Eymeric advised his associates, when an accuser appeared before them who was perfectly willing to accept the *pœna talionis* in case of failure, to urge the imprudent man to withdraw his demand. For he argued that the *accusatio* might prove harmful to himself, and besides give too much room for trickery.[3] In other words, the Inquisitors wished to be perfectly untrammeled in their action.

The secrecy of the Inquisition's procedure was one of the chief causes of complaint.

But the Inquisition, dreadful as it was, did not lack defenders. Some of their arguments were most extravagant and far-fetched. "Paramo in the quaint pedantry

---

et seq. Innocent III introduced the *inquisitio* into the canonical legislation as the regular method of procedure. Cf. Tanon, *op. cit.,* pp. 283–285.

[1] Bull *Præ cunctis* of July 28, 1262, in Ripoll, *Bullarium,* vol. i, p. 428; Sexto, *De Hæreticis,* cap. 20: Limborch, p. 268.

[2] *Practica,* 4ᵃ pars, ed. Douais, p. 192.

[3] "Inquisitor istum modum non libenter admittat, tum quia non est in causa fidei usitatus, tum quia est accusanti multum periculosus, tum quia est multum litigiosus. "*Directorium,*" p. 414, col. 1.

with which he ingeniously proves that God was the first
Inquisitor, and the condemnation of Adam and Eve the
first model of the Inquisitorial process, triumphantly
points out that he judges them in secret, thus setting the
example which the Inquisition is bound to follow, and
avoiding the subtleties which the criminals would have
raised in their defence, especially at the suggestion of the
crafty serpent. That he called no witnesses is explained
by the confession of the accused, and ample legal authority is cited to show that these confessions were sufficient
to justify the conviction and punishment." [1]

.　　　.　　　.　　　.　　　.　　　.　　　.　　　.

The subtlety of the casuists had full play when they
came to discuss the torture of the prisoner who absolutely
refused to confess. According to law the torture could
be inflicted but once, but this regulation was easily evaded.
For it was lawful to subject the prisoner to all the various
kinds of torture in succession; and if additional evidence
were discovered, the torture could be repeated. When
they desired, therefore, to repeat the torture, even after
an interval of some days, they evaded the law by calling it technically not a "repetition" but a "continuance
of the first torture": *Ad continuandum tormenta, non
ad iterandum*, as Eymeric styles it.[2] This quibbling

---

[1] Lea, *op. cit.*, vol. i, p. 406; Louis de Paramo, *De origine et progressu
officii sanctæ Inquisitionis ejusque utilitate et dignitate libri tres*, Madrid, 1598,
pp. 32, 33.

[2] "Quod si, questionatus decenter, noluerit fateri veritatem, ponanatur

of course gave full scope to the cruelty and the indiscreet zeal of the Inquisitors.[1]

But a new difficulty soon arose. Confessions, extorted under torture, had, as we have seen, no legal value. Eymeric himself admitted that the results obtained in this way were very unreliable, and that the Inquisitors should realize this fact.[2]

If, on leaving the torture chamber, the prisoner reiterated his confession,[3] the case was at once decided. But suppose, on the contrary, that the confession extorted under torture was afterwards retracted, what was to be done? The Inquisitors did not agree upon this point. Some of them, like Eymeric, held that in this case the prisoner was entitled to his freedom. Others, like the author of the *Sacro Arsenale*, held that "the torture should be repeated, in order that the prisoner might be forced to reiterate his first confession [4] which had evi-

---

alia genera tormentorum coram eo, dicendo quod oportet eum transire per omnia, nisi prodat veritatem; quod si nec sic, poterit ad terrorem, vel etiam ad veritatem secunda dies vel tertia assignari, *ad continuandum* tormenta, *non ad iterandum:* quia iterari, non debent, nisi novis supervenientibus indiciis contra eum; quia tunc possunt; sed continuari non prohibentur." Eymeric, *Directorium*, 3ª pars, p. 481, col. 2.

[1] In 1317, Bernard Gui, complaining of the Clementine restrictions, asks why the Bishops should be limited in applying torture to heretics, when they could apply it without limit in everything else. *Gravamina*, coll. Doat, xxx, 101; cf. Lea, *op. cit.*, vol. i, p. 557.

[2] "Scientes quod quæstiones sunt fallaces et inefficaces." *Op. cit.*, p. 481, col. 1.

[3] *Ibid.*, p. 481, col. 2.

[4] Masini, *Sacro Arsenale*, pp. 183–186.

dently compromised him." This seems to have been the traditional practice of the Italian tribunals.

But the casuists did not stop here. They discovered "that Clement V had only spoken of torture in general, and had not specifically alluded to witnesses, whence they concluded that one of the most shocking abuses of the system, the torture of witnesses, was left to the sole discretion of the Inquisitor, and this became the accepted rule. It only required an additional step to show that after the accused had been convicted by evidence or had confessed as to himself, he became a witness as to the guilt of his friends, and thus could be arbitrarily (?) tortured to betray them." [1]

. . . .

As a matter of course, the canonists and the theologians approved the severest penalties inflicted by the Inquisition. St. Raymond of Pennafort, however, who was one of the most favored counsellors of Gregory IX, still upheld the criminal code of Innocent III. The severest penalties he defended were the excommunication of heretics and schismatics, their banishment and the confiscation of their property.[2] His *Summa* was un-

[1] Lea, *op. cit.*, vol. i, p. 425.

[2] Lea writes (*op. cit.*, vol. i, p. 229, note): "Saint Raymond of Pennafort, the compiler of the decretals of Gregory IX, who was the highest authority in his generation, lays it down as a principle of ecclesiastical law that the heretic is to be coerced by excommunication and confiscation, and if they fail, *by the extreme exercise of the secular power.* The man who was doubtful in faith was to be held a heretic and so also was the schismatic who, while

doubtedly completed when the Decretal of Gregory IX appeared, authorizing the Inquisitors to enforce the cruel laws of Frederic II.

But St. Thomas, who wrote at a time when the Inquisition was in full operation, felt called upon to defend the infliction of the death penalty upon heretics and the relapsed. His words deserve careful consideration. He begins by answering the objections that might be brought from the Scriptures and the Fathers against his thesis. The first of these is the well-known passage of St. Matthew, in which our Savior forbids the servants of the householder to gather up the cockle before the harvest time, lest they root up the wheat with it.[1] St. John Chrysostom, he says, "argues from this text that it is wrong to put heretics to death." [2] But according to St. Augustine the words of the Savior: "Let the cockle grow until the harvest," are explained at once by what follows: "lest perhaps gathering up the cockle, you root up the wheat also with it." When there is no danger of uprooting the wheat and no danger of schism, violent measures may be used:

believing all the articles of religion, refused the obedience due to the Roman Church. All alike were to be forced into the Roman fold, and the fate of Core, Dathan and Abiron was invoked *for the destruction of the obstinate*." (*Summa*, lib. i, tit. v, 2, 4, 8; tit. vi, i). This is a travesty of the mind and words of Saint Raymond. He merely called attention to the lot of Core, Dathan and Abiron to show what a great crime schism was. He never asserted that heretics or schismatics, even when obdurate, ought to be "destroyed." *Summa*, lib. i, cap. *De Hæreticis* and *De Schismaticis*.

[1] Matt. xiii. 28, 30.

[2] *In Matthæum*, Homil. xlvi.

Cum metus iste non subest . . . non dormiat severitas disciplinæ.[1] We doubt very much whether such reasoning would have satisfied St. John Chrysostom, St. Theodore the Studite, or Bishop Wazo, who understood the Savior's prohibition in a literal and an absolute sense.

But this passage does not reveal the whole mind of the Angelic doctor. It is more evident in his exegesis of Ezechiel xviii. 32, *Nolo mortem peccatoris.* "Assuredly," he writes, "none of us desires the death of a single heretic. But remember that the house of David could not obtain peace until Absalom was killed in the war he waged against his father. In like manner, the Catholic Church saves some of her children by the death of others, and consoles her sorrowing heart by reflecting that she is acting for the general good."[2]

If we are not mistaken, St. Thomas is here trying to prove on the authority of St. Augustine that it is sometimes lawful to put heretics to death.

But it is only by garbling and distorting the context that St. Thomas makes the Bishop of Hippo advocate the very penalty which, as a matter of fact, he always denounced most strongly. In the passage quoted, St. Augustine was speaking of the benefit that ensues to the

---

[1] Augustine, *Contra epistol. Parmeniani*, lib. iii, cap. ii.   S. Thomas, *Summa*, IIa, IIae, quaest. x, art. 8, ad 4m.

[2] S. Thomas, *Summa, loc. cit.*, ad 4m.

church *from the suicide of heretics*, but he had no idea whatever of maintaining that the church had the right to put to death her rebellious children.[1] St. Thomas misses the point entirely, and gives his readers a false idea of the teaching of St. Augustine.

Thinking, however, that he has satisfactorily answered all the objections against his thesis, he states it as follows: "Heretics who persist in their error after a second admonition ought not only to be excommunicated, but also abandoned to the secular arm to be put to death. For, he argues, it is much more wicked to corrupt the faith on which depends the life of the soul, than to debase the coinage which provides merely for temporal life; wherefore, if coiners and other malefactors are justly doomed to death, much more may heretics be justly slain once they are convicted. If, therefore, they persist in their error after two admonitions, the Church despairs of their conversion, and excommunicates them to ensure the salvation of others whom they might cor-

[1] "Illi autem . . . quod sibi faciunt, nobis imputant. Quis enim nostrum velit non solum aliquem illorum perire, verumetiam aliquid perdere? Sed si aliter non meruit pacem habere domus David, nisi Absalon filius ejus in bello quod contra patrem gerebat, fuisset extinctus, quamvis magna cura mandaverit suis, ut eum quantum possent vivum salvumque servarent, ut esset cui pœnitenti paternus affectus ignosceret, quid ei restitit, nisi perditum flere et sui regni pace acquisita suam mæstitiam consolari? Sic ergo catholica mater Ecclesia, bellantibus adversus eam quibus allis quam filiis suis . . ., si aliquorum perditione cæteros tam multos colligit, præsertim quia *isti*, non sicut Absalon casu bellico, sed *spontaneo magis interitu pereunt*, dolorem materni cordis lenit et sanat tantorum liberatione populorum." *Ep.* clxxxv, ad *Bonifacium*, no. 32.

rupt; she then abandons them to the secular arm that they may be put to death." [1]

St. Thomas in this passage makes a mere comparison serve as an argument. He does not seem to realize that if his reasoning were valid, the Church could go a great deal further, and have the death penalty inflicted in many other cases.

The fate of the relapsed heretic had varied from Lucius III to Alexander IV. The bull *Ad Abolendam* decreed that converted heretics who relapsed into heresy were to be abandoned to the secular arm without trial.[2] But at the time this Decretal was published, the *Animadversio dedita* of the State entailed no severer penalty than banishment and confiscation. When this term, already fearful enough, came to mean the death penalty, the Inquisitors did not know whether to follow the ancient custom or to adopt the new interpretation. For a long time they followed the traditional custom. Bernard of Caux, who was undoubtedly a zealous Inquisitor, is a case in point. In his register of sentences from 1244 to 1248, we meet with sixty cases of relapse, not one of whom was punished by a penalty severer than imprisonment. But a little later on the strict interpretation of the *Animadversio*

[1] *Summa*, IIa IIae, quaest. xi, art. 3.

[2] "Illos quoque qui, post abjurationem præfati erroris . . . , deprehensi fuerint in abjuratam hæresim recidisse, seculari judicio sine ulla penitus audientia decernimus relinquendos." Decretals, in cap. ix, *De hæreticis*, lib. v, tit. vii.

debita began to prevail.[1] In St. Thomas's time it meant the death penalty; and we find him citing the bull *Ad Abolendam*[2] as his authority for the infliction of the death penalty upon the relapsed, penitent or impenitent, in ignorance of the fact that this document originally had a totally different interpretation.

His reasoning therefore rests on a false supposition. He advocates the death penalty for the relapsed in the name of Christian charity. For, he argues, charity has for its object the spiritual and temporal welfare of one's neighbor. His spiritual welfare is the salvation of his soul; his temporal welfare is life, and temporal advantages, such as riches, dignities, and the like. These temporal advantages are subordinate to the spiritual, and charity must prevent their endangering the eternal salvation of their possessor. Charity, therefore, to himself and to others, prompts us to deprive him of these temporal goods, if he makes a bad use of them. For if we allowed the relapsed heretic to live, we would undoubtedly endanger the salvation of others, either because he would corrupt the faithful whom he met, or because his escape from punishment would lead others to believe they could deny the faith with impunity. The inconstancy of the relapsed is, therefore, a sufficient reason why the Church,

---

[1] On the various views of the casuists regarding the relapsed, cf. Lea, *op. cit.*, vol. i, pp. 543–546.

[2] *Summa*, IIa IIae, quæst. ix, art. 4: *Sed contra.*

although she receives him to penance for his soul's salvation, refuses to free him from the death penalty.[1]

Such reasoning is not very convincing. Why would not the life imprisonment of the heretic safeguard the faithful as well as his death? Will you answer that this penalty is too trivial to prevent the faithful from falling into heresy? If that be so, why not at once condemn all heretics to death, even when repentant? That would terrorize the wavering ones all the more. But St. Thomas evidently was not thinking of the logical consequences of his reasoning. His one aim was to defend the criminal code in vogue at the time. That is his only excuse. For we must admit that rarely has his reasoning been so faulty and so weak as in his thesis upon the coercive power of the Church, and the punishment of heresy.

.   .   .   .

St. Thomas defended the death penalty without indicating how it was to be inflicted. The commentators who followed him were more definite. The *Animadversio debita*, says Henry of Susa (Hostiensis + 1271), in his commentary on the bull *Ad abolendam*, is the penalty of the stake (*ignis crematio*). He defends this interpretation by quoting the words of Christ: "If any one abide not in me, he shall be cast forth as a branch, and shall wither,

---

[1] "Sed quando recepti (ab Ecclesia) iterum relabuntur, videtur esse signum inconstantiæ eorum; et ideo ulterius redeuntes recipiuntur quidem ad pænitentiam, non tamen ut liberentur a sententia mortis." *Ibid.*

and they shall gather him *and cast him into the fire,* and he *burneth."* [1] Jean d'Andre (+ 1348), whose commentary carried equal weight with Henry of Susa's throughout the Middle Ages, quotes the same text as authority for sending heretics to the stake.[2] According to this peculiar exegesis, the law and custom of the day merely sanctioned the law of Christ. To regard our Savior as the precursor or rather the author of the criminal code of the Inquisition evidences, one must admit, a very peculiar temper of mind.

.   .   .   .

The next step was to free the Church from all responsibility in the infliction of the death penalty — truly an extremely difficult undertaking.

St. Thomas held, with many other theologians, that heretics condemned by the Inquisition should be abandoned to the secular arm, *judicio sæculari.* But he went further and declared it the duty of the State to put such criminals to death.[3] The State, therefore, was to carry out this sentence at least indirectly in the name of the Church.

---

[1] John, xv, 6; Hostiensis, on the decretal *Ad abolendum,* cap. xi, in Eymeric, *Directorium inquisitorum,* 2ª pars, pp. 149, 150.

[2] On the decretal *Ad abolendum,* cap. xiv, in Eymeric, *ibid.,* pp. 170, 171. Bartolo says the same of witches. "Mulier striga, de qua agitur, sive, latine Iamia, debet tradi ultimo supplicio et igne cremari. Fatetur enim Christo et baptismati renuntiasse; ergo debet mori, justa dictum Domini nostri Jesu Christi apud Joannem, cap. xv; *Si quis in me non manserit,* etc. Et lex evangelica prævalet omnibus aiis legibus, et debet servari etiam in foro contentioso." In Ziletti, *Consilia selecta,* 1577, vol. i, p. 8.

[3] *Summa,* IIa, IIae, quæst. xi, art. 3.

13

A contemporary of St. Thomas thus meets this difficulty: "The Pope does not execute any one," he says,
"or order him to be put to death; heretics are executed
by the law which the Pope tolerates; they practically
cause their own death by committing crimes which merit
death." [1] The heretic who received this answer to his
objections must surely have found it very far-fetched.
He could easily have replied that the Pope "not only
allowed heretics to be put to death, but ordered this done
under penalty of excommunication." And by this very
fact he incurred all the odium of the death penalty.

The casuists of the Inquisition, however, came to the
rescue, and tried to defend the Church by another subterfuge. They denounced in so many words the death
penalty and other similar punishments, while at the same
time they insisted upon the State's enforcing them. The
formula by which they dismissed an impenitent or a relapsed heretic was thus worded: "We dismiss you from
our ecclesiastical forum, and abandon you to the secular
arm. But we strongly beseech the secular court to mitigate its sentence in such a way as to avoid bloodshed or
danger of death." [2] We regret to state, however, that

[1] "Papa noster non occidit, nec præcipit aliquem occidi, sed lex occidit
quos papa permittit occidi, et ipsi se occidunt qui ea faciunt unde debeant
occidi." *Disputatio inter catholicum et Paterinum hæreticum*, cap. xii, in
Martène, *Thesaurus Anecdotorum*, vol. v, col. 1741.

[2] "De foro nostro ecclesiastico te projicimus et tradimus seu relinquimus
brachio sæculari ac potestati curiæ sæcularis, dictam curiam sæcularem
efficaciter deprecantes quod circa te citra sanguinis effusionem et mortis

the civil judges were not supposed to take these words literally. If they were at all inclined to do so, they would have been quickly called to a sense of their duty by being excommunicated. The clause inserted by the canonists was a mere legal fiction, which did not change matters a particle.

It is hard to understand why such a formula was used at all. Probably it was first used in other criminal cases in which abandonment to the secular arm did not imply the death penalty,[1] and the Inquisition kept using it merely out of respect to tradition. It seemed to palliate

periculum sententiam suam moderetur." *Forma tradendi hæreticum pertinacem, alias non relapsum, curiæ seculari.* Eymeric, *Directorium inquisitorum,* 3^a pars, p. 515, col. 2. Cf. *Forma ferendi sententiam contra eum qui in hæresim est relapsus, sed pænitens, et ut relapsus traditur curiæ seculari.* Ibid., p. 512, col. 1; *Forma tradendi seu relinquendi brachio sæculari eum, qui convictus est de hæresi per testes legitimos, et stat pertinaciter in negativa, licet fidem catholicam profiteatur, ibid.,* p. 524, col. 1. Bernard Gui quotes the Canons to justify this pretended appeal for clemency: "Relinquimus brachio et judicio curiae secularis, eamdem affectuose rogantes, *prout suadent canonicae sanctiones,* quatinus citra mortem et membrorum ejus mutilationem circa ipsum suum judicium et suam sententiam moderetur (*vel sic,* quatinus vitam et membra sibi illibata conservet). *Practica inquisitionis,* ed. Douais, p. 127; cf. pp. 128, 133-136; cf. Limborch, *Historia inquisitionis,* pp. 289-291. The *Canonicæ Sanctiones,* to which Bernard Gui refers, are undoubtedly the decretal *Novimus,* which we will quote in the following note, and the bull *Ad aboldendam* of Innocent IV.

[1] Cf. the decretal *Novimus,* in the Decretals, cap. 27, lib. v, tit. xl; "Et sic intelligitur tradi curiæ seculari, pro quo tamen debet Ecclesia efficaciter intercedere, ut citra mortis periculum circa eum sententia moderetur." Cf. also lib. ii, tit. i, cap. 10, *Cum ab homine:* "Cum Ecclesia non habeat ultra quid faciat, ne possit esse ultra perditio plurimorum, per secularem comprimendus est potestatem, ita quod ei deputetur exilium, vel alia legitima pæna inferatur." This law dealt with degraded clerics and forgers abandoned to the secular arm.

the too flagrant contradiction which existed between ecclesiastical justice and the teaching of Christ, and it gave at least an external homage to the teaching of St. Augustine, and the first fathers of the Church. Moreover, as it furnished a specious means of evading by the merest form the prohibition against clerics taking part in sentences involving the effusion of blood and death, and the irregularity resulting therefrom, the Inquisitors used it to reassure their conscience.

Finally, however, some Inquisitors, realizing the emptiness of this formula, dispensed with it altogether, and boldly assumed the full responsibility for their sentences. They deemed the rôle of the State so unimportant in the execution of heretics, that they did not even mention it. The Inquisition is the real judge; it lights the fires. "All whom we cause to be burned," says the famous Dominican Sprenger in his *Malleus Maleficarum*.[1] Although not intended as an accurate statement of fact,[2] it indicates

---

[1] "Experientia nos sæpe docuit, cum *omnes quas incinerari fecimus* ex eorum confessionibus patuit, ipsas fuisse involuntarias circa maleficia inferenda," etc. *Malleus maleficarum maleficas et earum hæresim framea conterens*, auct. Jacobo Sprengero, Lugduni, 1660, pars ii, quæst. i, cap. ii, p. 108, col. 2. The author quotes the *Formicarium de maleficis et eorum præstigiis ac deceptionibus* of the famous Jean Nider, who "recitat hoc ex inquisitore Eduensis diœcesis, qui etiam in ipsa diœcesi *multos de maleficiis reos inquisierat et incinerari fecerat.*" *Ibid.*, p. 106, col. 2. He also speaks of the Inquisitor Cumanus who, in 1485, "uno anno quadraginta et unam maleficam *incinerari fecit,*" *ibid.*, p. 105, col. 2.

[2] We must interpret in the same sense the decree of the Council of Constance pronouncing the penalty of the stake against the followers of John Huss, John Wyclif and Jerome of Prague: "Ut omnes et singuli spirituales

pretty well the current idea regarding the share of the ecclesiastical tribunals in the punishment of heretics.

.　　.　　.　　.　　.　　.　　.　　.

It is evident that the theologians and canonists were simply apologists for the Inquisition, and interpreters of its laws. As a rule, they tried, like St. Raymond Pennafort and St. Thomas, to defend the decrees of the Popes. We cannot say that they succeeded in their task. Some by their untimely zeal rather compromised the cause they endeavored to defend. Others, going counter to the canon law, drew conclusions from it that the Popes never dreamed of, and in this way made the procedure of the Inquisition, already severe enough, still more severe. especially in the use of torture.

et seculares qui errores vel hæreses Johannis Huss et Joannis Wiclif in sacro hoc concilio condemnatos prædicant, dogmatizant vel defendunt; et personas Joannis Huss et Hieronymi catholicas et sanctas pronuntiant vel tenent, et de hoc convicti fuerint, tanquam hæretici relapsi *puniantur ad ignem*." Session xliv, no. 23, Harduin, *Concilia*, vol. viii, col. 896 et seq. The Council here indicates only the usual punishment for the relapsed, without really decreeing it. This is evident from the words used in the condemnation of John Huss: "Hæc sancta synodus Joannem Huss, *attento quod Ecclesia Dei non habeat ultra quid agere valeat, judicio sæculari relinquit* et ipsum curiæ seculari relinquendum fore decernit." *Ibid.*, col. 410, sessio xv, anno 1415.

CHAPTER IX

THE INQUISITION IN OPERATION

WE do not intend to relate every detail of the Inquisition's action. A brief outline, a sort of bird's-eye view, will suffice.

Its field, although very extensive, did not comprise the whole of Christendom, nor even all the Latin countries. The Scandinavian kingdoms escaped it almost entirely; England experienced it only once in the case of the Templars; Castile and Portugal knew nothing of it before the reign of Ferdinand and Isabella. It was almost unknown in France — at least as an established institution — except in the South, in what was called the county of Toulouse, and later on in Languedoc.

The Inquisition was in full operation in Aragon. The Cathari, it seems, were wont to travel frequently from Languedoc to Lombardy, so that upper Italy had from an early period its contingent of Inquisitors. Frederic II had it established in the two Sicilies and in many cities of Italy and Germany.[1] Honorius IV (1285–1287) introduced it into Sardinia.[2] Its activity in Flanders and

---

[1] On the spread of the Inquisition, cf. Lea, *op. cit.*, passim.

[2] Potthast, no. 22307; *Registres d'Honorius IV*, published by Maurice Prou, 1888, no. 163.

Bohemia in the fifteenth century was very considerable. These were the chief centers of its operations.

Some of the Inquisitors had an exalted idea of their office. We recall the ideal portrait of the perfect Inquisitor drawn by Bernard Gui and Eymeric. But by an inevitable law of history the reality never comes up to the ideal.

We know the names of many Inquisitors, monks and bishops.[1] There are some whose memory is beyond reproach; in fact the Church honors them as saints, because they died for the faith.[2]

But others fulfilled the duties of their office in a spirit of hatred and impatience, contrary both to natural justice and to Christian charity. Who can help denouncing, for instance, the outrageous conduct of Conrad of Marburg. Contemporary writers tell us that when heretics appeared before his tribunal, he granted them no delay, but at once required them to answer yes or no to the accusations against them. If they confessed their guilt, they were granted their lives, and thrown into prison; if they refused to confess, they were at once condemned and sent to the stake.[3] Such summary justice strongly resembles injustice.

[1] Mgr. Douais, for example, gives a list, with biographical notes, of the Inquisitors of Toulouse from 1229 to 1329. *Documents*, vol. i, pp. cxxix–ccix.

[2] *v.g.* Peter of Verona, assassinated by heretics in 1252. Cf. Lea, *op. cit.*, vol. 2, p. 215.

[3] "Si testes, qui se confitebantur aliquantulum criminis eorum conscios et

But Robert the Dominican, known as Robert the Bugre, for he was a converted Patarin, surpassed even Conrad in cruelty. Among the exploits of this Inquisitor special mention must be made of the executions at Montwimer in Champagne. The Bishop, Moranis, had allowed a large community of heretics to grow up about him. Robert determined to punish the town severely. In one week he managed to try all his prisoners. On May 29, 1239, about one hundred and eighty of them, with their bishop, were sent to the stake. Such summary proceedings caused complaints to be sent to Rome against this cruel Inquisitor. He was accused of confounding in his blind fanaticism the innocent with the guilty, and of working upon simple souls so as to increase the number of his victims. An investigation proved that these complaints were well founded. In fact it revealed such outrages that Robert the Bugre was at first suspended from his office, and finally condemned to perpetual imprisonment.[1]

participes, in illorum absentia reciperentur et dictis eorum simpliciter crederetur, ita ut accusatis talis daretur optio, aut sponte confiteri et vivere aut innocentiam jurare et statim mori." Testimony of the Archbishop of Mainz and Bernard the Dominican in Aubri des Trois-Fontaines, *Mon. Germ. SS.*, vol. xxiii, p. 931. "Ut nullius, qui tantum propalatus esset, accusatio vel recusatio, nullius exceptio vel testimonium admitteretur, nec ullus defendendi locus daretur, sed nec induciae deliberationis darentur, sed in continenti oportebat eum vel reum se confiteri et in poenitentiam recalvari, vel crimen negare et cremari." *Gesta Trevirens* in *Mon. Germ. SS.*, vol. xiv, p. 400.

[1] Aubri des Trois Fontaines, ad ann. 1239, *Mon. Germ. SS.*, vol. xxiii, 944, 945; *Chronique* of Mathieu Paris in Raynaldi, *Annales eccles.*, ad ann. 1238, no. 52; cf. Tanon, *op. cit.*, pp. 114–117.

Other acts of the Inquisition were no less odious. In 1280 the Consuls of Carcassonne complained to the Pope, the King of France, and the episcopal vicars of the diocese of the cruelty and injustice of Jean Galand in the use of torture. He had inscribed on the walls of the Inquisition these words: *domunculas ad torquendum et cruciandum homines diversis generibus tormentorum.* Some prisoners had been tortured on the rack, and most of them were so cruelly treated that they lost the use of their arms and legs, and became altogether helpless. Some even died in great agony of their torments.[1] The complaint continues in this tone, and mentions five or six times the great cruelty of the tortures inflicted.

Philip the Fair, who was noble-hearted occasionally, addressed a letter May 13, 1291, to the seneschal of Carcassonne in which he denounced the Inquisitors for their cruel torturing of innocent men, whereby the living and the dead were fraudulently convicted; and among other abuses, he mentions particularly "tortures newly invented." [2] Another letter of his (1301), addressed to

---

[1] Nonnulli vero *ponuntur in equuleis*, in quibus *quamplurimi per tormentorum acerbitatem corporis destituuntur membris* et impotentes redduntur omnino. Nonnulli etiam propter impatientiam et dolorem nimium morte crudelissima finiunt dies suos. Vidal, *Jean Galand et les Carcassonnais*, Paris, Picard, 1903, p. 32, no. 2; cf. p. 40, nos. 3–5; p. 41, no. 9; *Le Tribunal d'inquisition de Pamiers, loc cit.*, 1905, pp. 151, 152.

[2] "Certiorati per aliquos fide dignos . . . eo quod innocentes puniant, incarcerent et multa gravamina eis inferant et per quaedam *tormenta de novo exquisita* multas falsitates . . . extorqueant." *Histoire de Languedoc*, vol. x, *Preuves*, col. 273.

Foulques de Saint-Georges, contained a similar denunciation.[1]

In a bull intended for Cardinals Taillefer de la Chappelle and Bérenger de Frédol, March 13, 1306, Clement V mentions the complaints of the citizens of Carcassonne, Albi, and Cordes, regarding the cruelty practiced in the prisons of the Inquisition. Several of these unfortunates "were so weakened by the rigors of their imprisonment, the lack of food, and the severity of their tortures (*sevitia tormentorum*), that they died."[2]

The facts in Savonarola's case are very hard to determine. The official account of his interrogatory declares that he was subjected to three and a half *tratti di fune*. This was a form of torture known as the *strappado*. The Signoria, in answer to the reproaches of Alexander VI at their tardiness, declared that they had to deal with a man of great endurance; that they had assiduously tortured him for many days with slender results.[3] Burchard, the papal prothonotary, states that he was put to the torture seven times.[4] It made very little difference whether

[1] "A captionibus, *quæstionibus et inexcogitatis tormentis* incipiens . . . *vi et metu tormentorum*, fateri compellit." *Histoire du Languedoc*, vol. x, *Preuves*, col. 379.

[2] "Adeo gravantur et hactenus sunt gravati carceris angustia, lectorum inedia, et victualium penuria, et *sevitia tormentorum*, quod spiritum reddere sunt coacti." Douais, *Documents*, vol. ii, p. 307.

[3] "Multa et assidua quæstione, multis diebus, per vim vix pauca extorsimus," etc. Villari, *La storia di Girolamo Savonarola*, Firenze, 1887, vol. ii, p. 197.

[4] *Diarium* in *Mémoires de Commynes*, Preuves, Bruxelles, 1706, p. 424.

these tortures were inflicted *per modum continuationis* or *per modum iterationis,* as the casuists of the Inquisition put it. At any rate, it was a crying abuse.[1]

We may learn something of the brutality of the Inquisitors from the remorse felt by one of them. He had inflicted the torture of the burning coals upon a sorceress. The unfortunate woman died soon afterwards in prison as a result of her torments. The Inquisitor, knowing he had caused her death, wrote John XXII for a dispensation from the irregularity he had thereby incurred.[2]

But the greatest excesses of the Inquisition were due to the political schemes of sovereigns. Such instances were by no means rare. Hardly had the Inquisition been established, when Frederic II tried to use it for political purposes. He was anxious to put the prosecution for heresy in the hands of his royal officers, rather than in the hands of the bishops and the monks. When, therefore, in 1233, he boasted in a letter to Gregory IX that he had put to death a great number of heretics in his kingdom, the Pope answered that he was not at all deceived by this pretended zeal.[3] He knew full well that the Em-

[1] On this question, cf. Lea, *op. cit.*, vol. iii, pp. 229, 230 and notes. Read a recent work of H. Lucas, *Fra Girolamo Savonarola, a biographical study*, London, Sands, 1905.

[2] "Fecisti plantas pedum ejusdem mulieris juxta carbones accensos apponi, quæ ipsorum calorem sentiens," etc., Document quoted par Vidal, *Le tribunal d'Inquisition de Pamiers, loc. cit.*, October, 1905, p. 5.

[3] Cf. Huillard-Bréolles, *Historia diplomatica Frederici II*, vol. iv, p. 462; cf. pp. 435, 444.

peror wished simply to get rid of his personal enemies, and that he had put to death many who were not heretics at all.

The personal interests of Philip the Fair were chiefly responsible for the trial and condemnation of the Templars. Clement V himself and the ecclesiastical judges were both unfortunately guilty of truckling in the whole affair. But their unjust condemnation was due chiefly to the king's desire to confiscate their great possessions.[1]

Joan of Arc was also a victim demanded by the political interests of the day. If the Bishop of Beauvais, Pierre Cauchon, had not been such a bitter English partisan, it is very probable that the tribunal over which he presided would not have brought in the verdict of guilty, which sent her to the stake;[2] she would never have been considered a heretic at all, much less a relapsed one.

---

[1] The tribunals of the Inquisition were perhaps never more cruel than in the case of the Templars. At Paris, according to the testimony of Ponsard de Gisiac, thirty-six Templars perished under torture. At Sens, Jacques de Saciac said that twenty-five had died of torment and suffering. (Lea, *op. cit.*, vol. iii, p. 262.) The Grand Master, Jaques Molay, owed his life to the vigor of his constitution. Confessions extorted by such means were altogether valueless. Despite all his efforts, Philip the Fair never succeeded in obtaining a formal condemnation of the Order. In his bull of July 22, 1773, Clement XIV says: "Etiamsi concilium generale Viennese, cui negotium examinandum commiserat, a formali et definitiva sententia ferenda consuerit se abstinere." *Bullarium Romanum*, Continuatio, Prati, 1847, vol. v, p. 620. On the trial of the Templars, cf. Lea, *op. cit.*, vol. iii, pp. 249–320; Langlois, *Histoire de France*, vol. iii, 2^e partie, 1901.

[2] The greatest crime of the trial was the substitution, in the documents, of a different form of abjuration from the one Joan read near the church of Saint-Ouen.

It would be easy to cite many instances of the same kind, especially in Spain. If there was any place in the world where the State interfered unjustly in the trials of the Inquisition, it was in the kingdom of Ferdinand and Isabella, the kingdom of Philip II.[1]

From all that has been said, we must not infer that the tribunals of the Inquisition were always guilty of cruelty and injustice; we ought simply to conclude that too frequently they were. Even one case of brutality and injustice deserves perpetual odium.

. . . .

The severest penalties the Inquisition could inflict (apart from the minor penalties of pilgrimages, wearing the crosses, etc.), were imprisonment, abandonment to the secular arm, and confiscation of property.

"Imprisonment, according to the theory of the Inquisition, was not a punishment, but a means by which the penitent could obtain, on the bread of tribulation and the water of affliction, pardon from God for his sins, while at the same time he was closely supervised to see that he persevered in the right path, and was segregated

[1] The complaints of various Popes prove this. Cf. Hefele, *Le cardinal Ximénes*, Paris, 1857, pp. 265–374. On the Spanish Inquisition consult with due precaution *L'histoire de l'Inquisition d'Espagne*, by Llorente, 1817, and the following works of Lea: *Chapters from the religious history of Spain connected with the Inquisition* (Philadelphia, 1890) and *The Moriscos of Spain* (Philadelphia, 1901). Cf. Ch. V. Langlois, *L'Inquisition d'après les travaux recents*, Paris, 1902, pp. 89–141; Bernaldez, *Historia de los Reyes: Cronicas de los reyes de Castilla, Fernandez y Isabel*, Madrid, 1878; Rodrigo, *Historia verdadera de la Inquisicion*, 3 vol., Madrid, 1876–1877.

from the rest of the flock, thus removing all danger of infection." [1]

Heretics who confessed their errors during the time of grace were imprisoned only for a short time; those who confessed under torture or under threat of death were imprisoned for life; this was the usual punishment for the relapsed during most of the thirteenth century. It was the only penalty that Bernard of Caux (1244–1248) inflicted upon them.

"There were two kinds of imprisonment," writes Lea, "the milder or *murus largus*, and the harsher, known as *murus strictus*, or *durus*, or *arctus*. All were on bread and water, and the confinement, according to rule, was solitary, each penitent in a separate cell, with no access allowed to him, to prevent his being corrupted, or corrupting others; but this could not be strictly enforced, and about 1306 Geoffroi d'Ablis stigmatizes as an abuse the visits of clergy and the laity of both sexes, permitted to prisoners." [2]

As far back as 1282, Jean Galand had forbidden the jailer of the prison of Carcassonne to eat or take recreation with the prisoners, or to allow them to take recreation, or to keep servants. [3]

Husband and wife, however, were allowed access to each other if either or both were imprisoned; and late

---

[1] Lea, *op. cit.*, vol. i, p. 484.
[2] Lea, *op. cit.*, vol. i, pp. 486, 487.
[3] Collection, Doat, vol. xxxii, fol. 1, 25.

in the fourteenth century Eymeric declared that zealous Catholics might be admitted to visit prisoners, but not women and simple folk who might be perverted, for converted prisoners, he added, were very liable to relapse, and to infect others, and usually died at the stake.[1]

"In the milder form or *murus largus*, the prisoners apparently were, if well behaved, allowed to take exercise in the corridors, where sometimes they had opportunities of converse with each other, and with the outside world. This privilege was ordered to be given to the aged and infirm by the cardinals who investigated the prison of Carcassonne, and took measures to alleviate its rigors. In the harsher confinement, or *murus strictus*, the prisoner was thrust into the smallest, darkest, and most noisome of cells, with chains on his feet, — in some cases chained to the wall. This penance was inflicted on those whose offences had been conspicuous, or who had perjured themselves by making incomplete confessions, the matter being wholly at the discretion of the Inquisitor. I have met with one case, in 1328, of aggravated false-witness, condemned to the *murus strictissimus*, with chains on both hands and feet. When the culprits were members of a religious order, to avoid scandal the proceedings were usually held in private, and the imprisonment would be ordered to take place in a convent of their own order. As these buildings, however, were unprovided with cells

[1] Eymeric, *Directorium*, p. 507.

for the punishment of offenders, this was probably of no great advantage to the victim. In the case of Jeanne, widow of B. de la Tour, a nun of Lespinasse, in 1246, who had committed acts of both Catharan and Waldensian heresy, and had prevaricated in her confession, the sentence was confinement in a separate cell in her own convent, where no one was to enter or see her, her food being pushed in through an opening left for the purpose — in fact, the living tomb known as the *in pace*." [1]

In these wretched prisons the diet was most meager. But "while the penance prescribed was a diet of bread and water, the Inquisition, with unwonted kindness, did not object to its prisoners receiving from their friends contributions of food, wine, money, and garments, and among its documents are such frequent allusions to this that it may be regarded as an established custom." [2]

The number of prisoners even with a life sentence was rather considerable. The collections of sentences that we possess give us precise information on this point.

[1] Lea, *op. cit.*, vol. i, p. 487. The *in pace* was a frightful punishment. In 1350 the Archbishop of Toulouse besought King John to mitigate its severity, and he consequently issued an *Ordonnance* that the superior of the convent should twice a month visit and console the prisoner, who moreover should have the right twice a month to ask for the company of one of the monks. Even this slender innovation provoked the bitterest resistance (?) of the Dominicans and Franciscans, who appealed to Pope Clement VI, but in vain. Lea, vol. i, p. 488, *note*; Vassete, *Histoire du Languedoc*, vol. iv, *Preuves*, p. 29.

[2] Lea, *op. cit.*, vol. i, p. 491.

We have, for instance, the register of Bernard of Caux, the Inquisitor of Toulouse for the years 1244–1246. Out of fifty-two of his sentences, twenty-seven heretics were sentenced to life imprisonment. We must not forget also that several of them contain condemnations of many individuals; the second, for instance, condemned thirty-three persons, twelve of whom were to be imprisoned for life; the fourth condemned eighteen persons to life imprisonment. On the other hand, the register does not record one case of abandonment to the secular arm, even for relapse into heresy.[1]

Bernard must be considered a severe Inquisitor. The register of the notary of Carcassonne, published by Mgr. Douais, contains for the years 1249–1255 two hundred and seventy-eight articles. But imprisonment very rarely figured among the penances inflicted. The usual penalty was enforced service in the Holy Land, *passagium, transitus ultramarinus.*[2]

Bernard Gui, Inquisitor at Toulouse for seventeen years (1308–1325), was called upon to condemn nine hundred and thirty heretics, of whom two were guilty of false witness, eighty-nine were dead, and forty were fugitives. In the eighteen *Sermones* or *Autos de fé* in which he rendered the sentences we possess to-day, he condemned three hundred and seven to prison,

---

[1] Douais, *Documents*, vol. i, pp. cclx–cclxi; vol. ii, pp. i–89.

[2] Douais, *Documents*, vol. i, pp. cclxvii–cclxxxiv; vol. ii, pp. 115, 243.

i.e. about one third of all the heretics brought before his tribunal.[1]

The tribunal of the Inquisition of Pamiers in the *Sermones* of 1318–1324, held ninety-eight heresy trials. The records declare that two were acquitted; and say nothing of the penalty inflicted upon twenty-one others who were tried. The most common penalty was life-imprisonment. In the *Sermo* of March 8, thirteen heretics were sentenced to prison, eight of whom were set at liberty on July 4, 1322; these latter were condemned to wear single or double crosses. Six out of ten, tried on August 2, 1321, were sentenced for life to the German prison. On June 19, 1323, six out of ten tried were condemned to prison (*murus strictus*); on August 12, 1324, ten out of eleven tried were condemned for life to the strict prison: *ad strictum muri Carcassonne inquisitionis carcerem in vinculis ferreis ac in pane et aqua.*[2] We gather from these statistics that the Inquisition of Pamiers inflicted the penalty of life imprisonment as often as, if not more than, the Inquisition of Toulouse.

We have seen above that the penalty of imprisonment was sometimes mitigated and even commuted. Life imprisonment was sometimes commuted into temporary imprisonment, and both into pilgrimages or wearing the

[1] Douais, *Documents*, vol. i, pp. ccv., cf. Appendix B.
Note that the register records 930 condemnations. Cf. Lea, *op. cit.*, vol. i, p. 550.
[2] Vidal, *op. cit.*, April, 1905, pp. 313–321.

cross. Twenty, imprisoned by the Inquisition of Pamiers, were set at liberty on condition that they wore the cross.[1] This clemency was not peculiar to the Inquisition of Pamiers. In 1328, by a single sentence, twenty-three prisoners of Carcassonne were set at liberty, and other slight penances substituted.

In Bernard Gui's register of sentences we read of one hundred and nineteen cases of release from prison with the obligation to wear the cross, and of this number, fifty-one were subsequently released from even the minor penalty.[2] Prisoners were sometimes set at liberty on account of sickness, *v.g.* women with child, or to provide for their families.

"In 1246 we find Bernard de Caux, in sentencing Bernard Sabbatier, a relapsed heretic, to perpetual imprisonment, adding that as the culprit's father is a good Catholic, and old and sick, the son may remain with him, and support him as long as he lives, meanwhile wearing the crosses."[3]

Assuredly this penalty of imprisonment was terrible, but while we may denounce some Inquisitors for having made its suffering more intense out of malice or indifference,[4] we must also admit that others sometimes mitigated its severity.

.   .   .   .

[1] Vidal, *op. cit.*, July, 1905, p. 376.
[2] Lea, *op. cit.*, vol. i, 495.
[3] Lea, *op. cit.*, vol. i, 486.
[4] Recall what was said above, and the reforms of Clement V.

The condemnation of obstinate heretics, and later on, of the relapsed, permitted no exercise of clemency. How many heretics were abandoned to the secular arm, and thus sent to the stake, is impossible to determine. However, we have some interesting statistics of the more important tribunals on this point. The portion of the register of Bernard de Caux which relates to impenitent heretics has been lost, but we have the sentences of the Inquisition of Pamiers (1318–1324), and of Toulouse (1308–1323.) In nine *Sermones* or *autos de fé*[1] of the tribunal of Pamiers, condemning sixty-four persons, only five heretics were abandoned to the secular arm.[2]

Bernard Gui presided over eighteen *autos de fé*, and condemned nine hundred and thirty heretics; and yet he abandoned only forty-two to the secular arm.[3] These Inquisitors were far more lenient than Robert the Bougre. Taking all in all, the Inquisition in its operation denoted a real progress in the treatment of criminals; for it not only put an end to the summary vengeance of the mob, but it diminished considerably the number of those sentenced to death.[4]

[1] The *Sermo generalis* after which the sentences were solemnly pronounced by the Inquisitors was called in Spain *auto de fé*.

[2] Cf. Vidal, *op. cit.*, July, 1905, p. 369.

[3] Cf. The sentences of Bernard Gui in Douais, *Documents*, vol. i, p. ccv, and Appendix B.

[4] Even while the Inquisition was in full operation, the heretics who managed to escape the ecclesiastical tribunals had no reason to congratulate themselves. For we read that Raymond VII, Count of Toulouse in 1248, caused

We notice at Pamiers that only one out of thirteen, while at Toulouse but one in twenty-two, was sentenced to death. Although terrible enough, these figures are far different from the exaggerated statistics imagined by the fertile brains of ignorant controversialists.[1]

It is true that many writers are haunted by the cruelty of the Spanish or German tribunals which sent to the stake a great number of victims, *i.e. conversos* and witches.

From the very beginning, the Spanish Inquisition acted with the utmost severity. "Twelve hundred *conversos,* penitents, obdurate and relapsed heretics were present at the *auto de fé* in Toledo, March, 1487; and, according to the most conservative estimate, Torquemada sent to the stake about two thousand heretics"[2] in twelve years.

eighty heretics to be burned at Berlaiges, near Agen, after they had confessed in his presence, without giving them the opportunity of recanting. As Lea says: *op. cit.,* vol. i, p. 537, "From the contemporary sentences of Bernard of Caux, it is probable that, had these unfortunates been tried before that ardent champion of the faith, not one of them would have been condemned to the stake as impenitent."

[1] Of course we do not here refer to honest historians like Langlois who estimates that one heretic out of every ten was abandoned to the secular arm (*op. cit.,* p. 106). Dom Brial erroneously states in his preface to vol. xix of the *Recueil des Historiens des Gaules* (p. xxiii) that Bernard Gui burned 637 heretics. This figure represented the number of heretics then known to be *condemned,* but only 40 of these were abandoned to the secular arm. Cf. Lea, *op. cit.,* vol. i, p. 550. The exact number is 42 out of 930. Cf. Douais, *Documents,* vol. i, p. ccv, and Appendix B.

[2] Langlois, *L'Inquisition d'après des tableaux récents,* 1902, pp. 105, 106. This number, without being certain, is asserted by contemporaries, Pulgar and Marineo Siculo. Cf. Héféle, *Le Cardinal Ximénes,* Paris, 1856, pp. 290, 291. Another contemporary, Bernaldes, speaks of over 700 burned

"During this same period," says a contemporary historian, "fifteen thousand heretics did penance, and were reconciled to the Church."[1] That makes a total of seventeen thousand trials. We can thus understand how Torquemada, although grossly calumniated, came to be identified with this period, during which so many thousands of *conversos* appeared before the Spanish tribunals.[2]

The zeal of the Inquisitors seemed to abate after a time.[3] Perhaps they thought it better to keep the Jews and the Mussulmans in the church by kindness. But kindness failed just as force had failed. After one hundred years, the number of obdurate *conversos* was as great as ever. Several ardent advocates of force advised the authorities to send them all to the stake. But the State determined to drive the Moriscos from Spain, as it had banished the Jews in 1492. Accordingly in September, 1609, a law was passed decreeing the banishment, under penalty of death, of all Moriscos, men, women, and chil-

from 1481–1488; cf. Gams, *Kirchengeschichte von Spanien*, vol. iii, 2, p. 69.

[1] Pulgar, in Héféle, *op. cit.*, p. 291.

[2] Torquemada established the Inquisition in the different cities of Castile, Aragon, Valencia, and Catalonia.

[3] "The Inquisition of Valencia condemned one hundred and twelve *conversos* in 1538 (of whom fourteen were sent to the stake); at the *auto de fé* of Seville, September 24, 1559, three were burned, and eight were reconciled and sentenced to life-imprisonment; on June 6, 1585, the Inquisitors of Saragossa in their account to Philip II speak of having reconciled sixty-three, and of having sent five to the stake." Langlois, *op. cit.*, p. 106.

dren. Five hundred thousand persons, about one sixteenth of the population, were thus banished from Spain, and forced to seek refuge on the coasts of Barbary.[1] "Behold," writes Brother Bléda, "the most glorious event in Spain since the times of the apostles; religious unity is now secured; an era of prosperity is certainly about to dawn." [2] This era of prosperity so proudly announced by the Dominican zealot never came. This extreme measure which pleased him so greatly in reality weakened Spain, by depriving her of hundreds of thousands of her subjects.

The witchcraft fever which spread over Europe in the fifteenth and sixteenth centuries stimulated to an extraordinary degree the zeal of the Inquisitors. The bull of Innocent VIII, *Summis desiderantes,* December 5, 1484, made matters worse. The Pope admitted that men and women could have immoral relations with demons, and that sorcerers by their magical incantations could injure the harvests, the vineyards, the orchards and the fields.[3]

---

[1] Langlois, *op. cit.,* p. 110.

[2] Cf. Bléda, *Defensio fidei in causa neophytorum sive Moriscorum regni Valentini totiusque Hispaniæ,* Valencia, 1610; *Tractatus de justa Moriscorum ab Hispania expulsione,* Valenciâ, 1610; cf. Llorente, *Histoire de l'Inquisition d'Espagne,* Paris, 1817, vol. iii, p. 430.

[1] "Sane nuper ad nostrum non sine ingenti molestia pervenit auditum, quod in nonnullis partibus Allemaniæ superioris . . . complures utriusque sexus personæ . . . a fide catholica deviantes, cum dæmonibus incubis et succubis abuti ac suis incantationibus et conjurationibus aliisque nefandis superstitionibus et sortilegiis, excessibus, criminibus et delictis, mulierum

He also complained of the folly of those ecclesiastics and laymen who opposed the Inquisition in its prosecution of heretical sorcerers, and concluded by conferring additional powers upon the Dominican Inquisitors, Institoris and Sprenger, the author of the famous *Malleus Maleficarum.*

Innocent VIII assuredly had no intention of committing the Church to a belief in the phenomena he mentioned in his bull, but his personal opinion [1] did have an influ-

partus, animalium fœtus, terræ fruges, vinearum uvas et arborum fructus, necnon homines, mulieres, pecora, pecudes, et alia diversorum generum animalia, vineas quoque, pomeria, prata, pascua, blada, frumenta et alia terræ legumina, perire, suffocari et extinguere." *Bullarium*, vol. v, p. 296 and seq., and Pegna's Bullarium in Eymeric, *Directorium Inquisit.*, p. 83. The notion of *dæmones succubi et incubi* comes from St. Augustine: "Et quoniam creberrima fama est, multique se expertos vel ab eis qui experti essent, de quorum fide dubitandum non est, audisse confirmant, Sylvanos et Faunos, quos vulgo incubos vocant, improbos sæpe extitisse mulieribus et earum appetisse ac peregisse concubitum, et quosdam dæmones, quos Dusios Galli nuncupant, hanc assidue immunditiam et tentare et efficere plures talesque asseverant, ut hoc negare impudentiæ videatur," etc. *De Civitate Dei*, lib. xv, cap. xxiii, no. 1. Cf. *Summa*, pars 1ª, quæst. li, art. 3, ad 6um. On witches, cf. the bulls *Honestis* of Leo X (February 15, 1521), *Dudum* of Adrian VI (July 20, 1522), *Cœli et terræ of* Sixtus V (January 5, 1586), in Eymeric, *loc. cit.*, pp. 99, 105, 142.

[1] Pastor writes (History of the Popes, vol. v, p. 349) concerning the reality of these facts: "The question whether the Pope believed in them has nothing to do with the subject. His judgment on this point has no greater importance than attaches to a papal decree in any other undogmatic question, *e.g.* in a dispute about a benefice." The learned historian is wrong, for the Pope's views made a great difference in this particular case. Many canonists cited it as proof, and the Inquisitors acted on it in their tribunals. "Præterea qui hoc asserunt somnia esse et ludibria, certe peccant contra reverentiam matri debitam," says the Jesuit Delrio, *Disquisitio magna*, ed. 1603, lib. II, quæst. xvi, p. 149; cf. p. 159; cf. *Malleus maleficarum* of Sprenger, and the *Novus malleus maleficarum* of Spina, Cologne, 1581, p. 146 and seq., etc.

ence upon the canonists and Inquisitors of his day; this
is clear from the trials for witchcraft held during this
period.[1] It is impossible to estimate the number of sorcerers condemned. Louis of Paramo triumphantly declared that in a century and a half the Holy Office sent to
the stake over thirty thousand.[2] Of course we must take
such round numbers with a grain of salt, as they always
are greatly exaggerated. But the fact remains that the
condemnations for sorcery were so numerous as to stagger
belief. The Papacy itself recognized the injustice of its
agents. For in 1637 instructions were issued stigmatizing the conduct of the Inquisitors on account of their
arbitrary and unjust prosecution of sorcerers; they were
accused of extorting from them by cruel tortures confessions that were valueless, and of abandoning them to
the secular arm without sufficient cause.[3]

.   .   .   .

[1] On this question, cf. Janssen-Pastor, *Geschichte des deutschen Volkes*,
vol. viii, Fribourg, 1894, p. 507 and seq.; Finke, *Historisches Jahrbuch*,
vol. xiv, p. 341 and seq.; Lea, *op. cit.*, vol. iii, pp. 492–549.

[2] *De Origine Officii sanctæ Inquisitionis*, p. 206. Lea says that "Protes-
tants and Catholics rivaled each other in the madness of the hour." *Op. cit.*,
vol. iii, p. 549.

[3] "Experientia rerum magistra aperte docet gravissimos quotidie committi
errores a diversis Ordinariis, Vicariis et Inquisitoribus, sed præcipue a secu-
laribus judicibus in formandis processibus contra striges sive lamias et
maleficas in grave præjudicium tam justitiæ quam hujusmodi mulierum
inquisitarum: cum longo tempore observatum fuerit, plures hujusmodi
processus non rite ac juridice formatos, imo plerumque necesse fuisse quam-
plures judices reprehendere et multos et impertinentes modos habitos in
formandis processibus, reis interrogandis, excessivis torturis inferendis ita,
ut quandoque contigerit injustas et iniquas proferri sententias, etiam ultimi

Confiscation, though not so severe a penalty as the stake, bore very heavily upon the victims of the Inquisition. The Roman laws classed the crime of heresy with treason, and visited it with a principal penalty, death, and a secondary penalty, confiscation. They decreed that all heretics, without exception, forfeited their property the very day they wavered in the faith. Actual confiscation of goods did not take place in the case of those penitents who had deserved no severer punishment than temporary imprisonment. Bernard Gui answered those who objected to this ruling, by showing that, as a matter of fact, there was no real pecuniary loss involved. For, he argued: "Secondary penances are inflicted only upon those heretics who denounce their accomplices. But, by this denunciation, they ensure the discovery and arrest of the guilty ones, who, without their aid, would have escaped punishment; the goods of these heretics are at once confiscated, which is certainly a positive gain." [1]   Actual confiscation took place in the

supplicii, sive traditionis brachio sæculari, et reipsa compertum est, multos judices ita faciles proclivesque fuisse ob leve aut minimum indicium credere aliquam talem esse strigem, et nihil omnino prætermisisse ab hujusmodi muliere, etiam modis illicitis, talem confessionem extorquere, cum tot tamen tantisque inverisimilitudinibus, varietatibus et contrarietatibus, ut super tali confessione nulla aut modica vis fieri posset." Pignatelli, *Consultationes novissimæ canonicæ*, Venetiis, 2 in fol., vol. i, p. 505, *Consultatio* 123.

[1] "Si autem aliquibus videatur absurdum, gratiam præcipue de confiscatione bonorum in prejudicium fisci aut domini temporalis per Inquisitores fieri non debere, attendant quod ex predicta gratia promissa et facta ex causa rationabili, ut præmittitur, revelantur personæ aliæ quæ latebant, et

case of all obdurate and relapsed heretics abandoned to the secular arm, with all penitents condemned to perpetual imprisonment, and with all suspects who had managed to escape the Inquisition, either by flight or by death. The heretic who died peacefully in bed before the Inquisition could lay hands upon him was considered contumacious, and treated as such; his remains were exhumed,[1] and his property confiscated. This last fact accounts for the incredible frequency of prosecutions against the dead. Of the six hundred and thirty-six cases tried by Bernard Gui, eighty-eight were posthumous.[2] As a general rule, the confiscation of the heretic's property, which so frequently resulted from the trials of the Inquisition, had a great deal to do with the interest they aroused. We do not say that the Holy Office systematically increased the number of its condemnations merely to increase its pecuniary profits. But abuses of this kind were inevitable. We know they existed, because

quod in uno videtur amitti recuperatur in pluribus cum augmento." *Practica*, 3 pars, p. 185.

[1] This was done with great solemnity. The bones and even the decomposed body of the heretic were carried through the city streets at the sound of a trumpet, and then burned. The names of the dead were read out, and the living were threatened with a like fate if they followed their example, "De cimeteriis . . . extumulati . . . et ossa eorum et corpora fætentia per villam tracta et voce tibicinatoris per vicos proclamata et nominata dicentis: Qui aytal fara, aytal perira." *Chronique of Guillem Pelhisse*, published by Douais, p. 110. Guillem Pelhisse was one of the first Inquisitors of Albi.

[2] Eighty-nine out of nine hundred and thirty. Cf. Douais, *Documents*, vol. i, p. ccv, and Appendix B.

the Popes denounced them strongly, although they were too rare to deserve more than a passing mention. But would the ecclesiastical and lay princes who, in varying proportions, shared with the Holy Office in these confiscations, and who in some countries appropriated them all, have accorded to the Inquisition that continual goodwill and help which was the condition of its prosperity, without what Lea calls "the stimulant of pillage"? We may very well doubt it. . . . That is why in point of fact their zeal for the faith languished whenever pecuniary gain was not forthcoming. "In our days," writes the Inquisitor Eymeric rather gloomily, " there are no more rich heretics, so that princes, not seeing much money in prospect, will not put themselves to any expense; it is a pity that so salutary an institution as ours should be so uncertain of its future," [1]

Most historians have said little or nothing about the money side of the Inqusition. Lea was the first to give it the attention it deserved. He writes: " In addition to the misery inflicted by these wholesale confiscations on the thousands of innocent and helpless women and children thus stripped of everything, it would be almost impossible to exaggerate the evil which they entailed upon all classes in the business of daily life." [2] There was indeed very

[1] Langlois, *op. cit.*, pp. 75–78. Cf. Lea, *op. cit.*, vol. i, pp. 501–524, cf. Tanon, *op. cit.*, pp. 523–538.

[2] Lea, *op. cit.*, p. 522.

little security in business, for the contracts of a hidden heretic were essentially null and void, and could be rescinded as soon as his guilt was discovered, either during his lifetime or after his death. In view of such a penal code, we can understand why Lea should write: "While the horrors of the crowded dungeon can scarce be exaggerated, yet more effective for evil and more widely exasperating was the sleepless watchfulness which was ever on the alert to plunder the rich and to wrench from the poor the hard-earned gains on which a family depended for support."[1]

.   .   .   .

This summary of the acts of the Inquisition is at best but a brief and very imperfect outline. But a more complete study would not afford us any deeper insight into its operation.

Human passions are responsible for the many abuses of the Inquisition. The civil power in heresy trials was far from being partial to the accused. On the contrary, it would seem that the more pressure the State brought to bear upon the ecclesiastical tribunals, the more arbitrary their procedure became.

We do not deny that the zeal of the Inquisitors was at times excessive, especially in the use of torture. But some of their cruelty may be explained by their sincere desire for the salvation of the heretic. They regarded

[1] Lea, *op. cit.*, p. 480

the confession of suspects as the beginning of their conversion. They therefore believed any means used for that purpose justified. They thought that an Inquisitor had done something praiseworthy, when, even at the cost of cruel torments, he freed a heretic from his heresy. He was sorry indeed to be obliged to use force; but that was not altogether his fault, but the fault of the laws which he had to enforce.

Most men regard the *auto de fé* as the worst horror of the Inquisition. It is hardly ever pictured without burning flames and ferocious looking executioners. But an *auto de fé* did not necessarily call for either stake or executioner. It was simply a solemn "Sermon," which the heretics about to be condemned had to attend.[1] The death penalty was not always inflicted at these solemnities, which were intended to impress the imagination of the people. Seven out of eighteen *autos de fé* presided over by the famous Inquisitor, Bernard Gui, decreed no severer penalty than imprisonment.

---

[1] On these "Sermons," cf. Tanon, *op. cit.*, pp. 425–431. In France the heretics were not dressed in any particular costume or mitred as in Spain during the sixteenth century. There is but one mention of mitred heretics, viz. at the *auto de fé* against sorcerers at Arras in 1459. "Et illec furent mitrés d'une mitre où estait peinct la figure du diable en telle manière qu'ils avaient confessé lui avoir fait hommage, et eulx à genoux peincts devant le diable; et illecq, par M. P. Le Broussart, Inquisiteur de la foy chrétienne, preschiez publiquement, présent tout le peuple; et y avoit tant de gens que ce estoit merveille, car de tous les villages d'entour Arras et de dix ou douze lieues allenviron et plus y avait de gens." Frédéricq, *Corpus documentorum inquisitionis Neerlandicæ*, vol. i, p. 353.

We have seen, moreover, that in many places, even in Spain at a certain period, the number of heretics condemned to death was rather small. Even Lea, whom no one can accuse of any great partiality for the Church, is forced to state: "The stake consumed comparatively few victims." [1]

In fact, imprisonment and confiscation were as a rule the severest penalties inflicted.

[1] *Op. cit.*, vol. i, p. 480. In making this statement, Lea of course means to exclude the witchcraft trials, which he treats in another part of his work. Cf. vol. iii, ch. vii, pp. 492–549.

CHAPTER X

A Criticism of the Theory and Practice of the Inquisition

Such was the development for over one thousand years (200–1300) of the theory of Catholic writers on the coercive power of the Church in the treatment of heresy. It began with the principle of absolute toleration; it ended with the stake.

During the era of the persecutions, the Church, who was suffering herself from pagan intolerance, merely excommunicated heretics, and tried to win them back to the orthodox faith by kindness and the force of argument. But when the emperors became Christians, they, in memory of the days when they were "*Pontifices maximi*," at once endeavored to regulate worship and doctrine, at least externally. Unfortunately, certain sects, hated like the Manicheans, or revolutionary in character like the Donatists, prompted the enactment of cruel laws for their suppression. St. Optatus approved these measures, and Pope St. Leo had not the courage to disavow them. Still, most of the early Fathers, St. John Chrysostom, St. Martin, St. Ambrose, St. Augustine, and many others,[1] protested strongly in the name of Christian charity against the infliction of the death penalty upon heretics. St. Augustine, who formed the mind of his age, at first favored the theory of absolute toleration. But afterwards, perceiving that certain good results followed from what he called "a salutary fear," he modified his views. He then maintained that the State could and ought to punish by fine, confiscation, or even exile, her rebellious children, in order to make them repent. This may be called his theory of moderate persecution.

The revival of the Manichean heresy in the eleventh century took the Christian princes and people by surprise, unaccustomed as they were to the legislation of the first Christian emperors. Still the heretics did not fare any better on that account. For the people rose up against them, and burned them at the stake. The Bishops and the Fathers of the Church at once protested against this lynching of heretics. Some, like Wazo of Liège, represented the party of absolute toleration, while others, under the leadership of St. Bernard, advocated the theory of

---

[1] Lea (*op. cit.*, vol. i, pp. 214, 215) says that St. Jerome was an advocate of force. "Rigor in fact," argues St. Jerome, "is the most genuine mercy, since temporal punishment may avert eternal perdition." Here St. Jerome merely says that God punishes in time that He may not punish in eternity. But he by no means "argues" that this punishment should be in the hands of either Church or State. "Scitote eum (Deum) ideo ad præsens reddidisse supplicia, ne in æternum puniret . . . Optandum est adulteris ut in præsentiarum brevi et cita pæna cruciatus frustrentur æternos." *Commentar.*, in Naum, i, 9, P. L., vol. xxv, col. 1238. This is the chief text quoted by Lea.

St. Augustine. Soon after churchmen began to decree the penalty of imprisonment for heresy — a penalty unknown to the Roman law, and regarded in the beginning more as a penance than a legal punishment. It originated in the cloister, gradually made its way into the tribunals of the Bishop, and finally into the tribunals of the State.

Canon law, helped greatly by the revival of the imperial code, introduced in the twelfth century definite laws for the suppression of heresy. This régime lasted from 1150 till 1215, from Gratian to Innocent III. Heresy, the greatest sin against God, was classed with treason, and visited with the same penalty. The penalty was banishment with all its consequences; *i.e.* the destruction of the houses of heretics, and the confiscation of their property. Still, because of the horror which the Church had always professed for the effusion of blood, she did not as yet inflict the death penalty which the State decreed for treason. Innocent III did not wish to go beyond the limits [1] set by St. Augustine, St. John Chrysostom, and St. Bernard.

But later Popes and princes went further. They began by decreeing death as a secondary penalty,[2] in case

---

[1] Cf. *supra*, pp. 62, 63.

[2] "Et si post tempus præfixum," says Pedro of Aragon, "aliqui in tota terra nostra eos invenerint . . . , corpora eorum ignibus crementur." De Marca, *Marca Hispanica*, col. 1484. In the statutes of Bologna of 1245, the podestà swore to banish heretics; if they refused to leave the city and were not con-

heretics rebelled against the law of banishment. But when the emperor Frederic had revived the legislation of his Christian predecessors of the fourth, fifth, and sixth centuries,[1] and had made the popular custom of burning heretics a law of the empire, the Papacy could not resist the current of his example. The Popes at once ordered the new legislation vigorously enforced everywhere, especially in Lombardy. This was simply the logical carrying out of the comparison made by Innocent III between heresy and treason, and was due chiefly to two Popes: Gregory IX who established the Inquisition under the Dominicans and the Franciscans, and Innocent IV who authorized the Inquisitors to use torture.

The theologians and casuists soon began to defend the procedure of the Inquisition. They seemed absolutely unaffected, in theory at least,[2] by the most cruel tor-

verted, they were to be arrested and sent to the stake. Ficker, *op. cit.*, pp. 205, 206.

[1] Cf. the law of Arcadius of 395 (*Cod. Theodos.*, xvi, v. 28), which says: "Qui vel levi argumento a judicio catholicæ religionis et tramite detecti fuerint deviare," and the Sicilian constitution *Inconsutilem tunicam* (in Eymeric, *Directorium inquisitorum*, Appendix, p. 14), where we read: "Si inventi fuerint a fide catholica saltem in articulo deviare," and again: "Prout veteribus legibus est indictum."

[2] Practically speaking, the Inquisitors often remained unmoved at the lot of heretics. The following fact is a proof. "It was in the year 1234, the day on which the news of St. Dominic's canonization reached Toulouse. The Bishop, Raymond du Felgar, had just said solemn mass in the Dominican convent, in honor of this canonization, and was on his way to the refectory with the brethren, when some one came from the city saying that they were about to 'hereticate' an old woman, sick with the fever. The Bishop at once went with the prior to this house, approached the sick woman, who,

ments. With them the preservation of the orthodox faith was paramount, and superior to all sentiment. In the name of Christian charity, St. Thomas, the great light of the thirteenth century, taught that relapsed heretics, even when repentant, ought to be put to death without mercy.

How are we to explain this development of the doctrine of the Church on the suppression of heresy, and granting that a plausible explanation may be given, how are we to justify it?

. . . .

Intolerance is natural to man. If, as a matter of fact, men are not always intolerant in practice, it is only because they are prevented by conditions born of reason and wisdom. Respect for the opinion of others supposes a temper of mind which takes years to acquire. It is a question whether the average man is capable of it. Intolerance regarding religious doctrines especially, with the cruelty

regarding him at first as a Catharan bishop, confessed her faith openly to him, and then persisted in her heresy when she learned who he was. Thereupon, he condemned her as a heretic, and handed her over to the Count's vicar, who had her transferred to Pré-le-Compte, where she was burned in her bed." After this, the Bishop and the Dominicans went to the refectory, where they joyfully ate their dinner, giving thanks to God and to St. Dominic: Episcopus vero et fratres et socii hoc completo venerunt ad refectorium et quæ parata erant cum lætitia comederunt, gratias agentes Deo et beato Dominico. G. Pelhisse, *Chronique*, ed. Douais, pp. 97, 98; Tanon, *op. cit.*, pp. 54, 55. The condemnation and execution of this sick woman did not interfere with their festivities in honor of St. Dominic, because they all thought that they had performed a pious duty. Such light-heartedness is very hard for us to understand to-day.

that usually accompanies it, has practicaly been the law of history. From this view-point, the temper of mind of the mediæval Christians differed little from that of the pagans of the empire. A Roman of the second or third century considered blasphemy against the gods a crime that deserved the greatest torments; a Christian of the eleventh century felt the same toward the apostates and enemies of the Catholic faith. This is clearly seen from the treatment accorded the first Manicheans who came from Bulgaria, and gained some adherents at Orléans, Mont-Wimer, Soissons, Liège, and Goslar. At once there was a popular uprising against them, which evidenced what may be called the instinctive intolerance of the people. The civil authorities of the day shared this hatred, and proved it either by sending heretics to the stake themselves, or allowing the people to do so. As Lea has said: "The practice of burning the heretic alive was thus not the creation of positive law, but arose generally and spontaneously, and its adoption by the legislator was only the recognition of a popular custom."[1] Besides, the sovereign could not brook riotous men who disturbed the established order of his dominions. He was well aware that public tranquillity depended chiefly upon religious principles, which ensured that moral unity desired by every ruler. Pagan antiquity had dreamed of this unity, and its philosophers, interpreting its mind,

[1] Lea, *op. cit.*, vol. i, p. 222.

showed themselves just as intolerant as the theologians of the Middle Ages.

"Plato," writes Gaston Boissier, "in his ideal Republic, denies toleration to the impious, *i.e.* to those who did not accept the State religion. Even if they remained quiet and peaceful, and carried on no propaganda, they seemed to him dangerous by the bad example they gave. He condemned them to be shut up in a house where they might learn wisdom (*sophronisteria*) — by this pleasant euphemism he meant a prison — and for five years they were to listen to a discourse every day. The impious who caused disturbance and tried to corrupt others were to be imprisoned for life in a terrible dungeon, and after death were to be denied burial." [1] Apart from the stake, was not this the Inquisition to the life? In countries where religion and patriotism went hand in hand, we can readily conceive this intolerance. Sovereigns were naturally inclined to believe that those who interfered with the public worship unsettled the State, and their conviction became all the stronger when the State received from heaven a sort of special investiture. This was the case with the Christian empire. Constantine, towards the end of his career, thought himself ordained by God, "a bishop in externals," [2] and his successors strove

---

[1] *La fin du paganism*, vol. i, pp. 47, 48. Cf. Plato's Republic, Book II; Laws, Book X.

[2] "Ego vero in eis quæ extra (Ecclesiam) geruntur *episcopus a Deo sum constitutus*." Eusebius, *Vita Constantini*, lib iv, cap. xxiv.

to keep intact the deposit of faith.   "The first care of the imperial majesty," said one of them, "is to protect the true religion, for with its worship is connected the prosperity of human undertakings." [1]   Thus some of their laws were passed in view of strengthening the canon law. They mounted guard about the Church, with sword in hand, ready to use it in her defence.[2]

The Middle Ages inherited these views. Religious unity was then attained throughout Europe.   Any attempt to break it was an attack at once upon the Church and the Empire.   "The enemies of the Cross of Christ and those who deny the Christian faith," says Pedro II, of Aragon, "are also our enemies, and the public enemies of our kingdom; they must be treated as such." [3] It was in virtue of the same principle that Frederic II punished heretics as criminals according to the common law; *ut crimina publica.*   He speaks of the "Ecclesiastical peace" as of old the emperors spoke of the "Roman peace."   As Emperor, he considered it his duty "to preserve and to maintain it," and woe betide the one who dared disturb it.   Feeling himself invested with both

---

[1] "Præcipuam imperatoriæ majestatis curam esse perspicimus veræ religionis indaginem, cujus si cultum tenere potuerimus iter prosperitatis humanis aperimus inceptis."   Theodosius II, *Novellæ,* tit. iii (438).

[2] Cf. *supra,* p. 29, n. 3.

[3] "Et omnes alios hæreticos . . . tanquam inimicos crucis Christi christianæque fidei violatores *et nostros etiam regnique nostri publicos hostes* exire ac fugere districte et irremeabiliter præcipimus."   Law of 1197, in De Marca, *Marca Hispanica,* col. 1384.

human and divine authority,[1] he enacted the severest laws possible against heresy. What therefore might have remained merely a threatening theory became a terrible reality. The laws of 1224, 1231, 1238, and 1239 prove that both princes and people considered the stake a fitting penalty for heresy.

It would have been very surprising if the Church menaced as she was by an ever increasing flood of heresy, had not accepted the State's eager offer of protection. She had always professed a horror for bloodshed. But as long as she was not acting directly, and the State undertook to shed in its own name the blood of wicked men, she began to consider solely the benefits that would accrue to her from the enforcement of the civil laws. Besides, by classing heresy with treason, she herself had laid down the premisses of the State's logical conclusion, the death penalty.[2] The Church, therefore, could hardly

---

[1] "Cum ad conservandum pariter et fovendum Ecclesiæ tranquillitatis statum ex commisso nobis imperii regimine defensores a Deo simus constituti . . ., utriusque juris auctoritate muniti, duximus sanciendum," etc. Constitution of 1224, *Mon. Germ.*, *Leges*, sect. iv, vol. ii, p. 126. Cf. the Constitution of March, 1232, *ibid.*, p. 196, and the Sicilian Constitution *Inconsutilem tunicam*, where we read: "Statuimus in primis, ut crimen hæreseos et damnatæ sectæ cujuslibet, quoqumque nomine censeantur (prout veteribus legibus est indictum) inter publica crimina numerentur." In Eymeric, *Directorum Inquisitorum*, Appendix, p. 14.

[2] "Cum enim secundum legitimas sanctiones *reis læsæ majestatis punitis* capite bona confiscentur eorum . . .; *cum longe sit gravius æternam quam temporalem lædere majestatem*," etc., said Innocent III in a letter of March 25, 1199, *Ep.* ii, 1. "Cum longe sit gravius æternam quam temporalem offendere majestatem," said Frederic II in his Constitution of 1220,

call in question the justice of the imperial laws, without in a measure going against the principles she herself had advocated.

Church and State, therefore, continually influenced one the other. The theory upheld by the Church reacted on the State and caused it to adopt violent measures, while the State in turn compelled the Church to approve its use of force, although such an attitude was opposed to the spirit of early Christianity.

The theologians and the canonists put the finishing touches to the situation. Influenced by what was happening around them, their one aim was to defend the laws of their day. This is clearly seen, if we compare the *Summa* of St. Raymond of Pennafort with the *Summa* of St. Thomas Aquinas. When St. Raymond wrote his work, the Church still followed the criminal code of Popes Lucius III and Innocent III; she had as yet no notion of inflicting the death penalty for heresy. But in St. Thomas's time, the Inquisition had been enforcing for some years the draconian laws of Frederic II. The Angelic doctor, therefore, made no attempt to defend the obsolete code of Innocent III, but endeavored to show that the imperial laws, then authorized by the Church, were conformable to the strictest justice. His one argument was to make

Mon Germ., *Leges*, sect. iv, vol. ii, p. 108. And he repeats this comparison in his Constitution of 1232, n. 8: "Si reos lesæ majestatis," etc., *ibid.*, p. 197. A law of 407 (*Cod. Theod.*, xvi, v. 40) had long before classed heresy with treason.

comparisons, more or less happy, between heresy and crimes against the common law.[1]

At a period when no one considered a doctrine solidly proved unless authorities could be quoted in its support, these comparisons were not enough. So the theologians taxed their ingenuity to find quotations, not from the Fathers, which would have been difficult, but from the Scriptures, which seemed favorable to the ideas then in vogue. St. Optatus had tried to do this as early as the fifth century,[2] despite the antecedent protests of Origen, Cyprian, Lactantius and Hilary. Following his example, the churchmen of the Middle Ages reminded their hearers that according to the sacred Scriptures, "Jehovah was a God delighting in the extermination of his enemies. They read how Saul, the chosen king of Israel, had been divinely punished for sparing Agag of Amalek; how the prophet Samuel had hewn him to pieces; how the whole-sale slaughter of the unbelieving Canaanites had been ruthlessly commanded and enforced; how Elijah had been commended for slaying four hundred and fifty priests of Baal; and they could not conceive how mercy to those who rejected the true faith could be aught but disobedience to God.[3] Had not Almighty God said:

---

[1] Cf. *supra*, p. 171 and seq.

[2] *De Schismate Donatistarum*, p. iii, cap. vii; cf. *supra*, pp. 16, 17.

[3] Lea, *op. cit.*, vol. i, p. 238. St. Pius V, in a letter to Charles IX, March 28, 1569, demanded the destruction of the Huguenots, *donec deletis omnibus*, and cited the destruction of Agag and the Amalekites. Cf. Vacandard, *Les*

"If thy brother, the son of thy mother, or thy daughter, or thy wife, that is in thy bosom, or thy friend, whom thou lovest as thy own soul, would persuade thee secretly, saying: 'Let us go and serve strange gods,' which thou knowest not, nor thy fathers . . . consent not to him, hear him not, neither let thy eye spare him to pity or conceal him, but thou shalt presently put him to death. Let thy hand be first upon him, and afterwards the hands of all the people."[1]

Such a teaching might appear, at first sight, hard to reconcile with the law of gentleness which Jesus preached to the world. But the theologians quoted Christ's words: "Do not think that I am come to destroy the law; I am not come to destroy but to fulfill," [2] and other texts of the gospels to prove the perfect agreement between the Old and the New law in the matter of penalties. They even went so far as to assert that St. John[3] spoke of the penalty of fire to be inflicted upon heretics.[4]

This strange method of exegesis was not peculiar to the founders and the defenders of the tribunals of the Inquisition. England, which knew nothing of the Inquisition save for the trial of the Templars, was just as cruel to heretics as Gregory IX or Frederic II.

Papes et la Saint-Barthélemy, in *Études de critique et d'histoire*, 3 ed., 1906, pp. 231–238.

[1] Deut. xiii. 6–9; cf. xvii. 1–6.
[2] Matt. v. 17.
[3] John xv. 16.
[4] Cf. *supra*, pp. 176, 177.

"The statute of May 25, 1382, directs the King to issue to his sheriffs commissions to arrest Wyclif's traveling preachers, and aiders and abettors of heresy, and hold them till they justify themselves *selon reson et la ley de seinte esglise.* After the burning of Sawtré by a royal warrant confirmed by Parliament in 1400, the statute ' *de hæreticis comburendis* ' for the first time inflicted in England the death penalty as a settled punishment for heresy. . . . It forbade the dissemination of heretical opinions and books, empowered the bishops to seize all offenders and hold them in prison until they should purge themselves or abjure, and ordered the bishops to proceed against them within three months after arrest. For minor offences the bishops were empowered to imprison during pleasure and fine at discretion, — the fine enuring to the royal exchequer. For obstinate heresy or relapse, involving under the canon law abandonment to the secular arm, the bishops and their commissioners were the sole judges, and on their delivery of such convicts, the sheriff of the county, or the mayor and bailiffs of the nearest town were obliged to burn them before the people on an eminence. Henry V followed this up, and the statute of 1414 established throughout the kingdom a sort of mixed secular and ecclesiastical Inquisition for which the English system of grand inquests gave special facilities. Under this legislation, burning for heresy became a not unfamiliar sight for English eyes, and Lollardy was readily suppressed. In 1533, Henry VIII repealed the statute of 1400, while retaining those of 1382 and 1414, and also the penalty of burning alive for contumacious heresy and relapse, and the dangerous admixture of politics and religion rendered the stake a favorite instrument of state-craft. One of the earliest measures of the reign of Edward VI was the repeal of this law, as well as those of 1382 and 1414, together with all the atrocious legislation of the Six Articles. With the reaction under Philip and Mary came a revival of the sharp laws against heresy. Scarce had the Spanish marriage been concluded when an obedient Parliament re-enacted the legislation of 1382, 1400, and 1414, which afforded ample machinery for the numerous burnings which followed. The earliest act of the first Parliament of Elizabeth was the repeal of the legislation of Philip and Mary, and of the old statutes which it had revived; but the writ *de hæretico comburendo* had become an integral part of English law, and survived, until the desire of Charles II for Catholic toleration caused him, in 1676, to procure its abrogation, and the restraint of the ecclesiastical courts in cases of atheism, blasphemy, heresy, and schism, and other damnable doctrines and opinions ' to the ecclesiastical remedies of excommunication, deprivation, degradation, and other ecclesiastical censures, not extending to death. ' [1]

These ideas of intolerance were so fixed in the public

[1] Lea, *op. cit.*, vol. i, pp. 352–354.

mind at the close of the Middle Ages, that even those who protested against the procedure of the Inquisition thought that in principle it was just. Farel wrote to Calvin, September 8, 1533: "Some people do not wish us to prosecute heretics. But because the Pope condemns the faithful (*i.e.* the Huguenots) for the crime of heresy, and because unjust judges punish the innocent, it is absurd to conclude that we must not put heretics to death, in order to strengthen the faithful. I myself have often said that I was ready to suffer death, if I ever taught anything contrary to sound doctrine, and that I would deserve the most frightful torments, if I tried to rob any one of the true faith in Christ. I cannot, therefore, lay down a different law to others." [1]

Calvin held the same views. His inquisitorial spirit was manifest in his bitter prosecution and condemnation of the Spaniard Michael Servetus.[2] When any one found fault with him he answered: "The executioners of the Pope taught that their foolish inventions were doctrines of Christ, and were excessively cruel, while I have always judged heretics in all kindness and in the fear of God;

---

[1] *Œuvres complètes de Calvin*, Brunswick, 1863–1900, vol. xiv, p. 612.

[2] Servetus was condemned October 26, 1533, to be burned alive, and was executed the next day. As early as 1545, Calvin had written: "If he (Servetus) comes to Geneva, I will never allow him to depart alive, as long as I have authority in this city: *Vivum exire numquam patiar. Œuvres complètes*, vol. xii, p. 283." Calvin, however, wished the death penalty of fire to be commuted into some other kind of death.

I merely put to death a confessed heretic." [1] Michael Servetus assuredly did not gain much by the substitution of Calvin for the Inquisition.[2]

Bullinger of Zurich, speaking of the death of Servetus, thus wrote Lelius Socinus: "If, Lelius, you cannot now admit the right of a magistrate to punish heretics, you will undoubtedly admit it some day. St. Augustine himself at first deemed it wicked to use violence towards heretics, and tried to win them back by the mere word of God. But finally, learning wisdom by experience, he began to use force with good effect. In the beginning the Lutherans did not believe that heretics ought to be punished; but after the excesses of the Anabaptists, they declared that the magistrate ought not merely to reprimand the unruly, but to punish them severely as an example to thousands." [3]

---

[1] Ferdinand Buisson, *Sébastien Castellio*, Paris, 1891, p. 151. To justify this execution, Calvin published his *Defensio orthodoxæ fidei de sacra Trinitate, contra prodigiosos errores Michælis Serveti Hispani, ubi ostenditur hæreticos jure gladii cœrcendos esse*, Geneva, 1554.

[2] In 1530, Michael Servetus wrote: "It is very unjust to put men to death simply because they err in interpreting certain texts of the Scriptures." Cf. M. N. Weiss, *Bulletin de la societé du protestantisme français*, December, 1903, p. 562. The author adds: "The imperial laws under which Servetus was tried were the decrees of Justinian and the laws of Frederic II. The reformers who desired a religious Renaissance through the Scriptures had not revised the existing legislation. Servetus well said that 'Justinian's code was not the law of the primitive church, which never prosecuted for scriptural teachings, or questions relating thereto.' This appeal to the apostolic traditions showed that he was more logical than the other reformers." *Ibid.*, p. 565.

[3] Cf. Ferdinand Buisson, *op. cit.*, ch. xi.

Theodore of Beza, who had seen several of his coreligionists burned in France for their faith, likewise wrote in 1554, in Calvanistic Geneva: "What crime can be greater or more heinous than heresy, which sets at nought the word of God and all ecclesiastical discipline? Christian magistrates, do your duty to God, who has put the sword into your hands for the honor of his majesty; strike valiantly these monsters in the guise of men." Theodore of Beza considered the error of those who demanded freedom of conscience "worse than the tyranny of the Pope. It is better to have a tyrant, no matter how cruel he may be, than to let everyone do as he pleases." He maintained that the sword of the civil authority should punish not only heretics, but also those who wished heresy to go unpunished.[1] In brief, before the Renaissance there were very few who taught with Huss[2] that a heretic ought not to be abandoned to the secular arm to be put to death.[3]

[1] *De hæreticis a civili magistratu puniendis*, Geneva, 1554; translated into French by Colladon in 1559.

[2] In his treatise *De Ecclesia*. This was the eighteenth article of the heresies attributed to him.

[3] In general, the Protestant leaders of the day were glad of the execution of Servetus. Melancthon wrote to Bullinger: "I am astonished that some persons denounce the severity that was so justly used in that case." Among those who did denounce it was *Nicolas Zurkinden* of Berne. Cf. his letter in the *Œuvres complètes of Calvin*, vol. xv, p. 19. Sébastien Castellio published in March, 1554, his *Traité des hérétiques, a savoir s'il faut les persécuter*, the oldest and one of the most eloquent pamphlets against intolerance. Cf. F. Buisson, *op. cit.*, ch. xi. This is the pamphlet that Theodore of Beza tried to refute. Castellio then attacked Calvin directly in a new work,

Such severity, nay, such cruelty, shown to what we would call "a crime of opinion," is hard for men of our day to understand. "To comprehend it," says Lea, "we must picture to ourselves a stage of civilization in many respects wholly unlike our own. Passions were fiercer, convictions stronger, virtues and vices more exaggerated, than in our colder and self-contained time. The age, moreover, was a cruel one. . . . We have only to look upon the atrocities of the criminal law of the Middle Ages to see how pitiless men were in their dealings with one another. The wheel, the caldron of boiling oil, burning alive, tearing apart with wild horses, were the ordinary expedients by which the criminal jurist sought to deter men from crime by frightful examples which would make a profound impression on a not over-sensitive population." [1]

Contra libellum Calvini in quo ostendere conatur hæreticos jure gladii cœrcendos esse, which was not published until 1612, in Holland. We know that the Calvinists of our day utterly repudiate the theory of Calvin. On November 1, 1903, the city of Geneva erected a statue in the Place de Champel where Servetus had been burned, with this inscription: A Michel Servet. Fils respectueux et reconnaissants de Calvin, mais condamnant une erreur qui fut celle de son siècle, et fermement attaches à la liberté de conscience selon les vrais principes de la Réformation et de l'Evangile, nous avons élevé ce monument expiatoire, le 27 octobre 1903.

[1] Lea, *op. cit.*, vol. i, pp. 234, 235. He continues: "An Anglo-Saxon law punishes a female slave convicted of theft, by making eighty other female slaves each bring three pieces of wood and burn her to death, while each contributed a fine besides; and in mediæval England, burning was the customary penalty for attempts on the life of the feudal lord. In the customs of Arques, granted by the Abbey of Saint-Bertin in 1231, there is a provision that if a thief have a concubine who is his accomplice, she is to be buried alive. . . . Frederic II,

When we consider this rigorous civil criminal code, we need not wonder that heretics, who were considered the worst possible criminals, were sent to the stake.

This explains why intelligent men, animated by the purest zeal for good, proved so hard and unbending, and used without mercy the most cruel tortures, when they thought that the faith or the salvation of souls was at stake. "With such men," says Lea, — and he mentions among others Innocent III and St. Louis,[1] — "it was not

the most enlightened prince of his time, burned captive rebels to death in his presence, and is even said to have encased them in lead in order to roast them slowly. In 1261, St. Louis humanely abolished a custom of Touraine by which the theft of a loaf of bread or a pot of wine by a servant from his master was punished by the loss of a limb. In Frisia, arson committed at night was visited with burning alive; and by the old German law, the penalty of both murder and arson was breaking on the wheel. In France, women were customarily burned and buried alive for simple felonies, and Jews were hung by the feet between two savage dogs, while men were boiled to death for coining. In Milan, Italian ingenuity exhausted itself in devising deaths of lingering torture for criminals of all descriptions. The *Carolina*, or criminal code of Charles V, issued in 1530, is a hideous calatogue of blinding, mutilation, tearing with hot pincers, burning alive, and breaking on the wheel. In England, prisoners were boiled to death even as lately as 1542, . . . and the barbarous penalty for high treason was hanging, drawing and quartering."

[1] "Dominic and Francis, Bonaventure and Thomas Aquinas, Innocent III and St. Louis were types in their several ways, of which humanity in any age might well feel proud, and yet they were as unsparing of the heretic as Ezzelin da Romano was of his enemies." Lea, *op. cit.*, vol. i, p. 234. Lea seems very fond of making such exaggerated statements. We know that neither St. Francis nor Innocent III was ever present at any bloody executions, nor did they ever approve of them. The case of St. Dominic is not so clear. It would be difficult to prove that he ever put any heretics to death, but many trustworthy authors like the Dominicans Benôit (Histoire des Albigeois, 1691, vol. ii, p. 129) and Percin (*Monumenta Conventus Tholosani*, 1693, pp. 84–89) agree in giving him the title of "the first Inquisitor." Ber-

hope of gain, or lust of blood or pride of opinion, or wanton exercise of power, but sense of duty, and they but represented what was universal public opinion from the thirteenth to the seventeenth century." [1]

It was, therefore, the spirit of the times, the *Zeitgeist* as we would call it to-day, that was responsible for the rigorous measures formerly used by both Church and State in the suppression of heresy. The other reasons we have mentioned are only subsidiary. This is the one reason that satisfactorily explains both the theories and the facts.

But an explanation is something far different from a defence of an institution. To explain is to show the relation of cause to effect; to defend is to show that the effect corresponds to an ideal of justice. Even if we grant that the procedure of the Inquisition did correspond to a certain ideal of justice, that ideal is certainly not ours to-day. Let us go into this question more thoroughly.

It is obvious that we must strongly denounce all the abuses of the Inquisition that were due to the sins of individuals, no matter what their source. No one, for instance, would dream of defending Cauchon, the iniquitous

---

nard Gui declares that he exercised *Inquisitionis officium contra labem hæreticam auctoritate legati Apostolicæ sedis sibi commissum in partibus Tholosanis.* If he were not actually an Inquisitor, he at least was employed by Gregory IX to prepare the way for the Inquisition, which was definitely established in 1231.

[1] Lea, *op. cit.*, vol. i, p. 234.

judge of Joan of Arc, or other cruel Inquisitors who like him used their authority to punish unjustly suspects brought before their tribunal. From this standpoint, it is probable that many of the sentences of the Inquisition need revision.

But can we rightly consider this institution "a sublime spectacle of social perfection," and "a model of justice" ? [1]

To call the Inquisition a model of justice is a manifest exaggeration, as every fair student of its history must admit.

The Inquisitorial procedure was, in itself, inferior to the *accusatio*, in which the accuser assumed the burden of publicly proving his charges. That it was difficult to observe this method of procedure in heresy trials can readily be understood; for the *pœna talionis* awaiting the accuser who failed to substantiate his charges was calculated to cool the ardor of many Catholics, who otherwise would have been eager to prosecute heretics. But we must grant that the *accusatio* in criminal law allowed a greater chance for justice to be done than the *inquisitio*. Besides, if the ecclesiastical *inquisitio* had proceeded like the civil *inquisitio*, the possibility of judicial errors might have been far less. "In the *inquisitio* of the civil law, the secrecy for which the Inquisition has been justly criticised, did not exist; the suspect was cited, and a

[1] "Uno sublime spectacolo di perfezione sociale," says the author of an article in the *Civilta Cattolica*, 1853, vol. i, p. 595 seq., cited by Döllinger, *La papauté*, 1904, p. 384, n. 684.

copy of the *capitula* or *articuli* containing the charges was given to him. When questioned, he could either confess or deny these charges. The names of the witnesses who were to appear against him, and a copy of their testimony, were also supplied, so that he could carry on his defence either by objecting to the character of his accusers, or the tenor of their charges. Women, minors aged fourteen, serfs, enemies of the prisoner, criminals, excommunicates, heretics, and those branded with infamy were not allowed to testify. All testimony was received in writing. The prisoner and his lawyers then appeared before the judge to rebut the evidence and the charges." [1]

In the ecclesiastical procedure, on the contrary, the names of the witnesses were withheld, save in very exceptional cases; any one could testify, even if he were a heretic; the prisoner had the right to reject all whom he considered his mortal enemies, but even then he had to guess at their names in order to invalidate their testimony; he was not allowed a lawyer, but had to defend himself in secret. Only the most prejudiced minds can consider such a procedure the ideal of justice. On the contrary it is unjust in every detail wherein it differs from the *inquisitio* of the civil law.

Certain reasons may be adduced to explain the attitude of the Popes, who wished to make the procedure of the Inquisition as secret and as comprehensive as possible.

---

[1] Tanon, *op. cit.*, pp. 287, 288.

They were well aware of the danger that witnesses would incur, if their names were indiscreetly revealed. They knew that the publicity of the pleadings would certainly hinder the efficiency of heresy trials. But such considerations do not change the character of the institution itself; the Inquisition in leaving too great a margin to the arbitrary conduct of individual judges, at once fell below the standard of strict justice.

All that can and ought to be said in the defence and to the honor of the Roman pontiffs is that they endeavored to remedy the abuses of the Inquisition. With this in view, Innocent IV and Alexander IV obliged the Inquisitors to consult a number of *boni viri* and *periti;* [1] Clement V forbade them to render any grave decision without first consulting the bishops, the natural judges of the faith; [2] and Boniface VIII recommended them to reveal the names of the witnesses to the prisoners, if they thought that this revelation would not be prejudicial to any one. [3] In a word, they wished the laws of justice to be scrupulously observed, and at times mitigated. [4] But

[1] Cf. *supra*, p. 139.

[2] Clementinæ, *De hæreticis*, Decretal *Multorum Querela*, cap. i, sect. 1.

[3] "Cessante vero periculo supradicto, accusatorum et testium nomina (prout in aliis fit judiciis) publicentur. Cæterum in his omnibus præcipimus, tam episcopos quam inquisitores puram et providam intentionem habere, ne ad accusatorum vel testium nomina supprimenda, ubi est securitas, periculum esse dicant." Sexto, *De hæreticis*, cap. xx; cf. Tanon, *op. cit.*, p. 391.

[4] Döllinger is very unjust when he says: "From 1200 to 1500 there is a long uninterrupted series of papal decrees on the Inquisition; these decrees

examined in detail, these laws were far from being perfect.

. . . .

Antecedent imprisonment and torture, which played so important a part in the procedure of the Inquisition, were undoubtedly very barbarous methods of judicial prosecution. Antecedent imprisonment may be justified in certain cases; but the manner in which the Inquisitors conceived it was far from just. No one would dare defend to-day the punishment known as the *carcer durus,* whereby the Inquisitors tried to extort confessions from their prisoners.[1] They rendered it, moreover, all the more odious by arbitrarily prolonging its horrors and its cruelty.[2]

It is harder still to reconcile the use of torture with any idea of justice. If the Inquisitors had stopped at flogging, which according to St. Augustine was administered at home, in school, and even in the episcopal tribunals of the early ages, and is mentioned by the Council of Agde, in 506 and the Benedictine rule,[3] no one

---

increase continually in severity and cruelty." *La Papauté,* p. 102. Tanon (*op. cit.,* p. 138) writes more impartially: "Clement V, instead of increasing the powers of the Holy Office, tried rather to suppress its abuses."

[1] We say nothing here of the ruses adopted to obtain the arrest of heretics, or to discover their secrets. Cf. Tanon, *op. cit,* pp. 356–358; Vidal, *Revue des Questions Historiques,* January, 1906, pp. 102–105.

[2] "Non est aliqualiter relaxandus, sed detinendus per annos plurimos ut vexatio det intellectum." Bernard Gui, *Practica Inquisitionis,* 5 pars, formula 13, p. 302. Cf. Lea, *op. cit.,* vol. i, pp. 419, 420, Tanon, *op. cit.,* pp. 361, 362.

[3] Cf. *supra,* p. 32, n. 3.

would have been greatly scandalized. We might perhaps have considered this domestic and paternal custom a little severe, but perfectly consistent with the ideas men then had of goodness.[1] But the rack, the *strappado*, and the stake were peculiarly inhuman inventions.[2] When the pagans used them against the Christians of the first centuries, all agreed in stigmatizing them as the extreme of barbarism, or as inventions of the devil. Their character did not change when the Inquisition began to use them against heretics. To our shame we are forced to admit that, notwithstanding Innocent IV's appeal for moderation,[3] the brutality of the ecclesiastical tribunals was often on a par with the tribunals of the pagan persecutors. Pope Nicolas I thus denounced the use of torture as a means of judical inquiry: "Such proceedings," he says, "are contrary to the law of God and of man, for a confession ought to be spontaneous, not forced; it ought to be free and not the result of violence. A prisoner may endure all the torments you inflict upon him without confessing anything. Is not that a disgrace to the judge, and an evident proof of his inhumanity! If, on the contrary, a prisoner, under stress of torture, acknowledges

---

[1] It must be noted that flogging could be and was sometimes administered in a cruel and barbarous manner, so that it became a frightful punishment. Cf. Tanon, *op. cit.*, p. 372.

[2] This was the view of St. Augustine, *Ep.* cxxxiii, 2.

[3] "Citra membri diminutionem et mortis periculum." Bull *Ad extirpanda*, in Eymeric, *Directorium inquisitorum*, Appendix, p. 8.

himself guilty of a crime he never committed, is not the one who forced him to lie, guilty of a heinous crime?" [1]

.   .   .   .

The penalties which the tribunals of the Inquisition inflicted upon heretics are harder to judge. Let us observe first of all that the majority of the heretics abandoned to the secular arm merited the most severe punishment for their crimes. It would surely have been unjust for criminals against the common law to escape punishment under cover of their religious belief. Crimes committed in the name of religion are always crimes, and the man who has his property stolen or is assaulted cares little whether he has to deal with a religious fanatic or an ordinary criminal. In such instances, the State is not defending a particular dogmatic teaching, but her own most vital interests. Heretics, therefore, who were criminals against the civil law were justly punished. An antisocial sect like the Cathari, which shrouded itself in mystery and perverted the people so generally, by the very fact of its existence and propaganda called for the vengeance of society and the sword of the State.

"However much," says Lea, "we may deprecate the means used for its suppression, and commiserate those who suffered for conscience' sake, we cannot but admit that the cause of orthodoxy was in this case the cause

[1] *Responsa ad consulta Bulgarorum*, cap. lxxxvi; Labbe, *Concilia*, vol. viii, col. 544. Cf. *supra*, p. 148, n. 3.

of progress and civilization. Had Catharism become dominant, or even had it been allowed to exist on equal terms, its influence could not have failed to prove disastrous. Its asceticism with regard to commerce between the sexes, if strictly enforced, could only have led to the extinction of the race. . . . Its condemnation of the visible universe, and of matter in general as the work of Satan rendered sinful all striving after material improvement, and the conscientious belief in such a creed could only lead man back, in time, to his original condition of savagism. It was not only a revolt against the Church, but a renunciation of man's domination over nature." [1] Its growth had to be arrested at any price. Society, in prosecuting it without mercy, was only defending herself against the working of an essentially destructive force. It was a struggle for existence.

We must, therefore, deduct from the number of those who are commonly styled the victims of ecclesiastical intolerance, the majority of the heretics executed by the State; for nearly all that were imprisoned or sent to the stake, especially in northern Italy and southern France, were Cathari.[2]

This important observation has so impressed certain

[1] Lea, *op. cit.*, vol. i, p. 106.

[2] Jean Guiraud has proved that the Waldenses, Fraticelli, Hussites, Lollards, etc., attacked society, which acted in self-defence when she put them to death. *La répression de l'hérésie au moyen âge*, in the *Questions d'histoire et d'archéologie Chrétienne*, p. 24 and seq.

historians, that they have been led to think the Inquisition dealt only with criminals of this sort. "History," says one of them, "has preserved the record of the
outrages committed by the heretics of Bulgaria, the Gnostics, and the Manicheans; the death sentence was inflicted
only upon criminals who confessed their murders, rob-
beries, and acts of violence. The Albigenses were treated
with kindness. The Catholic Church deplores all acts
of vengeance, however strong the provocation given by
these factious mobs." [1]

Such a defence of the Inquisition is not borne out by
the facts. It is true, of course, that in the Middle Ages
there was hardly a heresy which had not some connection
with an anti-social sect. For this reason any one who
denied a dogma of the faith was at once suspected,
rightly or wrongly, of being an anarchist. But as a
matter of fact, the Inquisition did not condemn merely
those heresies which caused social upheaval, but all
heresies as such: "We decree," says Frederic II, "that
the crime of heresy, no matter what the name of the
sect, be classed as a public crime . . . and that every
one who denies the Catholic faith, even in one article,
shall be liable to the law: *si inventi fuerint a fide catholica
saltem in articulo deviare*.[2] " This was also the view of

---

[1] Rodrigo, *Historia verdadera de la Inquisicion*, Madrid, 1876, vol. i,
pp. 176, 177.
[2] Constitution *Inconsutilem tunicam*. Cf. *supra*, p. 114, n. 1.

the theologians and the canonists. St. Thomas Aquinas, for instance, who speaks for the whole *schola,* did not make any distinction between the Catharan heresy and any other purely speculative heresy; he put them all on one level; every obdurate or relapsed heretic deserved death.[1] The Inquisitors were so fully persuaded of this truth that they prosecuted heretics whose heresy was not discovered until ten or twenty years after their death, when surely they were no longer able to cause any injury to society.[2]

We need not wonder at these views and practices, for

[1] Summa IIa, IIae, q. x, art. 8; q. xi, art. 3 and 4. Mgr. Douais is of a different opinion. Recently he wrote: "A heretic is one who obstinately persists in his error. A heretic was not liable to the Inquisition for holding or expressing opinions which were more or less contrary to the teaching of the Church. He was prosecuted only when he obstinately persisted in holding doctrines, which were utterly subversive not only of dogma but of church unity. The *Insabbatati* (Waldenses) held views of this character, etc. . . . The heretic also was one who believed such errors (Waldensian) and who — be it understood — manifested them externally." Douais, *Saint Raymond de Pennafort et les hérétiques. Directoire a l'usage des inquisiteurs aragonais* (1242), in *Le Moyen Age,* vol. iii (1899), p. 306. But unfortunately the text quoted by Mgr. Douais makes no such distinction: "Et videtur quod hæretici sint qui in suo errore perdurant sicut Insabbatati," etc. "Credentes vero dictis erroribus (errors of the Insabbatati) similiter hæretici sunt dicendi." *Ibid.* In making special mention of the Waldenses, the *Directorium* by no means excluded other heretics. The Waldenses are merely cited as an example. St. Raymond of Pennafort indeed held that "whoever obstinately persists in his error is a heretic." In fact, the commentary of Mgr. Douais, which we have given above, is a modern view entirely, which we have never seen expressed by the writers of the Middle Ages. Cf. *supra,* p. 160 and notes.

[2] Cf. Tanon, *op. cit.,* pp. 407–412; Lea, *op. cit.,* p. 448; Molinier, *L'Inquisition dans le Midi de la France au XIIIe et au XIVe siècle,* pp. 358–367.

they were fully in accord with the notion of justice current at the time.   The rulers in Church and State felt it their duty not only to defend the social order, but to safeguard the interests of God in the world.   They deemed themselves in all sincerity the representatives of divine authority here below.   God's interests were their interests; it was their duty, therefore, to punish all crimes against his law.   Heresy, therefore, a purely theological crime, became amenable to their tribunal.   In punishing it, they believed that they were merely fulfilling one of the duties of their office.[1]   We have now to examine and judge the penalties inflicted upon heresy as such.

The first in order of importance was the death penalty of the stake, inflicted upon all obdurate and relapsed heretics.

Relapsed heretics, when repentant, did not at first incur the death penalty.   Imprisonment was considered an adequate punishment,[2] for it gave them a chance to

[1] This was the view held as late as the seventeenth century. After the revocation of the edict of Nantes, Jurieu, who had protested most strongly against this measure, called upon the princes to use their power for *the true religion*, and the pure doctrine. He writes: "Princes and magistrates are the anointed of God, and his lieutenants on earth. . . . But they are strange lieutenants indeed, if as magistrates they feel no special obligation to God; how then can we imagine a Christian magistrate, the lieutenant of God, fulfilling all the duties of his state, if he does not feel called upon to prevent rebellion against God, that the people go not after another God, or serve the true God in a way He does not will."   Cf. Baudrillart, *L' Église Catholique la Renaissance, le Protestantisme*, 1904, pp. 234, 235.

[2] Cf. Lea, *op. cit.*, vol. i, pp. 543–547.

expiate their fault. The death penalty inflicted later on placed the judges in a false position. On the one hand, by granting absolution and giving communion to the prisoner, they professed to believe in the sincerity of his repentance and conversion, and yet by sending him to the stake for fear of a relapse, they acted contrary to their convictions. To condemn a man to death who was considered worthy of receiving the Holy Eucharist, on the plea that he might one day commit the sin of heresy again, appears to us a crying injustice.

But should even unrepentant heretics be put to death? No, taught St. Augustine, and most of the early Fathers, who invoked in favor of the guilty ones the higher law of "charity and Christian gentleness." [1] Their doctrine certainly accorded perfectly with our Savior's teaching, in the parable of the cockle and the good grain. As Wazo, Bishop of Liège said: "May not those who are to-day cockle become wheat to-morrow?" [2] But in decreeing the death of these sinners, the Inquisitors at once did away with the possibility of their conversion. Certainly this was not in accordance with Christian charity. Such severity can only be defended by the authority of the old law, whose severity, according to the early Fathers, had been abolished by the law of Christ.[3]

[1] Cf. *supra*, pp. 3, 4, 17, 28.

[2] *Vita Vasonis*, cap. xxv, in Migne, P. L., vol. cxlii, col. 753.

[3] St. Optatus (*De Schismate Donatistarum*, lib. iii, cap. vi and vii) was one of the first of the Fathers to quote the Old Testament as his authority for

Advocates of the death penalty, like Frederic II and St. Thomas, tried to defend their view by arguments from reason. Criminals guilty of treason, and counterfeiters are condemned to death. Therefore, heretics who are traitors and falsifiers merit the same penalty. But a comparison of this kind is not necessarily a valid argument. The criminals in question were a grave menace to the social order. But we cannot say as much for each and every heresy in itself. It was unjust to place a crime against society and a sin against God on an equal footing. Such reasoning would prove that all sins were crimes of treason against God, and therefore merited death.[1] Is not a sacrilegious communion the worst possible insult to the divine majesty? Must we argue, therefore, that every unworthy communicant, if unrepentant, must be sent to the stake?

It is evident, therefore, that neither reason, Christian tradition, nor the New Testament call for the infliction of the death penalty upon heretics. The interpretation of

the infliction of the death penalty upon heretics. But in this he was not followed either by his contemporaries or his immediate successors. Before him, Origen and St. Cyprian had protested against this appeal to the Mosaic law. Cf. *Supra*, pp. 3 and 4.

[1] Mgr. Bonomelli, Bishop of Cremona, writes: "In the Middle Ages, they reasoned thus: If rebellion against the prince deserves death, *a fortiori* does rebellion against God. Singular logic! It is not very hard to put one's finger upon the utter absurdity of such reasoning. For every sinner is a rebel against God's law. It follows then that we ought to condemn all men to death, beginning with the kings and the legislators"; quoted by Morlais in the *Revue du clergé français*, August 1, 1905, p. 457. Cf. *supra*, p. 5, n. 1.

St. John xv. 6: *Si quis in me non manserit, in ignem mittent et ardet,* made by the mediæval canonists,[1] is not worth discussing. It was an abuse of the accommodated sense which bordered on the ridiculous, although its consequences were terrible.

.   .   .   .

Modern apologists have clearly recognized this. For that reason they have tried their best to show that the execution of heretics was solely the work of the civil power, and that the Church was in no way responsible.

"When we argue about the Inquisition," says Joseph de Maistre, "let us separate and distinguish very carefully the rôle of the Church and the rôle of the State. All that is terrible and cruel about this tribunal, especially its death penalty, is due to the State; that was its business, and it alone must be held to an accounting. All the clemency, on the contrary, which plays so large a part in the tribunal of the Inquisition must be ascribed to the Church, which interfered in its punishments only to suppress and mitigate them."[2] "The Church," says another grave historian, "took no part in the corporal punishment of heretics. Those executed were simply punished for their crimes, and were condemned by judges acting under the royal seal."[3] "This," says Lea, "is a

[1] Cf. *supra*, p. 177.

[2] *Lettres à un gentilhomme russe sur l'Inquisition espagnole,* ed. 1864, pp. 17, 18, 28, 34.

[3] Rodrigo, *Historia verdadera de la Inquisicion,* 1876, vol. i, p. 176.

typical instance in which history is written to order.[1]
. . . It is altogether a modern perversion of history to
assume, as apologists do, that the request for mercy was
sincere, and that the secular magistrate and not the Inquisition was responsible for the death of the heretic.
We can imagine the smile of amused surprise with which
Gregory IX and Gregory XI would have listened to the
dialectics with which Count Joseph de Maistre proves
that it is an error to suppose, and much more to assert,
that a Catholic priest can in any manner be instrumental
in compassing the death of a fellow creature." [2]

The real share of the Inquisition in a condemnation involving the death penalty is indeed a very difficult question to determine. According to the letter of the papal
and imperial Constitutions of 1231 and 1232, the civil
and not the ecclesiastical tribunals assumed all responsibility for the death sentence;[3] the Inquisition merely
decided upon the question of doctrine, leaving the
rest to the secular Court. It is this legislation that
the above named apologists have in mind, and the
text of these laws is on their side.

[1] Lea, *op. cit.*, vol. i, p. 540.

[2] *Ibid.*, pp. 227, 228.

[3] "Dampnati vero per Ecclesiam, *seculari judicio relinquantur*, animadversione debita puniendi." Decretals, cap. xv, *De hæreticis*, lib. v, tit. vii.
"Hæretici . . . , ubicumque per imperium dampnati ab Ecclesia fuerint et
seculari judicio assignati," etc., *Mon. Germ.*, *Leges*, sect. iv, vol. ii, p. 196.
The *Processus Inquisitionis*, written between 1244 and 1254, also says: "Per
sententiam *definitivam hæreticum judicamus*, *relinquentes ex nunc judicio
seculari*." Cf. Appendix A.

17

But when we consider how these laws were carried out in practice, we must admit that the Church did have some share in the death sentence. We have already seen that the Church excommunicated those princes who refused to burn the heretics which the Inquisition handed over to them.[1] The princes were not really judges in this case; the right to consider questions of heresy was formally denied them.[2] It was their duty simply to register the decree of the Church, and to enforce it according to the civil law.[3] In every execution, therefore, a twofold authority came into play: the civil power which carried out its own laws, and the spiritual power which forced the State to carry them out. That is why Peter Cantor declared that the Cathari ought not to be put to death after an ecclesiastical trial, lest the church be compromised: "*Illud ab eo fit, cujus auctoritate fit,*" he said, to justify his recommendation.[4]

---

[1] Cf. *supra* p. 147 and note.

[2] Boniface VIII declares expressly that the judgment of heretics is purely ecclesiastical: "Prohibemus quoque districtius potestatibus, dominis temporalibus et rectoribus eorumdemque officialibus supradictis ne ipsi de hoc crimine (cum mere sit ecclesiasticum) quoquo modo cognoscant et judicent." The sentence of the Inquisitors put an end to the trial: *donec eorum nogotium per Ecclesiæ judicium terminetur.* Cf. Sexto, v. ii, cap. xi. and xviii, *De hæreticis*, in Eymeric, *Directorum*, p. 110. Cf. Lea, *op. cit.*, vol. i, pp. 539, 540.

[3] This is what Boniface expressly says; *loc cit.*

[4] "Sed nec convicti ab hujusmodi judicio (the ordeals were in question) tradendi essent morti, quia hoc judicium quodammodo est ecclesiasticum, quod non exercetur sine præsentia sacerdotis, per quod, cum traditur morti, a sacerdote traditur; quia illud ab eo fit cujus auctoritate fit." *Verbum abbreviatum*, cap. lxxviii, P. L., vol. ccv, col. 231.

It is therefore erroneous to pretend that the Church had absolutely no part in the condemnation of heretics to death. It is true that this participation of hers was not direct and immediate; but even though indirect, it was none the less real and efficacious.[1]

The judges of the Inquisition realized this, and did their best to free themselves of this responsibility which weighed rather heavily upon them. Some maintained that in compelling the civil authority to enforce the existing laws, they were not going outside their spiritual office, but were merely deciding a case of conscience. But this theory was unsatisfactory. To reassure their consciences, they tried another expedient. In abandoning heretics to the secular arm, they besought the state officials to act with moderation, and avoid "all bloodshed and all danger of death."[2] This was unfortunately an empty formula which deceived no one. It was intended to safeguard the principle which the Church had taken for her motto: *Ecclesia abhorret a sanguine*. In strongly asserting this traditional law, the Inquisitors imagined that they thereby freed themselves from all responsibility, and

[1] In Spain, the manner in which the Inquisition abandoned heretics to the secular arm denoted a real participation of the State in the execution of heretics. The evening before the execution the Inquisitors brought the King a small fagot tied with ribbons. The King at once requested "that this fagot be the first thrown upon the fire in his name." Cf. Baudrillart, *A propos de l'Inquisition*, in the *Revue pratique d'Apologétique*, July 15, 1906, p. 354, note.

[2] Cf. *supra*, p. 178.

kept from imbruing their hands in bloodshed. We must take this for what it is worth. It has been styled "cunning" and "hypocrisy";[1] let us call it simply a legal fiction.[2]

•   •   •   •   •   •   •   •   •   •

[1] Lea, *op. cit.*, vol. i, p. 224.

[2] The following text, taken from a *Liber Penitentialis* of the thirteenth century, shows what efforts the canonists made to free the Church from all responsibility in condemning heretics to death. We quote it from Döllinger, *Beiträge*, vol. 2, pp. 621, 622. "Cum secundum prædicta constat ecclesiam non debere sanguinem effundere neque manu neque lingua, videtur esse reprobabile quod cum hæretici et Publicani convincuntur in foro ecclesiastico de infidelitate sua, statim traduntur curiæ, id est seculari potestati ad comburendum vel occidendum, et quod pejus est non possunt evadere quin occidantur, vel judicium subeant ferri candentis. Si enim veros se dicunt esse Christianos, non creditur eis, nisi per judicium ferri candentis probent: si vero dixerint se fuisse hæreticos, sed veros modo pœnitentes, non creditur eis nisi simili modo hoc probent, cum tamen non sit tutum viro ecclesiastico hoc modo tentare Deum. Si autem in tali judicio deprehensi fuerint et se esse hæreticos et pœnitere nolle confessi, statim occiduntur. Videtur tamen eadem observatio de eis esse consideranda quæ observatur de Judæis, de quibus scriptum est: Ne occidas eos, ne quando obliviscantur. Si enim volunt esse sub jugo nostræ servitutis in pace neque fidem nostram impugnare neque nos, sustinendi sunt inter nos et deputandi ad sordida officia, ne se possint extollere super Christianos. Verumtamen ideo præcipue sustinentur Judæi, quia capsarii nostri sunt, et portant testimonium legis contra se pro nobis. A multis etiam bonis viris audivimus quod si hæretici vel excommunicati contra Christianos velint insurgere vel impugnare fidem publicis persuasionibus et prædicationibus, non est peccatum eos occidere, sed si quieti velint esse et pacifici, non sunt occidendi, quod videtur posse haberi ex canone ita dicente: Excommunicatorum interfectoribus, prout in ordine Rom. ecclesiæ didicisti secundum intentionem modum congruum satisfactionis injunge. Non enim eos homicidas arbitramur, quos, adversus excommunicatos catholicæ zelo matris ecclesiæ ardentes, aliquos eorum trucidasse contigerit (cf. Gratiani *Decretum*, Causa 23, q. 5, cap. 47). Nec credimus quod hæretici super infidelitate sua in foro ecclesiastico condemnati curiæ sunt tradendi, ita quod a sacerdotibus dicatur judicibus: Occidite istos hæreticos: sed sustinet ecclesia ut statim rapiantur a viris sæcularibus ad supplicium, nec aliquod eis præstat patrocinium sicut Judæis, et sicut etiam præstat clericis degradatis."

The penalty of life imprisonment and the penalty of confiscation inflicted upon so many heretics, was like the death penalty imposed only by the secular arm. We must add to this banishment, which was inscribed in the imperial legislation, and reappeared in the criminal codes of Lucius III and Innocent III. These several penalties were by their nature vindicative. For this reason they were particularly odious, and have been the occasion of bitter accusations against the Church.

· With the exception of imprisonment, which we will speak of later on, these penalties originated with the State.[1] It is important, therefore, to know what crimes they punished. As a general rule it must be admitted that they were only inflicted upon those heretics who seriously disturbed the social order. If the death penalty could be justly meted out to such rioters, with still greater reason could the lesser penalties be inflicted.

The penalty of confiscation was especially cruel, inasmuch as it affected the posterity of the condemned heretics. According to the old Roman law, the property

---

[1] "Gratian, in qu. 7, Causa 23 of the *Decretum*, proves that the property of heretics should be confiscated on the authority of St. Augustine, who himself founds it on the Roman law; his interpreters unanimously refer it to this law, as its true origin," etc. Tanon, *op. cit.*, p. 524. "His auctoritatibus liquido monstratur, quod ea quæ ab hæreticis male possidentur, a catholicis juste auferuntur." Gratian, *Decretum*, 4, causa xxiii, quæst. vii, in fine. "Imperatorum siquidem jure statutum est, ut quicumque a catholica unitate inventus fuerit deviare, suarum rerum debeat omnimodam præscriptionem perferre." *Summa Rolandi*, ed. Thaner, Inspruck, 1874, p. 96. Roland became Pope under the name of Alexander II.

of heretics could be inherited by their orthodox sons, and even by their agnates and cognates.[1] The laws of the Middle Ages declared confiscation absolute; on the plea that heresy should be classed with treason, orthodox children could not inherit the property of their heretical father.[2] There was but one exception to this law. Frederic II and Innocent IV both decreed that children could inherit their father's property, if they denounced him for heresy.[3] It is needless to insist upon the odious character of such a law. We cannot understand to-day how Gregory IX could rejoice on learning that fathers did not scruple to denounce their children, children their parents, a wife her husband or a mother her children.[4]

Granting that banishment and confiscation were just penalties for heretics who were also State criminals, was it right for the church to employ this penal system for the suppression of heresy alone?

[1] 4 and 19, cap. *De hæreticis*, iv, 5, *Manichæos* and *Cognovimus*.

[2] Decretal *Vergentis* of Innocent III. Decretals, cap. x, *De hæreticis* lib. v, tit. vii.

[3] Law of Frederic: *Commissis nobis cælitus* of March, 1232, incorporated into the Decretal of Innocent IV, October 31, 1243: "Nec quidem a misericordiæ finibus duximus excludendum, ut, si qui paternæ hæresis non sequaces, latentam patrum perfidiam revelaverint, quacumque reatus illorum animadversione plectantur, prædictæ punitioni non subjaceat innocentia filiorum." *Mon. Germ., Leges*, vol. ii, sect. iv, p. 197; Ripoll, *Bullarium ordinis Prædicat.*, vol. i, p. 126.

[4] "Ita quod pater filio vel uxori, filius ipse patri, uxor propriis filiis aut marito vel consortibus ejusdem criminis, in hac parte sibi aliquatenus non parcebant." Bull *Gaudemus*, of April 12, 1233, in Ripoll, vol. i, p. 56.

It is certain that the early Christians would have strongly denounced such laws as too much like the pagan laws under which they were persecuted. St. Hilary voiced their mind when he said: "The Church threatens exile and imprisonment; she in whom men formerly believed while in exile and prison, now wishes to make men believe her by force."[1] St. Augustine was of the same mind. He thus addressed the Manicheans, the most hated sect of his time: "Let those who have never known the troubles of a mind in search for the truth, proceed against you with rigor. It is impossible for me to do so, for I for years was cruelly tossed about by your false doctrines, which I advocated and defended to the best of my ability. I ought to bear with you now, as men bore with me, when I blindly accepted your doctrines."[2] Wazo, Bishop of Liège, wrote in a similar strain in the eleventh century.[3]

But continued St. Augustine, retracting his first theory — and nearly all the Middle Ages agreed with him, — "these severe penalties are lawful and good when they serve to convert heretics by inspiring them with a salutary fear."[4] The end here justifies the means.

---

[1] *Liber contra Auxentium*, cap. iv; cf. *supra*, p. 6.

[2] *Contra epistolam Manichæi, quam vocant Fundamenti*, n. 2 and 3, *supra*, p. 12.

[3] *Vita Vasonis*, cap. xxv and xxvi, Migne, P. L., vol. cxlii, col. 752, 753; cf. *supra*, p. 51.

[4] Cf. *supra*, p. 21, n. 1.

Such reasoning was calculated to lead men to great extremes, and was responsible for the cruel teaching of the theologians of the school, who were more logically consistent than the Bishop of Hippo. They endeavored to terrorize heretics by the specter of the stake. St. Augustine, bold as he was, shrank from such barbarity. But if, on his own admission, the logical consequences of the principle he laid down were to be rejected, did not this prove the principle itself false?

If we consider merely the immediate results obtained by the use of brute force, we may indeed admit that it benefited the Church by bringing back some of her erring children. But at the same time these cruel measures turned away from Catholicism in the course of ages many sensitive souls, who failed to recognize Christ's Church in a society which practiced such cruelty in union with the State. According, therefore, to St. Augustine's own argument, his theory has been proved false by its fatal consequences.

We must, therefore, return to the first theory of St. Augustine, and be content to win heretics back to the true faith by purely moral constraint. The penalties, decreed or consented to by the Church, ought to be medicinal in character, viz., pilgrimages, flogging, wearing the crosses, and the like. Imprisonment may even be included in the list, for temporary imprisonment has a well-defined expiatory character. In fact that is why in the beginning the monasteries made it the punishment for heresy.[1]   If later on the Church frequently inflicted the penalty of life imprisonment, she did so because, by a legal fiction, she attributed to it a purely penitential character.[2]   Anyone of these punishments, therefore, may be considered lawful, provided it is not arbitrarily inflicted.   This theory does not permit the Church to abandon impenitent heretics to the secular arm.   It grants her only the right of excommunication, according to the penitential discipline and the primitive canon law of the days of Tertullian, Cyprian, Origen, Lactantius, and Hilary.[3]

.   .   .   .

But is this return to antiquity conformable to the spirit of the Church?   Can it be reconciled in particular with one of the condemned propositions of the Syllabus: *Ecclesia vis inferendæ potestatem non habet?*[4]   The *Church has no right to use force.*

Without discussing this proposition at length, let us

[1] Cf. *supra*, pp. 32, 33.

[2] "The penal code of the Inquisition . . . is worth studying as the concept of a peculiar system which tried to reconcile the severest methods of suppression with the principles of ecclesiastical penalty and discipline, by fictitiously attributing a purely penitential character to all penalties except death, even to life imprisonment," etc.   Tanon, *op. cit.*, p. iii.

[3] "Nunc autem, quia circumcisio spiritalis esse apud fideles servos Dei cœpit," says St. Cyprian, "*spiritali gladio superbi et contumaces necantur dum de Ecclesia ejiciuntur.*"   Cypriani, *Ep.* lxii, ad Pomponium, no 4, P. L., vol. iii, col. 371.   Cf. *supra*, pp. 2–7.

[4] Proposit, xxiv.

first state that authorities are not agreed on its precise meaning. Every Catholic will admit that the Church has a coercive power, in both the external and the internal forum. But the question under dispute — and this the *Syllabus* does not touch — is whether the coercive power comprises merely spiritual penalties, or temporal and corporal penalties as well.[1] The editor of the Syllabus did not decide this question; he merely referred us to the letter *Ad apostolicæ Sedis* of August 22, 1851. But this letter is not at all explicit; it merely condemns those who pretend "to deprive the Church of the external jurisdiction and coercive power, which was given her to win back sinners to the ways of righteousness." We would like to find more light on this question elsewhere. But the theologians who at the Vatican Council prepared canons 10 and 12 of the schema *De Ecclesia* on this very point of doctrine did not remove the ambiguity. They explicitly affirmed that the Church had the right to exercise over her erring children "constraint by an external judgment and salutary penalties," but they said nothing about the nature of these penalties.[2] Was not such

[1] Gayraud, Discourse delivered in the Chamber of Deputies, January 28, 1901.

[2] "Cum vero Ecclesiæ potestates alia sit et dicatur ordinis, alia jurisdictionis: de hac altera speciatim docemus, eam non esse solum fori interni et sacramentalis, sed etiam fori externi ac publici, absolutam atque omnino plenam, nimirum legiferam, judiciariam, coercitivam. Potestatis autem hujusmodi subjectum sunt Pastores et Doctores a Christo dati, qui eam libere et a quavis sæculari dominatione independenter exercent; adeoque cum omni imperio regunt Ecclesiam Dei tum necessaris et conscientiam

silence significant? It authorized, one may safely say, the opinion of those who limited the coercive power of the Church to merely moral constraint. Cardinal Soglia, in a work approved by Gregory XVI and Pius IX, declared that this opinion was "more in harmony with the gentleness of the Church."[1] It also has in its favor Popes Nicholas I[2] and Celestine III,[3] who claimed for the Church of which they were the head the right to use only the spiritual sword. Without enumerating all the modern authors who hold this view, we will quote a work which has just appeared with the *imprimatur* of Father Lepidi, the Master of the Sacred Palace, in which we find the two following theses proved: 1. "Constraint, in the sense of employing violence to enforce ecclesiastical

quoque obligantibus legibus, tum decretoriis judiciis, tum denique *salutaribus pœnis* in sontes etiam invitos, nec solum in iis quæ fidem et mores, cultum et sanctificationem, sed etiam in iis quæ externam Ecclesiæ disciplinam et administrationem respiciunt." Can. 10. "Si quis dixerit, a Christo Domino et Salvatore nostro Ecclesiæ suæ collatam tantum fuisse potestatem dirigendi per consilia et suasiones, non vero jubendi per leges, ac devios contumacesque *exteriori judicio ac salubribus pœnis* coercendi atque cogendi," etc. Can. 12.

[1] "Sunt enim qui docent potestatem coercitivam divinitus Ecclesiæ collatam pænis tantummodo spiritualibus contineri . . . Sententia (hæc) prior magis Ecclesiæ mansuetudini consentanea videtur." *Institutiones juris publici ecclesiastici*, 5 ed., Paris, vol. i, pp. 169, 170.

[2] "Ecclesia gladium non habet nisi spiritualem." *Nicolai, Ep.* ad Albinum archiepiscop., in the *Decretum*, Causa xxxiii, quæst. ii, cap. *Inter hæc.* Note, however, that the Pope was not treating this particular question *ex professo*.

[3] Celestine, according to the criminal code of his day, declared that a guilty cleric, once excommunicated and anathematized, ought to be abandoned to the secular arm, *cum Ecclesia non habeat ultra quid faciat.* Decretals, cap. x, *De judiciis*, lib. ii, tit. i. This was the common teaching. Cf. *supra*, p. 136, n. 3.

laws, originated with the State." 2. "The constraint of ecclesiastical laws is by divine right exclusively moral constraint." [1]

Indeed, to maintain that the Church should use material force, is at once to make her subject to the State; for we can hardly picture her with her own police and gendarmes, ready to punish her rebellious children. Every Catholic believes that the Church is an independent society, fully able to carry out her divine mission without the aid of the secular arm. Whether govern-

[1] "La coazione, nel senso di intervento della forza materiale per la esecuzione di leggi ecclesiastiche, ha origine da poteri umani." "La coazione delle leggi ecclesiastiche per dirritto divino è solamente coazione morale." Salvatore di Bartolo. *Nuova espozitione dei criteri teologici,* Roma, 1904, pp. 303 and 314. The first edition of this work was put upon the Index. The second edition, revised and corrected, and published with the approbation of Father Lepidi, has all the more weight and authority. Salvatore di Bartolo quoted a number of authors in favor of his thesis, among them the *Abbé Bautain.* "Catholic discipline," he said, "is eminently liberal, because it is altogether spiritual, and altogether moral; it uses only those methods which are conformable to its nature, and therefore the more conformable to the spirit of true liberty, which acts upon human wills through the intellect, and the heart, *and never by external violence or constraint.* . . . The Church directs her children *by laws which she imposes without constraint,* and which she asks the faithful conscientiously to obey. Everyone obeys them, if he wills and as he wills, according to his conscience. *She forces no one by external means, and if others use force in her name, she denounces them.* The cruelty of the secular arm is not due to the Church, and if at times the temporal sword has been associated with the spiritual sword, under the pretext of winning back souls more readily, and of extending more vigorously and more rapidly the Kingdom of God, the Church which is absolutely opposed to brute force, and which wishes to gain souls, cannot be held responsible, even though the imprudence of her ministers was the cause of this excess." *La Religion et la Liberté,* Conference 6, Paris, 1865. From the historical standpoint, the author's thesis is inaccurate and naïve. But his view of the Church's coercive power is clearly stated.

ments are favorable or hostile to her, she must pursue her course and carry on her work of salvation under them all.

.   .   .   .

"Heresy," writes Jean Guiraud, "in the Middle Ages was nearly always connected with some anti-social sect. In a period when the human mind usually expressed itself in a theological form, socialism, communism, and anarchy appeared under the form of heresy. By the very nature of things, therefore, the interests of both Church and State were identical; this explains the question of the suppression of heresy in the Middle Ages."[1]

We are not surprised, therefore, that when Church and State found themselves menaced by the same peril, they agreed on the means of defence. If we deduct from the total number of heretics burned or imprisoned the disturbers of the social order and the criminals against the common law, the number of condemned heretics will be very small.

Heretics in the Middle Ages were considered amenable to the laws of both Church and State. Men of that time could not conceive of God and His revelation without defenders in a Christian kingdom. Magistrates were considered responsible for the sins committed against the law of God. Indirectly, therefore, heresy was amenable

[1] Jean Guiraud, *La répression de l'hérésie au moyen âge*, in the *Questions d'archéologie et d'histoire*, p. 44.

to their tribunal. They felt it their right and duty to punish not only crimes against society, but sins against faith.

The Inquisition, established to judge heretics, is, therefore, an institution whose severity and cruelty are explained by the ideas and manners of the age. We will never understand it, unless we consider it in its environment, and from the view-point of men like St. Thomas Aquinas and St. Louis, who dominated their age by their genius. Critics to whom the Middle Ages is an unknown book may feel at liberty to shower insult and contempt upon a judicial system whose severity is naturally repugnant to them. But contempt does not always imply a reasonable judgment, and to abuse an institution is not necessarily a proof of intelligence. If we would judge an epoch intelligently, we must be able to grasp the view-point of other men, even if they lived in an age long past.

But even if we grant the good faith and good will of the founders and judges of the Inquisition — we speak only, be it understood, of those who acted conscientiously — we must still maintain that their idea of justice was far inferior to ours. Whether taken in itself or compared with other criminal procedures, the Inquisition was, so far as the guarantees of equity are concerned, undoubtedly unjust and inferior. Such judicial forms as the secrecy of the trial, the prosecution carried on independently of the prisoner, the denial of advocate and defence, the use of torture, etc., were certainly despotic and barbarous. Severe penalties, like the stake and confiscation, were the legacy which a pagan legislation bequeathed to the Christian State; they were alien to the spirit of the Gospel.

The Church in a measure felt this, for to enforce these laws she always had recourse to the secular arm. In time, all this criminal code was to fall into desuetude, and no one to-day wishes it back again. Besides, the crying abuses committed by some of the Inquisitors have made the institution forever odious.

But in abandoning the system of force, which she formerly used in union with the State, does not the Church seem to condemn to a certain degree her past?

Even if to-day she were to denounce the Inquisition, she would not thereby compromise her divine authority. Her office on earth is to transmit to generation after generation the deposit of revealed truths necessary for man's salvation. That to safeguard this treasure she uses means in one age which a later age denounces, merely proves that she follows the customs and ideas in vogue around her. But she takes good care not to have men consider her attitude the infallible and eternal rule of absolute justice. She readily admits that she may sometimes be deceived in the choice of means of government.[1] The system of defence and protection that she adopted in the Middle Ages succeeded, at least to some extent. We cannot maintain that it was absolutely unjust and absolutely immoral.

Undoubtedly we have to-day a much higher ideal of justice. But though we deplore the fact that the Church did not then perceive, preach or apply it, we need not be surprised. In social questions she ordinarily progresses with the march of civilization, of which she is ever one of the prime movers.

But perhaps men may blame her for having abandoned and betrayed the cause of toleration, which she so ably defended in the beginning. Do not let us exaggerate. There was, undoubtedly, a period in which she did not deduce from the principle she was the first to teach, all its logical consequences. The laws she enforced against heretics prove this. But it is false to say that, while in the beginning she insisted strongly on the rights of conscience, she afterwards totally disregarded them. In

[1] This is also a thesis of Salvatore di Bartolo: "Nè la Chiesa è infallibile nel suo governo." *Op. cit.*, p. 307. And he declares the three following propositions theologically certain: 1. Puo il R. Pontefice promulgare leggi disconvenienti. 2. Puo il Sommo Pontefice governar la Chiesa in modo disconveniente. 3. I Romani Pontefici non furono infallibili nell' istituire i tribunali di Suprema Inquisizione contro l'eretica pravità, i quali infliggevano pene violente ai rei. *Op. cit.*, pp. 120 and 124. Melchior Cano wrote in the same sense: "Non ego omnes Ecclesiæ leges approbo," etc. *De locis theologicis*, lib. v, cap. v, concl. 2. Apologists freely admit these principles; but they often hesitate to apply them, when they come to judge certain facts of history.

fact, she exercised constraint only over her own stray children. But while she acted so cruelly toward them, she never ceased to respect the consciences of those outside her fold. She always interpreted the *compelle intrare* to imply with regard to unbelievers moral constraint, and the means of gentleness and persuasion.[1] If respect for human liberty is to-day dominant in the thinking world, it is due chiefly to her.

In the matter of tolerance, the Church has only to study her own history.[2] If, during several centuries, she treated her rebellious children with greater severity than those alien to her fold, it was not from a want of consistency. And if to-day she manifests to every one signs of her maternal kindness, and lays aside for ever all physical constraint, she is not following the example of non-Catholics, but merely taking up again the interrupted tradition of her early Fathers.

[1] This is an important distinction, which an historian, otherwise accurate, has forgotten to make. "How," he asks, "was a religion of love and toleration, which is founded on the Gospel, led to burn alive *those who did not accept its teachings*. That is the problem." Paul Frédéricq, introduction to the French translation of Lea, vol. i, p. v. Lea himself does not make this mistake. He shows, on the contrary, that the Church never prosecuted non-Christians, and that she "exercised no constraint over unbelievers." *Op. cit.*, vol. i, p. 240. But he deems this inconsistent. To be perfectly consistent, he holds that the church should have burned the unbelievers as well as the heretics. To our mind, the contrary is true; to be consistent, she ought to treat her own children differently.

[2] Cf. *De la tolerance religieuse.* Vacandard, Paris, Bloud. Science et Religion.

APPENDIX A

UNDER this title we reproduce the oldest known copy of a manual of the Holy Office, discovered by the Dominican François Balme, in the University Library of Madrid, and published by Tardif in the *Nouvelle Revue historique de droit français et étranger*, Paris (Larose et Forcel), 1883, pp. 670–678. The date of the first formula is 1244. The work was evidently written about this time.

Although very brief, it gives a rather complete insight into the procedure and the penal code of the Inquisition. In several passages, especially in the *Formula interrogatorii*, the heretic in question is called a Waldensian, although the heretical doctrine mentioned is Catharan.

Littere commissionis

Viris religiosis et discretis dilectis in Christo fratribus Guilelmo Raymondi et Petro Duranti, Ordinis Predicatorum Fr. Pontius fratrum ejusdem ordinis in Provincia Provincie servus inutilis et indignus, salutem et spiritum caritatis.

De zelo discretionis et devotionis vestre plenarie confidentes, Vos in provincia Narbonensi, exceptis Villelonge et Villemuriensi archdiaconatibus, diocesis Tholosani, et in Albiensi, Ruthenensi, Mimatensi et Aniciensi diocesibus ad inquirendum de hereticis, credentibus, fautoribus, receptatoribus, et defensoribus eorum et etiam infamatis, auctoritate Domini Pape nobis in hac parte commissa, in remissionem peccatorum vestrorum duximus transmittendos, eadem vobis auctoritate mandantes quatenus juxta mandatum et ordinationem Sedis Apostolice in negotio procedatis eodem viriliter et prudenter. Quod si ambo hiis exequendis interesse non potueritis, alter vestrum ea nichilominus exequatur.

Datum Narbone, XII Kal. novembris Anno Domini 1244.

Processus inquisitionis

Processus talis: Infra terminos inquisitionis nobis per Priorem Provincie auctoritate prædicta, commisse ac limitate, locum eligimus, qui ad hoc commodior esse videtur, de quo vel in quo de locis aliis inquisitionem faciamus, ubi, Clero et populo convocatis, generalem faciamus predicationem, Litteris tam Domini Pape quam Prioris provincialis de Inquisitionis forma et commissione publice legimus, et sicut convenit explanamus, et exinde generaliter citamus vel verbo presentes, vel absentes per litteras in hunc modum:

Modus citandi

"Inquisitores heretice pravitatis Capellano tali . . .

salutem in Domino. Auctoritate qua fungimur districte vobis precipiendo mandamus quatenus parochianos sive habitatores omnes illius ecclesie sive loci, masculos a XIV, feminas a XII et inferioris (?) etatis, si forte deliquerint, et ex parte et ex auctoritate nostra citetis ut, tali die et tali loco responsuri de hiis quæ contra fidem commiserint et heresim abjuraturi compareant coram nobis; et si de loco illo alia Inquisitio facta non fuerit, omnibus de ipso loco qui nominatim citati vel aliter venia digni non essent, immunitatem carceris indulgemus, si, infra tempus assignatum, sponte venientes et peni-tentes tam de se quam de aliis puram et plenam dix-erint veritatem."

Quod et tempus gratie sive indulgentie appellamus.

Modus abjurandi et forma jurandi

Omnem quemque, dum se ad confitendum presentat, facimus abjurare omnem heresim et jurare quod dicat plenam et puram veritatem, de se et aliis vivis et mortuis, super facto seu crimine heresis et Valdensie; quod fidem catholicam servabit ac defendet, et Hereticos, cujuscum-que secte, non solum aut recipiet aut defendet, eisque favebit aut credet, quin potius eos eorumve nuntios bona fide persequetur et capiet, vel saltem Ecclesie aut princip-ibus eorumve bajulis, qui eos capere velint et valeant, revelabit, et Inquisitionem non impediet, imo eam im-pedientibus se opponet.

Formula interrogatorii

Deinde requiritur si vidit hereticum vel Valdensem et ubi et quando, et quoties et cum quibus, et de aliis circumstantiis diligenter. — Si eorum predicationes aut monitiones audivit, et eos hospitio recepit aut recipi fecit. — Si de loco ad locum duxit seu aliter associavit, aut duci vel associari fecit. — Si cum eis comedit aut bibit, vel de pane benedicto ab eis. — Si dedit vel misit eis aliquid. — Si fuit eorum questor aut nuntius, aut minister. — Si eorum depositum vel quid aliud habuit. — Si ab eorum libro, aut ore, aut cubito pacem accepit. — Si hereticum adoravit, vel caput inclinavit, vel genua flexit, vel dixit Benedicite coram eis; vel si eorum consolamentis aut appareillamentis interfuit. Si cene Valdensi affuit, si peccata sua fuit eis confessus, vel accepit penitentiam vel didicit aliquid ab eis. — Si aliter habuit familiaritatem seu participationem cum hereticis vel Valdensibus, seu quoquo modo. — Si pactum vel preces vel munera recepit, aut fecit super veritate de se aut de aliis non dicenda. — Si quemquam monuit vel induxit seu induci fecit ad aliquid de predictis. — Si scit alium vel aliam fecisse aliquid de premissis. — Si credidit hereticis seu Valdensibus, aut erroribus eorumdem.

Tandem de hiis omnibus et quandoque de pluribus non sine causa rationabili requisitus, scriptis fideliter que de se confessus fuerit vel deposuerit de aliis, coram nobis ambobus vel altero et aliis duobus ad minus viris idoneis ad hec sollicitius exequenda adjunctis, universa que scribi fecerit recognoscet, atque hoc modo acta Inquisitionis ad confessiones et depositiones sive per notarium confecta, sive per scriptorem alium, roboramus.

Et quando terra est generaliter corrupta, generaliter de omnibus inquisitionem secundum modum facimus pretaxatum: nomina omnium redigentes in actis et illorum qui se nihil scire de aliis vel in nullo se asserunt deliquisse, ut, sive mentiti fuerint sive postea delinquerint, sicut frequenter de pluribus reperitur, et eos abjurasse constet, et de singulis requisitos (fuisse).

Modus singulos citandi

Quando autem citamus aliquem singulariter, scribimus sub hac forma:

"Talem, ex parte et auctoritate nostra uno pro omnibus peremptorio citetis edicto, ut tali die, tali loco, de fide sua, vel de tali culpa compareat responsurus vel recepturus carceris (pænam), aut simpliciter penitentiam pro commissis; vel defensurus parentem mortuum, vel sententiam de se aut de mortuo cujus heres existit auditurus."

In singulis quam plurimum citationibus, exprimentes auctoritatem ex qua citamus et quam notoria est in terra, et in dignitate positis deferentes personis, et loca et citationis causam declaramus, et loca tuta et contemptos dilationis sive terminos assignamus, et nulli negamus defensiones legitimas neque a juris ordine deviamus, nisi quod testium non publicamus nomina, propter ordinationem Sedis Apostolice sub Domino Gregorio provide factam et ab Innocentio, beatissimo Papa nostro, postmodum innovatam in privilegium et necessitatem fidei evidentem, super quo habemus testimoniales litteras Cardinalium aliquorum. Circa hoc tamen sufficienter providemus et caute tam eis contra quos Inquisitio fit quam testibus, juxta sanctum consilium Prelatorum.

Hanc autem formam servamus in injungendis penitentiis et condempnationibus faciendis. — Eos qui redire volunt ad ecclesiasticam unitatem ex causa iterum facimus heresim abjurare, et ad fidei observationem ac defensionem et hereticorum persecutionem et inquisitiones per promotionem, ut supra, et penitentie pro nostro arbitrio injungende receptionem et impletionem, solemniter et cum publicis instrumentis obligare: deinde, juxta formam Ecclesie, beneficio absolutionis impenso, injungimus penitenti et recipienti penitentiam carceris in hunc modum:

Modus et forma reconciliandi et puniendi redeuntes ad ecclesiasticam unitatem

"In nomine Domini Nostri Jesu Christi, Amen. Nos inquisitores heretice pravitatis, etc. Per inquisitionem quam de hereticis et infamatis ex mandato facimus apos-

tolico, invenimus quod tu talis, sicut confessus es in
judicio coram nobis, hereticos plures adorasti, receptasti,
visitasti, et eorum erroribus credidisti. Idcirco tibi
taliter deprehenso ad ecclesiasticam tamen unitatem, de
corde bono et fide non ficta, prout asseris, revertenti et
abjuranti ut supra, et te, si contra feceris, ad penam
hereticis debitam sponte obliganti, et recognoscenti quod
ab excommunicatione qua tenebaris pro premissis astric-
tus, absolutus es sub ea conditione et retentione quod si
veritatem, vel de te vel de aliis, inventus fueris suppress-
isse, et si penitentiam et mandata que tibi injungimus non
servaveris et impleveris, ex tunc tibi absolutio præfata
non prosis, sed pro non facta penitus habeatur. Adjunctis
et assistentibus nobis talibus prelatis jurisque discretis,
de ipsorum et aliorum consilio, ad agendam penitentiam
de premissis, quibus Deum et Ecclesiam nequiter offen-
disti, tibi in virtute prestiti juramenti, juxta mandatum
precipimus Apostolicum ut in carceram tolerabilem et
humanum tibi, in civitate illa, paratum sine mora intendas,
facturus ibidem salutarem et perpetuam mansionem.
Sane si hoc mandatum nostrum implere nolueris, aut
ingredi differendo, aut post ingressum forsitan exeundo,
aut alias contra superius a te abjurata et jurata sive
promissa, quocumque tempore veniendo, aut per hoc
fictam conversionem tuam . . . et in penitentiam decla-
mando, te ex tunc tanquam inpenitentem punimus, cul-
pisque astrictum perjoribus, et omnes qui te scienter aut

receperint aut defenderint aut tibi nostra non implenti mandata, vel ne impleas, consilium, auxilium qualitercumque impenderint vel favorem, tanquam hereticorum fautores, receptatores et defensores, excommunicationis vinculo, auctoritate qua fungimur innodamus, decernentes reconciliationem et misericordiam tibi factam ulterius prodesse non posse, et te justissime pariter ex tunc seculari judicio, velut hereticum, relinquentes."

Littere de penitentiis faciendis

De penitentiis vero, quas non immurandis injungimus, damus litteras sub hac forma:

"Universis Christi fidelibus præsentes litteras inspecturis, tales inquisitores, etc. . . . Cum talis lator . . . sicut ex ipsius confessione coram nobis in judicio facta in crimine labis heretice sic deliquit, nos eidem sponte atque humiliter ad sinum Sancte Matris Ecclesie reverenti, et labem prorsus hereticam abjuranti ac demum ab excommunicationis vinculo juxta formam Ecclesie absoluto, injungimus ut in detestationem (sui) erroris duas cruces coloris crocei, longitudinis duarum palmarum, latitudinisque duarum, et in se trium digitorum amplitudinem habentes, portet, et in superiore veste perpetuo, unam anteriorem in pectore et alteram posterius in spatulis; vestem in qua cruces portaverit coloris crocei nunquam habens. Intersit diebus dominicis et festivis, dum vixerit,

misse et vesperis et sermoni generali, si fiat in villa in qua
fuerit, nisi impedimentum habuerit, sine fraude; proces-
siones per tot annos sequatur, virgas largas in manu inter
Clerum et populum portans, et cui processioni affuerit
presentans se in statione aliqua, ut exponat populo quod
hic propter illa que contra fidem commissit, penitentiam
istam agit. Visitet quoque, per tot annos, limina tot
sanctorum, et in singulis peregrinationibus supradictis
presentet litteras nostras quas ipsum habere volumus et
portare, ostendere teneatur prelato Ecclesie quam visi-
taverit et eidem de sua peregrinatione debito modo per-
fecta ejusdem testimoniales nobis litteras reportare.
Eapropter, karissimi, vos rogamus quod ei prefatum talem
has nostras habentem litteras crucesque portantem et ea
servantem que injunximus eidem ac per omnia catholice
conversantem invenistis, occasione illorum que ipsum
contra fidem superius commisisse invenimus, nullatenus
molestetis nec sustineatis ab aliis molestari, vestras ei
testimoniales litteras liberaliter concedendo. Sin autem
secus eum facientem aut etiam attemptantem videritis,
ipsum tanquam perjurum, excommunicatum et culpis
astrictum perjoribus habeatis. Ex tunc enim et reconciliationem et misericordiam sibi factam eidem prodesse
non posse decernimus, et tam ipsum velut hereticum quam
omnes qui eum scienter, aut receperint aut defenderint,
aut aliter ei consilium auxilium vel favorem impenderint,
velut hereticorum fautores, receptatores, seu defensores

excommunicationis vinculo, auctoritate qua fungimur, innodamus."

Forma sententie relinquendi brachio seculari

Hereticos eorumque credentes, premissis et expressis culpis et erroribus, et aliis que in hujusmodi processibus solent sententiis, sic dampnamus.

"Nos inquisitores prefati, auditis et diligenter attentis culpis et demeritis dicti talis et illis precipue circumstantiis que ad extirpendam de terra labem hereticam fidemque plantandam, sive plectemdo, sive ignoscendo, debent potissime nos movere, adjunctis et assistentibus nobis Reverendis Patribus, etc., supradictum talem, quia hereticorum erroribus credidit, et adhuc credere convincitur, cum examinatus et convictus sive confessus reverti et absolute mandatis ecclesia obedire contempnat, per sententiam definitivam hereticum judicamus, relinquentes ex nunc judicio seculari et tam ipsum velut hereticum contempnamus quam omnes qui eum scienter de cetero aut receperint, aut defenderint, aut eidem consilium, auxilium aut favorem impenderint, velut hereticorum fautores, receptatores, defensores excommunicationis vinculo auctoritate qua fungimur innodantes."

Forma sententie contra eos qui heretici decesserint

Mortuos quoque hereticos et credentes, expressis eorum erroribus et culpis et aliis, dampnamus similiter isto modo:

"Nos inquisitores, etc., visis ac diligenter inspectis et attentis culpis ac demeritis talis superius notati, et defensionibus propositis pro eodem, et circumstantiis quas circa personas et dicta testium et alia considerari oportuit et attendi, adjunctis et assistentibus nobis talibus, etc., eumdem talem, etc., definitive pronunciando, judicamus hereticum decessisse atque ipsum et ipsius memoriam pari severitate dampnantes, ossa ejus si ab aliis discerni poterunt, de cemeterio ecclesiastico exhumari simulque comburi decernimus in detestationem criminis tam nefandi."

Condemnationes et penitentias memoratas facimus et injungimus, clero et populo convocatis solemniter et mature, facientes eos quibus penitentias injungimus memoratas, prius ibidem abjurare atque jurare prout superius continetur; et de hujusmodi condempnationibus et carcerum penitentiis fiunt publica instrumenta sigillorum nostrorum assessorum testimoniis roborata.

Forma vero litterarum que de aliis penitentiis conceduntur retinetur in actis.

Ad nullius vero condempnationem, sine lucidis et apertis probationibus vel confessione propria processimus nec, dante Domino, procedemus. Et omnes condempnationes et pentitentias quas majores fecimus et facere proponimus non solum de generali sed etiam de speciali sigillato consilio prelatorum.

Plura quidem alia facimus in processu et aliis, que scripto facile non possent comprehendi, per omnia juris tenentes ordinem aut sedis ordinationem apostolice specialem. Bona hereticorum tam dampnatorum quam immuratorum publicare facimus et compellimus ut debemus, et per hoc est quod specialiter confundit hereticos et credentes, et, si bene fieret justitia de damnatis et relapsis, et bona publicarentur fideliter, et incarceratis provideretur in necessariis competenter, in fructu Inquisitionis gloriosus Dominus et mirabilis appareret.

APPENDIX B

CONDEMNATIONS OF THE INQUISITOR, BERNARD GUI, 1308–1323

	March 3, 1308	May 25, 1309	October 23, 1309	April 5, 1310	April 9, 1310	April 23, 1312	April 30, 1312	September 20, 1313	March 7, 1316	September 30, 1319	November 28, 1319	December 8, 1319	June 29, 1321	July 14, 1321	August 2, 1321	July 3 and 4, 1322	September 12, 1322	June 19, 1323	
Ad gratiam de crucibus		4		3		11	1		21	20						11	61		= 132
Ad peregrinationes sine cruce							1			5							3		= 9
Educti de muro	2	6		1		3	16		5	57						8	41		= 139
Cruce signati		16		20		50			15	20					2	1	7	12	= 143
Immurati		59		62		88			21	28		1			6	20	13	9	= 307
Immurati, si viverent						10				7									= 17
Relicti curie seculari	3	1	1	17	1	5		1	1	4					3		5		= 42
Relinquendi cur. sec., si viverent	2						1												= 3
Exhumandi et comburendi		5		6		36			9	3						2	6		= 69
Fugitivi, condemnati ut heretici						5			3	14						1	16	1	= 40
Exponendi in scala						1			1										= 2
Degradandi										1		1							= 2
Exulatus														1					= 1
Domus diruende	2			4		16													= 22
Talmutz comburendi											1								= 1
Reconciliatio castri de Cordua													1						= 1
	9	91	1	113	1	225	19	1	76	161	1	2	1	1	11	43	152	22	= 930

BIBLIOGRAPHY

THIS volume does not contain any unpublished documents. Every reference in the footnotes may be verified in books that have already been published. We have, however, gone conscientiously to the sources, although occasionally we cite works at second hand. Among the best of these are the works of Lea, Tanon, Douais, and Döllinger.

We have already given our estimate of Lea and Tanon in the preface.

Mgr. Douais is chiefly an editor of documents; his critical ability is usually beyond reproach. I would make one exception, however, with regard to his edition of Bernard Gui's *Practica inquisitionis hæreticæ pravitatis.* There are four manuscripts of this work, two of which (Nos. 387, 388) are in the library of Toulouse. Tanon (loc. cit., p. 163) "regrets that Mgr. Douais, instead of giving us a critical edition of the text, simply copied Manuscript 387, whereas No. 389 is the better. For, according to Molinier, this manuscript is the older; it belonged to the Inquisition of Toulouse, where, as its condition shows, it was in constant use; and finally, it contains important marginal notes in the fourth part."

The documents published by Döllinger, although of unequal value, are on the whole very useful. It is a great pity, however, that he edited them with so little care. Molinier has criticised him rather severely, pointing out many errors, omissions, and inconsistencies. (Revue Historique LIV, p. 155, seq.) His treatise introducing these documents is also rather untrustworthy. Still we do not hesitate to use this work, such as it is, for, from our view-point the mistakes are unimportant.

The following bibliography is far from being complete. For other works I would refer the reader to

Molinier, Les Sources de l'Histoire de France, vol. 3, pp. 58–77, Paris, 1903.

Vernet, Article *Cathares* in the *Dictionnaire de théologie Catholique*, vol. 2, col. 1997–99 (1905).

Fredericq, Historiographie de l'Inquisition, the preface to Reinach's French translation of Lea's History of the Inquisition in the Middle Ages.

. . . .

Alain, De fide catholica contra hæreticos sui temporis, Migne, *Pat. lat.*, vol. ccx, 305–430.

Alphandéry, Les idées morales chez les hétérodoxes latins au début du XIIIe siècle, Paris, 1903, pp. 34–99.

Bernard De Come, Lucerna inquisitorum hæreticæ pravitatis, Rome, 1584.

Bernard Gui, Practica officii inquisitionis hereticæ pravitatis, éd. Douais, Paris, 1886.

Bonacursa, Manifestatio heresis Catarorum, Migne, *Pat. lat.*, cciv, 775–792; d'Achéry, *Spicilegium*, in fol. i, 208–215.

Clédat, Le nouveau Testament traduit au XIIIe siècle en langue provençale, suivi d'un Rituel cathare, Paris, 1888.

Doat (collection), *Documents relatifs à Inquisition, à la Bibliothèque nationale*, 17 vol. (vol. xxi–xxxvii). Vols. xxix and xxx contain a copy of Bernard Gui's *Practica*.

Doctrina de modo procedendi contra hæreticos, in Martène, *Thesaurus novus Anecdotorum*, v, 1797–1822, a treatise composed about 1275.

Döllinger, Beiträge zur Sektengeschichte des Mittelalters, Munich, 1890, 2 vol. in 8º. The second volume is made up of documents.

Douais, Documents pour servir a l'histoire de l'Inquisition dans le Languedoc, Paris, 1900, 2 vol. The documents of the second volume are: 1st. The Sentences of Bernard de Caux and of Jean de Saint Pierre (1244–1248). 2d. Testimony against Pierre Garcias of Bourguet-Nau of Toulouse, received by Bernard de Caux and Jean de Saint Pierre (Aug. 22 to Dec. 10, 1247). 3d. The register of the notary of the Inquisition of Carcassonne. 4th. The Pontifical commission of Cardinal Taillefer de la Chapelle and Berenger Frédol (April 15 to May, 1306).

La formule Communicato bonorum virorum Consilio des sentences inquisitoriales in the *Compte rendu du quatrième congrès scientifique international des catholiques*, Fribourg (Switzerland), 1898, sect. *des Sciences historiques*, pp. 316–367, and in *Le Moyen Age*, 1898, pp. 157–192, 286–311.

Saint Raymond de Pennafort et les hérétiques, Directoire à l'usage des inquisiteurs aragonais, 1242, in *Le Moyen Age*, xii (1899), 305–325.

Du Plessis d'Argentré, Collectio judiciorum de novis erroribus, etc., Paris, 1728 et seq., 3 vol. in fol.

Egbert (Ekkebertus, +1185), *Sermones* xiii contra Catharos in Migne, *Pat. lat.*, cxcv, 13–102.

Eymeric (Nicolas). *Directorium inquisitorum*, written about 1376. We quote the Venetian edition of 1607, with Pegna's commentary.

Ficker, Die gesetzliche Einführung der Todesstrafe für Ketzerei, in the *Mittheilungen des Instituts für Oesterreichische Geschichtsforschung*, Innspruck, 1880, vol. i, pp. 177–226, 430–431.

Frédéricq (Paul), *Corpus documentorum inquisitionis hæreticæ pravitatis Neerlandicæ* (1205–1525), vol. i, 1889; vol. ii, 1896; vol. iii, 1906; vol. iv, 1900.

Grégoire de Fano, about 1240, *Disputatio inter Catholicum et Paterinum hæreticum*, in Martène, *Thesaurus novus anecdotorum*, vol. v, col. 1715–1758.

Guillem Pelhisse, Chronicon (1230–1237), edited by Ch. Molinier, *De fratre Guillelmo Pelisso veterrimo inquisitionis historico*, Paris,

19

1880, and by Mgr. Douais in *Les Sources de l'histoire de l'inquisition dans le midi de la France*, Paris, 1882.

Guiraud (Jean), *Questions d'histoire et archéologie chrétienne*, Paris, 1906.

Havet (Julien) *L'hérésie et le bras séculier au moyen âge jusqu'au XIIIe siècle*, in the *Bibliothèque de l'Ecole des Chartes XLI*, 488–517; 570–607, and in *Œuvres complètes*, Paris, 1896, vol. ii, pp. 117–180.

Henner (Camille), *Beiträge zur Organisation und Competenz der päpstlichen Ketzergeschichte*, Leipzig, 1890.

Huillard-Bréolles, *Historia diplomatica Frederici II*, Paris, 1854–1861, 12 vol. in 4°.

Labbe et Cossart, *Concilia* (sacrosancta), Paris, 1671–1672, 18 vol. in-fol.

Langlois (ch. v), *L'Inquisition d'après les travaux récents*, Paris, 1902.

Lea (Henry-Charles), *A history of the inquisition in the Middle Ages*, 1888, 3 vol.; a French translation by Salomon Reinach, 1900–1902.

Limborch, *Historia inquisitionis*, Amsterdam, 1692. This work contains the *Liber sententiarum inquisitionis Tolosanæ* of Bernard Gui.

Louis De Paramo, *De origine et progressu officii sanctæ Inquisitionis ejusque utilitate et dignitate libri tres*, Madrid, 1598.

Lucas De Tuy (1239–1288), *De altera vita fideique controversiis adversus Albigenses*, written about 1240, in the Bibliotheca Patrum, 4th ed., vol. iv[b], pp. 575–714.

Martène and *Durand*, *Amplissima collectio veterum scriptorum*, etc., Paris, 1724–1743, 9 vol. in-fol.

Thesaurus novus anecdotorum, Paris, 1717, 5 vol. in-fol.

Masini (Eliseo), *Sacro Arsenale ovvero Prattica dell' Officio della Santa Inquisizione*, Bologna, 1665.

Migne, *Patrologia latina*, 218 vol. in-4°.

Molinier (Ch.), *L'Inquisition dans le midi de la France au XIIIe et au XIVe siècle. Étude sur les sources de son histoire*, Paris, 1880.

L'endura, coutume religieuse des derniers sectaires albigeois, in the *Annales de la Faculté de Bordeaux*, vol. iii, 1881.

Rapport sur une mission exécutée en Italie, in the *Archives des missions scientifiques et litteraires*, Paris, 1888, 3d series, vol. xiv.

Moneta, of Cremona (Inquisitor from 1231 to 1250), *Adversus Catharos et Valdenses libri quinque*, ed. Richini, Rome, 1743.

Monumenta Germaniæ historica, *Scriptores*, 31 vol. in-fol.

Monumenta Germaniæ historica, *Leges*, in-4°.

Müller (K.), *Die Valdenses und ihre einzelne Gruppen bis zum Anfang* *des XIV*en *Jahrhunderts*, an important work, in the *Theologische Studien und Kritiken*, 1886, pp. 665–732, and 1887, pp. 45–146.

Percin (J.-J.), *Monumenta Conventus Tholosani ordinis FF. Prædicatorum primi*, Toulouse, 1693.

Potthast, Regesta pontificum Romanorum inde ab anno post Christum natum MCXCVIII ad annum MCCCIV, Berlin, 1874–1875, 2 vol. in-4°.

Processus Inquisitionis, a manual of the year 1244, in the *Nouvelle Revue historique de droit français et étranger*, 1883, pp. 669–678. See Appendix A.

Questiones domini Guidonis Fulcodii et responsiones ejus, a treatise on procedure for Inquisitors, written about 1254, edited by Cesare Carena, *Tractatus de officio sanctissimæ inquisitionis*, 1669, p. 367–393. Gui Foucois became Pope under the name of Clement IV.

Raoul Ardent, about 1100, *Sermo in dominica VIII post Trinitatem*, Migne, *Pat. lat.*, clv, 2007–2013.

Registres d'Alexandre IV, published by La Roncière, Paris, 1895–1902.

Registres d'Honorius IV, published by Maurice Prou, Paris, 1888.

Registres de Nicolas IV, published by Langlois, Paris, 1886–1893.

Ripoll, Bullarium ordinis FF. Prædicatorum, Paris, Biblioth. Nationale, Inventaire H 1671.

Rodrigo, Historia verdadera de la Inquisicion, 3 vol., Madrid, 1876–1877

Sacconi (Rainier or Raineri), a converted heretic and Inquisitor about 1258, *Summa de Catharis et Leonistis et Pauperibus de Lugduno*, in Martène, Thesaurus novus anecdotorum, vol. v, pp. 1457–1776.

Salve Burce, of Piacenza, about 1235, *Supra Stella*, in Döllinger's Beiträge, quoted above, vol. ii, pp. 52–84.

Schmidt (C.), *Histoire et doctrine de la secte des Cathares ou Albigeois*, Paris, 1849, 2 vol. in-8°.

Tanon, Histoire des tribunaux de l'Inquisition en France, Paris, 1893, in-8°.

Vaissete, Histoire générale du Languedoc, old edition, 1730–1745; new edition, 1872–1892.

Vidal (J. M.), *Un inquisiteur jugé par ses victimes, Jean Galland et les Carcassonnais*, Paris, 1903.

Le tribunal de l'Inquisition de Pamiers, in the *Annales de Saint-Louis-des-Français*, Rome and Paris, 1904–1906.

Zanchino Ugolini, De hæreticis tractatus aureus, Mantua, 1567; Rome, 1579.

INDEX

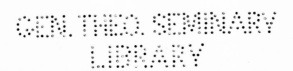